CRISIS MANAGEMENT IN SPORT

ENDORSEMENTS

Sport is intense, often the subject of great passion and seldom devoid of struggle. Crisis management is part and parcel of the sporting landscape. Jacques's new book is a must-read for those in the sports industry.

Graeme Smith, Former Proteas Captain; SA 20 Commissioner

I have worked with Jacques during the 2012 CSA crisis. He is one of the leading sports administrators and the go-to man during a crisis. This book reflects his knowledge and experience and will help sportspeople deal with a crisis clinically and practically. This is a significant contribution to the field of Sports Management. We don't do enough to train sports administrators, and this is a very welcome publication.

Max Fuzani, Special advisor to the Minister of Sports, Arts and Culture

I like Jacques and respect his intellect. He is a critical thinker. We have discussed sport and what the zeitgeist should and could be for sport in South Africa. We have both experienced the power of sport. It can change the world and unite people like little else does, paraphrasing Madiba. Why would sport face a crisis when you have talent in abundance? Who are the leaders, and what are the vision, culture and governance? Jacques's experience in managing crises in sports gave him valuable insight and understanding. Thank you for sharing it with us.

Francois Pienaar, World Cup-winning Springbok Captain 1995; Varsity Cup Founder & CEO

I have worked with Dr Faul for longer than a decade. During this time, cricket faced many challenges. He provided guidance and leadership to resolve many of these challenges. He is well-educated, and the book combines his knowledge and practical experience. The book will be beneficial for sports boards. Dealing with a crisis in sport can be a daunting task. It could be traumatic for those involved. To quote Dr Faul, "We are temporary custodians of the game". This book will help us serve better.

Tebogo Siko, Titans Cricket President; Cricket South Africa Board member

Crisis Management in Sport provides invaluable insights and strategies for navigating the complex world of sports management. Filled with practical advice and case studies, this book is a must-read for anyone involved in the sports industry. It is a comprehensive guide to handling crises effectively and maintaining a positive reputation.

Prof. Rian Cloete, Chairperson: South African Sports Law Association;
Editor: Introduction to Sports Law in South Africa; Sports Lawyer

As someone involved in planning and executing sporting and other events, I have encountered unique challenges in this industry. This insightful work offers a pragmatic approach to the subject matter, making it an invaluable resource for anyone in the sports industry. One of the standout features of this book is its insightful exploration of the various types of crises we frequently encounter in sports management. I extend my highest commendation to Dr Jacques Faul for making an exceptional contribution to the sports industry. I wholeheartedly endorse "Crisis Management in Sport" as an essential read for individuals in the sports industry.

Bertie Grobbelaar, CEO Stadium Management South Africa;
Founding member of the South African Sports Law Association

The beauty of working in the sports industry is that no day is the same, but inevitably, it seems you are going from managing one crisis to the next due to the ever-changing environment. Nobody knows these intricacies better than Jacques, but he has always come out on top of the crisis. This is a great read for any aspiring sports administrator…if you can master the crisis…you can master the sport, and Jacques is a master at it!

Edgar Rathbone, CEO of Bulls Rugby

They often say 'don't waste a good crisis'. Whilst it can be torturous for all stakeholders to endure a crisis, there are always valuable opportunities to reflect on. Jacques's outstanding book provides vital insights in an area of the sports industry which is often overlooked.

David Becker, former General Counsel International Cricket Council;
Partner at Becker Kemp Attorneys.

Congratulations on the publication of this book. South African sport is constantly subjected to various crises that weaken sporting bodies and prejudice our athletes. A key issue that plagues our sport is the lack of leadership in dealing with these crises, and this book is to be welcomed as it focuses on all the elements that leaders must master to change this reality. Faul calls on various experts to provide the necessary input to ensure that every element of crisis management is covered – this provides a comprehensive perspective on the subject. This is compulsory reading for all involved in sports administration.

Andrew Breetzke, CEO South African Cricketers' Association

Congratulations, Jacques, on producing this fantastic resource for sports administrators, players, and scholars in sport. The book is based on your long and distinguished career in sports, your legal training, and your absolute passion for the advancement of sport in our country. Sports management has changed drastically in our lifetime from when it was run by ranked amateurs who were committed volunteers to the professional era where good governance, fiduciary duties, legal disputes, and match-fixing became the buzzwords. This book is a must-have for every serious sports administrator.

Gregory Fredericks, Former Gauteng Lions CEO

Jacques Faul may be a professor, but a more no-nonsense, humble, effective man and, thus, writer you will not find. In this ode…no, make that "bible" to sports management, he postulates: "If you can afford it, make use of experts". It's probably because he is an expert administrator. Here, he straight bats stakeholders, crises and change management, dispute resolution and even presents a game plan to prevent being caught out on the boundary. But here's the real point of this book: you may think a googly is a new type of search engine or a reverse sweep is a pool cleaning mechanism, but the principles of this fine advisory and instructive writing, gleaned from cricket, can be applied to big business, churches, committees, family and even on a personal growth and development level. I know I will.

Arnold Geerdts, Broadcaster and Media Professional

This is the culmination of 27 years in one book, which is commendable. Jacques has become a pioneer upon whose shoulders many will stand. Crisis management is a skill that is crucial in sports administration.

This book offers a plethora of thoughts on challenges faced by different stakeholders in sport. Further, it presents solutions that can be applied effectively by leaders and those who seek to leave a lasting impression on the footsteps of history. I am certain that this book will play an important role in sports development in general.

Lesedi Mphahlele, Director Fairbridges Wertheim Becker Attorneys

Crisis Management in Sport is a must-read if you want to understand the crises and challenges that sports have faced. Jacques Faul shares his two decades of leadership experience and advises how to lead an organisation when the morale is low and the environment is uncertain. In this book, Faul emphasises the importance of leadership, creating trustworthy relationships with stakeholders and true to his character, he focuses on the practice of governance in the sports industry.

Birgitta Wasserfall, Radio Broadcaster, Commercial Sports Specialist

"We are merely temporary custodians of this beautiful game, and we need to leave it in a better space than what we found it in." These are the profound words of my mentor and dear friend, Professor Jacques Jacobs Faul, or simply "Jaaks". He has been a courageous leader throughout his life, and I have been privileged to walk this administrative journey with him for the last 15 years. There is no better person to share experiences of successfully navigating different forms of adversity. This is the book I want my team to read to learn more about dealing with challenges. Jaaks' leadership is based on choosing right over wrong, ethics over convenience, and truth over popularity. Travel the path of integrity without looking back, for there is never a wrong time to do the right thing.

Heinrich Strydom, CEO Dolphins Cricket

I have worked for many years representing players and running players' associations at both country and global levels, primarily in cricket.

Here in South Africa, I worked with and alongside Jacques a lot when we were dealing with fundamental cricket issues and as a counterpart sitting on the opposite side of the negotiating table. I always appreciated his very clear understanding that players are important stakeholders in the game and he always applied this consistently. The most forward-thinking sports administrators know that many crises can be averted or better managed when the players or their representatives are around the table.

Tony Irish, Former CEO of the South African Cricketers' Association; Former CEO of the Professional Cricketers' Association (UK); Former Chairman of the Board of My Players Rugby organisation; Current Director of Federation of International Cricketers' Associations

Copyright © KR Publishing and Professor Jacques Faul

All reasonable steps have been taken to ensure that the contents of this book do not, directly or indirectly, infringe any existing copyright of any third person and, further, that all quotations or extracts taken from any other publication or work have been appropriately acknowledged and referenced. The publisher, editors and printers take no responsibility for any copyright infringement committed by an author of this work.

Copyright subsists in this work. No part of this work may be reproduced in any form or by any means without the written consent of the publisher or the author.

While the publisher, editors and printers have taken all reasonable steps to ensure the accuracy of the contents of this work, they take no responsibility for any loss or damage suffered by any person as a result of that person relying on the information contained in this work.

First published in 2024.

ISBN: 978-1-991272-09-6 (Printed)
eISBN: 978-1-991272-10-2 (PDF Ebook)

Published by KR Publishing
Republic of South Africa
Tel: (011) 706-6009
E-mail: orders@knowres.co.za
Website: www.kr.co.za

Typesetting, layout and design: Cia Joubert, cia@knowres.co.za
Cover design: Marlene de'Lorme, marlene@knowledgekr.co.za
Editing and Proofreading: Marica West, maricarichter@gmail.com
Project management: Cia Joubert, cia@knowres.co.za

CRISIS MANAGEMENT IN SPORT

Dealing with Challenges
On and Off the Field

by

PROFESSOR JACQUES FAUL

2024

DEDICATION

This book is dedicated to all the unsung heroes of the sporting world who manage sporting organisations, host sporting events, and other contributors in the world of sport. As well as the unsung heroes and behind-the-scenes actors who make it possible for sports stars to shine and inspire nations. On a personal note, I would like to dedicate this book to my family and especially to my late brother, Werner Faul, who was a sports administrator and coach – I miss you every day.

I worked in sports for most of my professional life, which makes it an absolute privilege to, in a small, humble way, share my experiences with others. I hope you will benefit from it.

Jacques

TABLE OF CONTENTS

Foreword by Dr Ali Bacher iii
Acknowledgements iv
About the Author v
About the Contributors vi
About the Book ix
CCEOs In Sport Conference on Crisis Management, Sun City 2023 xi
Acronyms Used xiii

Chapter 1: My 20-year Career In (Trying) To Manage Crises in Sports
    by *Jacques Faul* 1

Chapter 2: What Is a Crisis in Sport? by *Jacques Faul* 17

Chapter 3: Managing Crises in Sport – Lessens from CEOs in Sport
    by *Suané Nortje* and *Ivanke Broodryk* 27

Chapter 4: Leading Through a Crisis by *Jacques Faul* 37

Chapter 5: Stakeholder Management During a Crisis by *Jacques Faul* ... 45

Chapter 6: Crisis Communication by *Johan van Zyl, Luke Alfred* and
    Jacques Faul 53

Chapter 7: Governance in Sport by *Rian Cloete* 67

Chapter 8: Compliance and Risk Management by *Janie Marais* 77

Chapter 9: The Crisis Management of Sporting Events by *Jacques Faul* ... 87

Chapter 10: Mental Wellness by *Monique de Klerk* 97

Chapter 11: Legal Considerations During a Crisis in Sport by *Bertie Grobler*
    and *Rian Cloete* 111

Chapter 12: Alternative Dispute Resolution in Sports by *Jacques Faul* ... 123

Chapter 13: Racism and Discrimination in Sports by *Jacques Faul* 135

Chapter 14 Crisis Management Plan by *Jacques Faul* 155

Annexure A: Crisis Management Template 157
Endnotes 165
Bibliography 169
Index 176

Tables

Table 1: Possible Crises in Sport 19
Table 2: Crises: Sporting Organisation 23
Table 3: Possible Sports Stakeholders 45
Table 4: King IV: Principles 69
Table 5: Compliance Universe 82
Table 6: Compliance Risk Management Plan 83
Table 7: Reports on Racism in Sport 136

Figures

Figure 1: Mendelow's Power/Interest Matrix 50
Figure 2: Corporate Governance 79
Figure 3: Model On Practical Guidelines for Managing a Crisis 100
Figure 4: Crisis Management Strategic Plan 156

Photos/Illustrations

Photo of Dr Ali Bacher, Benoni City Times, 13 September 2022, Facebook iii

Chief Executives Meeting 2013. I was the Acting CEO at CSA xvi

Titans men's Team 2-17/2018 Season. This is one of the strongest domestic teams in the world outside the T20 circuit. (Rayder Media) xvi

Titans women's team 2024 (Rayder Media) xvii

Lords, UK. Acting CEO of CSA. The Proteas became the one team in all three formats. (CricTracker) xvii

Professors Leenta Grobler, and Ronnie Lotriet, colleagues at NWU Business School (Jake Media) xviii

SA 20 After party, Cape Town with Janie Marais and Steven Cook xviii

Celebrating 10 Years at Titans in 2023. SuperSport Park (Rayder Media) xix

Illustration, 'DANKIE MAAR NEE DANKIE! EK LOOP LIEWER!', Niël van Vuuren, Beeld 1 August 2020 14

FOREWORD BY DR ALI BACHER

Congratulations on your handbook.

This is much needed to add to the body of knowledge in Sports Management. Many sports organisations have experienced crises over the years; sadly, not all have been dealt with effectively. I was blessed to play sports at the international level and manage national and international sports. I know the challenges a manager or board must deal with. This can be traumatic and have a very negative impact on an organisation and sporting code. Having guidance on a more effective way of dealing with them is important. I was also privileged to learn from experienced administrators at the start of my administrative career.

People like Joe Pamensky guided me as a young person just after my playing career. This was of tremendous value to me. I needed to deal with challenges such as match-fixing scandals and political challenges, especially when I was aiming to unify cricket in South Africa. It is probably my biggest achievement that we were able to transition from a divided cricket community to a United Cricket Board in South Africa.

I must mention the late Steve Tshwete's role in this and how he saved me from many difficult situations. We all need help in challenging times. I also remember how many consultations you had when you were seconded to cricket South Africa yourself and had to deal with these challenges. I am sure that the sporting fraternity will benefit tremendously from this book.

ACKNOWLEDGEMENTS

Thank you to Wilhelm Crous and Cia Joubert for enabling me to write this book; I appreciate it. Thank you to my employer, Titans Cricket, for allowing me to write the book.

To all the contributors to the book, thank you. Without your assistance, this would not have been possible. Your chapters add to the value offering of this publication. To Knowledge Resources, thank you for your willingness to publish the book. Thank you to CEOs in Sport for allowing us to include two significant conferences in the book. This will add tremendous value to practitioners in sports.

I had the opportunity to interview industry legends and would like to recognise the following contributions:

Dr Ali Bacher
Hugo Kemp
David Becker
Anant Sarkaria

Technical Assistance:

Cia Joubert
Elvira Faul
Janie Marais

ABOUT THE AUTHOR

Professor Jacques Faul is a well-known cricket administrator and has been a CEO in cricket for 20 years. During this time, he has consulted on behalf of the International Cricket Council with members of the Council to provide strategic direction. Prof Faul is regarded as a turnaround specialist in sports and is credited for successful turnaround strategies. His field of study includes stakeholder management, law, and mega and major sporting events. He is a trained mediator and founded the Centre for Alternative Dispute Resolution in Sport. He is a co-founding member of CEOs in Sport; which focuses on the continuous professional development of executives in sports. He is also a founding member of the South African Sports Law Association.

Professor Faul started his administrative career in 2003 when he was appointed CEO of North West Cricket. He was the acting CEO of Cricket South Africa in 2012 and again in 2020. He was appointed the CEO of Titans Cricket in 2013. The Titans Cricket Franchise is considered the most successful cricket franchise in the modern era. He is an associate professor at the North-West University Business School and a guest lecturer at many other tertiary institutions. In 2007 he was Student of The Year at the University of the Witwatersrand's Business School Executive Sports Management Programme. He has completed an executive certificate in major event management at the Sydney University of Technology. Professor Faul holds various qualifications, including a PhD, MBA and LLM.

ABOUT THE CONTRIBUTORS

Johan van Zyl

As a specialist in media relations and corporate communication for the past 19 years, Johan gained valuable experience from various organisations where he was employed. From junior reporter to senior journalist, editor, spokesperson and marketing and communications specialist. This includes media platforms such as newspapers, magazines, national radio, digital social media, higher education, and agricultural sectors. He is a multiple awards winner. He has received international training from renowned and reputable institutions such as the London College of Media and Journalism and Harvard University Business School in Boston, USA.

In 2018, he took a massive leap of faith to see the birth of JAKE Media, a media agency with experience across the broad spectrum of the media industry. It provides a one-stop service for organisations' corporate marketing and communication needs.

Luke Alfred

Luke is a seasoned journalist and author of books, having worked at the Sunday Independent, the Sunday Times and, briefly, at Cricket South Africa under Jacques.

He still loves cricket, although he doesn't get as excited about it as he once did. He looks forward to when the Proteas might reach a World Cup final. As for winning it, well, that's a different story.

He lives in Cape Town, with a fine view of False Bay.

Dr Monique de Klerk

Dr Monique de Klerk is an HPCSA-registered Counselling Psychologist at the Centre for Health & Human Performance: Psychology & Wellbeing. She is part of a multi-disciplinary team of professionals who deliver various services, including psychotherapy sessions and psychometric evaluations, coaching sessions to parents and corporate entities, webinars, and training. Dr Monique de Klerk also serves as the internship coordinator for interns and project coordinator of a short learning programme focused on building knowledge and skills in practice. She recently completed her doctoral studies in psychology on crisis containment to empower individuals to handle various crises. Crisis containment and trauma-focused work greatly interest her, along with following a Schema Therapy approach.

Bertie Grobbelaar

Bertie Grobbelaar is the Managing Director at Stadium Management South Africa (SMSA). He was admitted as an attorney in the High Court of South Africa in February 1997 and obtained a postgraduate qualification in Sport Law in 2003.

As a sports lawyer, he represented amateur and professional players, coaches, referees and officials, the sports industry's governing bodies, sports administrators, educational institutions, and sports facility owners and operators.

He has experience in the contentious area of sports doping, the World Anti-Doping Code, which contains an unusual mix of public and private regulations and appeared in matters before the Court for Arbitration in Sport.

SMSA is South Africa's leading stadium management group managing the City of Johannesburg-owned venues: FNB Stadium, Orlando Stadium, Dobsonville Stadium and the Rand Stadium. In addition, he has overseen multiple high-profile events hosted at the stadiums, from Superhero Sunday to the Soweto Derbies and numerous international music concerts.

Professor Rian Cloete

Rian Cloete obtained BLC and LLB degrees from the University of Pretoria, while the University of South Africa (UNISA) conferred the doctoral degree on him in 2001. In 2014, he obtained his master's degree in International Sports Law and Practice from the De Montfort University (DMU) in the United Kingdom.

Rian was admitted as an attorney of the High Court of South Africa in 1992. Professor Cloete joined the Department of Procedural Law at the University of Pretoria in January 1993, rose to professor in 2004, and has been the Head of the Department of Procedural Law since 2012.

Rian established the Centre for Sports and Entertainment Law at the University of Pretoria in 2002 and serves as director. The mission of the centre is to provide a centre of excellence in delivering high-quality services, research and courses to the sporting world at large.

As a sports lawyer, he has advised and represented most sporting bodies in South Africa, such as Cricket South Africa (CSA), Athletics South Africa (ASA), the South African Rugby Union (SARU), Basketball SA, Boxing SA, Netball SA and the South African Institute for Drug-Free Sport (SAIDS).

Ivanke Broodryk

In 2018, Ivanke completed her degree in Human Movement Science with Psychology and became a Golden Key International Honor Society member. Ivanke continued her educational pursuits and graduated with an honours degree in Child Development from North-West University in 2019.

From November 2019 to July 2021, she was the practice manager, Kinderkineticist, and Vision and Reading Therapist at Spectacle Warehouse Atterbury and Miraculum Kinetics. Her primary focus was on child development, programme management, and practice expansion.

In November 2020, Ivanke became involved with the CEOs in Sport Association as an association coordinator and administrator, a role she continues to hold. She is dedicated to new business development, conference and event management, webinars and meetings, speaker coordination, media and content management, collaborative partnerships, and administrative support.

Ivanke was recently appointed as the Vodacom Blue Bulls' Event Manager by SAIL, a testament to her commitment to event management and working with people. Ivanke will be pivotal at the Blue Bulls, covering administration, event management, financial oversight, business development, and health and safety management.

Suané Nortje

Suané Nortje earned her undergraduate degree at the University of Pretoria, where she completed her Bachelor of Arts degree. She proceeded to complete her postgraduate degree, Honours in Psychology.

After her studies, Suané worked for the CEOs in Sport Association, where she masterfully handled administration, event planning, member relations, and the strategic advancement of organisational objectives. Suané proceeded to gain experience in London, where she served as the personal assistant to the membership director at the renowned Marylebone Cricket Club. Her enthusiastic demeanour and passion for networking render her an invaluable asset to any team.

Janie Marais

Janie Marais is the Human Resources and Compliance Manager at Northerns Cricket Union, where she has worked for 18 years. She obtained her Post Graduate Diploma in Management from the North-West University, with distinction, before she embarked on her current studies of Master's in Business Management. Janie conducted training and presented at a conference focussed on sustainability on the topic of sustainability compliance. Janie is actively managing compliance and risk management at Northerns Cricket Union, in which she also holds accredited certificates.

ABOUT THE BOOK

The book will benefit students and practitioners in sports management, media and communication, risk/compliance management and law. The first chapter deals with my 20 years as a CEO in cricket and the various challenges I faced. The book will benefit governing bodies in sports dealing with significant crises. This includes chairpersons tasked to guide the organisation in stormy times. The chapter on leadership provides specific guidelines.

The reader will be provided with the characteristics of a crisis and the various crises in sports, including case studies. I firmly believe that ongoing effective stakeholder management establishes trust relationships with key stakeholders and forces you to scan the environment and map role-players. It equips the organisation to survive challenges. Stakeholder management is one of my fields of study, and the chapter on the subject will provide ample insight into stakeholder management.

Communication during a crisis is of the utmost importance, and the input from Luke Alfred and Johan van Zyl will enable the reader to compile a communication plan. I included my perception of a specific communication strategy for a sporting organisation.

Governance and the law are covered in three chapters by legendary figures in sports: Prof Rian Cloete and Bertie Grobler. Both lawyers have immense experience in their fields related to sports. Compliance is covered by Janie Marais, a highly qualified individual who shaped compliance management at the Titans.

I have included a chapter on mental wellness. I suffered from depression during my career and have witnessed the same with other colleagues and people in the industry. This chapter will be significant to all facing trauma-related challenges.

I have become an advocate for alternative dispute resolutions (ADR) and could not resist including my "gospel" in this book. Money in sports should be spent on sports and not on the courts. Administrators need continuous education in this regard.

Racism and discrimination are societal problems, and sports are not immune to this. At some stage, this will become a challenge and, if not dealt with correctly, may destroy your organisation. I participated in the Social Justice and Nation Building hearings and provided my insights into what must have been the most challenging time of a two-decade career.

I co-founded the CEOs in Sport, an organisation aiming to continuously develop practitioners. I am very proud of the conferences held by the organisation, and the two included in the book are on crisis management. There is much wisdom provided by those who had to deal with it all in these two chapters. The CEOs share their expertise and wisdom in managing crises. The chapters include contributions from international practitioners such as James Sutherland, the previous CEO of Australian Cricket and the current CEO of Golf Australia.

The book covers mainly sports, but I firmly believe that all industries will be able to benefit from the knowledge and insights provided. I teach at a business school and realised that each sector has uniqueness; however, all can benefit from generic management best practices. I sincerely hope that more than just the sports industry will benefit from the book.

Jacques Faul

CCEOs IN SPORT CONFERENCE ON CRISIS MANAGEMENT SUN CITY 2023

I would like to acknowledge the individuals who attended the CCEOs in Sport Conference on Crisis Management at Sun City in 2023. Your valuable insights and contributions have greatly enriched the discussions on crisis management in the realm of sports.

Attendees

Bennie de Bruyn – Trade Marketing Director at SAB

Suane Nortje – CEOs in Sport

Ivanke Broodryk – CEOs in Sport

Johan van Heerden – CEO at FSCU

Jaco Beukes – CEO at SAIL

Heinrich Strydom – CEO at Dolphins Cricket

LJ Swart – Managing director at Oxigen

Rian Cloete – University of Pretoria

Werner Kruger – Director at Impact Sport

Bertie Grobbelaar – CEO at Stadium Management SA

Ajee Valentine – Owner of AJEEV Commercial Consultants

Pieter Visser – General Manager at Golden Lions Rugby Union

Caesar Bond Nayoto – Managing Director at Sports Guru

Charlotte Serwadi – Cricket Services Manager at Titans

Pierre Joubert – Commercial Manager at Titans

Samuel Prinsloo – Financial Manager/Titans Cricket (Pty) Ltd

Campbell Jamieson – Professor of Practice Sport Management at Deakin University

Jabulani Kubheka – Stadium Manager at SSP

Marise Banks – Key Accounts Manager at Lift

Raymond Langa – Sponsorship & Marketing Professional

Jono Leaf-Wright – Lions Cricket CEO

Shukri Toefy – Migration

AB Basson – Migration

Kira Louw – Migration

Koyal Singh – Migration

Hugo Kemp – Operations Manager Loftus Versfeld

Garann Kriek – Sponsorship Manager at The Jester Sports and Entertainment

Lesedi Mphahlele – Director, Fairbridges Wertheim Becker

Shane Wafer – Attorney/Director at Javelin Sports

John Wright – Directorate Sport & Recreation

Eddy Fwamba – Marketing & Commercial Consultant at Heroes Athletic

Sphe Vundla – Corporate Brand Director at SAB

Laurelle Simonetti – DRAFTLINE Director at SAB

Christo Cronje – National Events Manager at SAB

Rassie Pieterse – TK Sports

Michael Canterbury – Western Province Cricket CEO

Tebogo Siko – Titans

Hugo Maree – XCO Sport

Rudi Kotze – XCO Sport

Deon de Klerk – Special Project Director Masakhane Seating

Susan de Klerk – CEO Masakhane Seating

Lizell Brown – Senior Project Manager Masakhane Seating

Marizane Lewis – PA Masakhane Seating

Carlos Laffitte – Technical Engineer & Export Manager EuroSeating

Erika Robredo Crespo – Business Development Manager EuroSeating

Beatriz Tecedor Mingo – EuroSeating

Final thank you

Janie Marais helped tremendously with the reference checks.

Elvira Faul compiled the introduction section and helped design the cover.

Lastly, to my family, thank you for your support.

ACRONYMS USED

ADR	Alternative Dispute Resolutions
AFCON	African Cup of Nations
ASA	Athletics South Africa
BLM	Black Lives Matter
CAF	Confederation of African Football
CCEOs	Certified Chief Executive Officers
CCMA	Commission for Conciliation, Mediation and Arbitration
CDC	Centres for Disease Control and Prevention
CDC	Cricket Discipline Commission
CEO	Chief Executive Officer
CFR	Council on Foreign Relations
COO	Chief Operating Officer
COSAFA	Council of Southern Africa Football Associations
CRMP	Compliance Risk Management Plan
CSA	Cricket South Africa
DBT	Dialectic Behaviour Therapy
DCMS	Department for Digital, Culture, Media & Sport
DMU	De Montfort University
DOC	Director of Cricket
ECB	England Cricket Board
EDI	Equity Diversity Inclusive
EE	Employment Equity
ESS	Environmentally Sustainable Stadiums
ESSPC	Event Safety and Security Planning Committee
FA	Football Association
FIFA	Federation of International Football Association
FINA	Fédération Internationale de Natation

GSAS	Global Sustainability Assessment System
IBA	International Boxing Association
ICC	International Cricket Council
ICEC	Independent Commission for Equity in Cricket
IDSA	Institute of Directors in South Africa
IOC	International Olympic Committee
ISE	International Sporting Event
ISV	International Sporting Venue
KHS	Klerksdorp High School
LEED	Leadership in Energy and Environmental Design
LGBTQ	Lesbian, Gay, Bisexual, Transgender, and Questioning
LOC	Local Organising Committee
MC	Members Council
MCC	Melbourne Cricket Club
NCA	National Credit Act
NCTSN	National Child Traumatic Stress Network
NCU	Northerns Cricket Union
NSA	Netball South Africa
NWU	North-West University
PFC	Prefrontal Cortex
PMR	Progressive Muscle Relaxation
PPP	Public-Private Partnerships
PSED	Public Sector Equality Duty
PSL	Premier Soccer League
RFU	Rugby Football Union
SACA	South African Cricketers Association
SAFA	South African Football Association
SAIDS	South African Institute for Drug-Free Sport

SAPS	South African Police Service
SARU	South African Rugby Union
SASCOC	South African Sports Confederation and Olympic Committee
SASREA	Safety at Sports and Recreational Events Act
SJN	Social Justice and Nation Building hearings
SOP	Standard Operating Procedure
UNISA	University of South Africa

Chief Executives Meeting 2013. I was the Acting CEO at CSA

Titans men's Team 2-17/2018 Season. This is one of the strongest domestic teams in the world outside the T20 circuit. (Rayder Media)

Titans women's team 2024 (Rayder Media)

Lords, UK. Acting CEO of CSA. The Proteas became the one team in all 3 formats. (CricTracker)

Professors Leenta Grobler, and Ronnie Lotriet, colleagues at NWU Business School (Jake Media)

SA 20 After party, Cape Town with Janie Marais and Steven Cook

Celebrating 10 Years at Titans in 2023. SuperSport Park (Rayder Media)

CHAPTER 1

MY 20-YEAR CAREER IN (TRYING) TO MANAGE CRISES IN SPORT

Jacques Faul

Introduction

I have been blessed to serve in sports in various capacities for 27 years. It has been memorable, with more good times than bad. I have experienced challenges on all levels. This book aims to provide a resource I wish I had when I started my career in sports. I have been depressed and had burnout syndrome during my career. I am still thankful to be involved in an industry that I love. I hope to offer, with my co-contributors, a book that will help people in sports to deal with the many challenges they will face. They will be learning from my own experiences. Dealing with the various challenges can be daunting.

My life in sport

I have always loved sports; as a young child, I participated in most sports at school. I excelled in cricket. I started playing club cricket at 13 years old. I was on a club committee in my early 20s; I served on a provincial federation board at 27 and was appointed a professional sports CEO at 34. I became the acting Cricket South Africa (CSA) CEO in March 2012 and again in December 2019. At the time of writing the book, I have been blessed to be a CEO in cricket for 20 years. I have attended cricket committee and board meetings from Klerksdorp Cricket Club to the International Cricket Council and everything in between.

I worked as a coach and administrator in the cricket industry. Ironically, all I ever wanted was to be a professional cricket player. I represented various provincial teams for North West Cricket; however, I now realise I was not good enough to become a full-time professional player. The fact that I played at a reasonable level and coached cricket did help me in my career. It is easier to manage a sports organisation if you know the sporting code and its inner workings. Becoming an effective leader or manager within a sporting code without previous involvement is however, not impossible. But I have benefitted tremendously from my involvement as a player, coach and management participant on various levels.

In hindsight, I realised that the management structures I served on were not always effective; even though these structures were influential within the sporting fraternity, how they dealt with a crisis reflected the leadership required at their level. The ineffective management mainly resulted from inexperience, lack of urgency or, on the other hand, a total overreaction. Personal agendas, including vested interest, played a role. My experience is that a lack of intellect seldom played a role in failing to address a crisis. I have seen intelligent people getting it wrong. I was blessed to be part of sporting structures that often effectively dealt with solving problems. There are lessons to be learnt from both failures and successes.

In my 20-year career, I had to deal with staff being murdered and a young player drowning, defend myself against allegations of racism, deal with fraud and theft, and lead CSA when almost all sponsors withdrew. The COVID-19 pandemic was a crisis. These are not all I had to deal with but merely the crises that came to mind immediately. Hindsight is a perfect science; reflecting on my handling of these crises, it is easy to see what we did right and what we did not. This book aims to record 20 years of lessons so others can learn from it.

Club Cricket

I started playing club cricket as a 13-year-old and was blessed to be able to play for 20 years. I was in the management structure of a club in my early 20s. The crises were related to the on-field performance, facilities, and funding. Succession planning was not a focus, and the clubs sometimes depended on only one person. There was always a lack of a long-term vision for the club. Club cricket administrators at this level are foot soldiers of the game and serve at the grassroots level. Their ability to solve challenges relied on experience and wisdom.

North West Cricket Board (NWC)

I was elected to the NWC board in 1996. I was 27 years old at the time and still playing. Lourens Vorster and I started a cricket academy at my alma mater, Klerksdorp High School (KHS). The same year, I was elected as a board member of the North West Cricket Board. We had an entrepreneurial president in Mickey Gordon and a first full-time CEO in John Openshaw. Both gentlemen worked tirelessly to advance the union. We built a new stadium in Potchefstroom and hosted the 2003 World Cup. Even as a young board member, I noticed the danger of vested interest and the threat of unregulated power. I also came across people who serve the game of cricket unconditionally.

My time on the board was a good learning experience for me. Cricket administration was mainly unstructured, with no focus on governance. The challenge for the North West Cricket Union came when CSA suggested introducing a 6-structure team instead of an 11- structure team. I clearly remember how emotionally we reacted to it. We saw it as the end for us, and it would nullify everything we had worked for. John Openshaw resigned because of the new proposed structure.

North West Cricket CEO

In 2003, I was appointed General Manager and later CEO of the union. The first challenge was that we lost our status as a professional team and needed to join Gauteng to have a combined team. I made a conscious decision to embrace the new franchise system.

As a young CEO, I realised I was out of my depth. I studied part-time for 17 years and continued to gain knowledge. This equipped me better for my new role. I must emphasise the value of training at all levels. I grew every time I studied. North West cricket flourished, and I appointed young go-getters who later graduated to become senior staff. My CFO, Heinrich Strydom, succeeded me at North West and later became a successful CEO at Dolphins Cricket.

My first real crisis at North West came when a young school player drowned. We had a training camp at Potchefstroom Boys High. Two players went to the school pool at night, and one drowned. I was shocked when I received the news. I did not know how to react. We were not negligent in any way; however, this tragic event happened on my watch. The father told me over the phone, "I sent you a healthy boy, and you sent him back in a box". The incident still haunts me.

North West Cricket implemented a successful strategy that saw Potchefstroom become a sought-after training venue for cricket teams. My early days in the administration were marked with bravery and innovation. It was not always well thought through, but it was ambitious. I realise how daunting it is for a young CEO to take charge of a union struggling with resources. This can be a crisis. I worked hard to sign up sponsors during my eight years at North West Cricket. It changed the perception of the cricket union from struggling to thriving.

Lions cricket

My appointment as CEO at NWC meant that I was the General Manager of the Lions franchise. Our partner was Gauteng Cricket. I had to work with Alan Kourie, the CEO of Gauteng Cricket. Alan was one of my heroes who played for the Transvaal "Mean Machine" team of the eighties. I also met Barry Skjoldhammer, a champion individual who served the game as an administrator. Both gentlemen had a positive impact on me. Alan never treated me less than his administrative equal. Barry taught me that serving the game of cricket is the most crucial focus. Gauteng Cricket had many high-profile administrators at the time. They did not always get on with each other. I realised the importance of stability at a union for a strategy to flourish and to allow the organisation to deal with challenges.

We were desperate for the team to win. This only happened in the third year of the new franchise system. Desperation is not a great state of mind, and I recall we fired a coach who won a trophy in the same season and came second in the competition. He won the coach of the year award, making us look even more stupid. We jumped the gun after the first competition, where we ended last, only to end second and first in the next two competitions. The winning coach, Gordon Parsons, extended his middle finger on the podium. We deserved it.

Emotions drive many decisions in sports. Losing in a televised match only brings about rational reasoning from some involved and not for many others who get blinded by the raw emotion. I was also the acting CEO in 2010 when the Lions CEO parted ways with the Gauteng Board. We were scheduled to play in the Champions Cricket League hosted in South Africa. I was also the team manager. A prominent South African company sponsored our jersey for the competition. They were upset that the previous CEO had parted ways with us. It was a complex negotiation, and I realised how important it was to engage with key stakeholders early and often. They made us reprint their logo twice. I did not attend the opening concert in order to oversee the process the night before our opening game. I always reserved significant challenges for myself and wanted to avoid delegating them. It is only fair that leaders are tasked with the most important and difficult matters.

Alan Kourie was an ex-Transvaal and Springbok cricketer. After his playing career he was involved in administration and coaching and was ultimately appointed as the CEO of Gauteng Cricket. In 2004, North West Cricket and Gauteng Cricket formed the Lions Cricket franchise, Alan was appointed the CEO and I took on the role of General Manager whilst remaining the CEO of Nort West Cricket.

I learned from Alan Kourie, he treated me as his equal, and we made a good team. Alan told me that we must always be assertive. He was never the person in the room who got bullied. His passion for the Lions cricket team was unmatched. Alan was street smart and a character. He also taught me not to sell myself short. I took this to heart.

I was also privileged to work with corporate leaders on the Gauteng Lions Board. I recall how well-prepared someone like Roger Hogarth was for board meetings and his thorough understanding of the compliance universe.

CSA 2012 - 2013

Until around 2009, Cricket South Africa (CSA) was the poster boy of sports administration in South Africa. This all changed with the bonus scandal in 2010. The CEO received a bonus for hosting the IPL in South Africa. At the time, the president, Dr Nyoka questioned the CEO, Gerald Majola, and in a public disagreement, the two attacked each other. The president was removed via a vote of no confidence; however, the courts overturned this due to not following the correct process. The process was rectified, and the president was removed. North West chose to abstain during the vote. Some of the board members disagreed with how the then-CEO was behaving. CSA lost most of their sponsors, and there was an outcry from the media insisting that the minister of sport intervene, and for the board and CEO to resign. The minister, Fikile Mbalula, appointed the Nicholson Commission. The commission suggested, among other things, a board consisting of directors that are more independent than the union presidents. Further to this, they recommended that the chairperson must be independent. It highlighted that union presidents have an inherent vested interest, and independent directors add objectivity and specific skill sets. The CEO was eventually dismissed. It was not possible for CSA to fully implement the Nicholson Commission recommendations as SASCOC threatened to suspend CSA as the recommendations contradicted the SASCOC constitution. The SASCOC constitution requires a majority cricket union presidents and a chairperson who is a union president. An independent nominations committee appointed the independent director. This was a drastic departure from the past. The board suspended the CEO after being threatened by the Minister of Sport, Minister Fikile Mbalula. I was appointed CEO on 1 March 2012.

My life as an administrator would drastically change as I faced many complex crises. I got a call from Atul Gupta on the day I was appointed. He said that we must have an urgent meeting about the Friendship Cup. The Sahara group sponsored a 50-over match between India and the Proteas. He informed me that India was angry because the CEO had been suspended and threatened not to honour the game. I am proud of the way I dealt with the Guptas. I protected the integrity of the game and, on my watch, did not allow the game to be captured by a prominent family. At the time, I was oblivious to the fact that the Gupta family was already an undue influence in most state organisations.

I decided that the game of cricket belongs to each fan, coach, player, scorer and whoever works for cricket, and influential individuals will not control it. Maybe it was my humble upbringing or passion for the game, but I always resisted these attempts. I got a death threat and informed Rory Steyn, our security liaison. Rory suggested we sweep my office for listening devices. It was a good idea. The death threat shook me; Rory told me that if people want to kill you, they don't warn you, and the threats were a form of intimidation. Rory Steyn is a security expert, an ex-policeman who was tasked to protect Nelson Mandela after his release. If you can afford it, always make use of experts.

Dr Willie Basson was appointed as the acting president. He was a Northerns stalwart. He started his career predemocracy and became an adamant fighter for racial transformation after unification in cricket. He was honestly devoted to racially transforming sports in South Africa. He was a brilliant man with great intellect. We had a rocky start as he tried to bully and micromanage me. He also became very operational. After four months as acting CEO, I resigned, citing issues with the board. Dr Basson met with me and promised to let me get on with my job and not interfere operationally. I withdrew my resignation, and he kept his promise.

Corporate South Africa turned its back on Cricket SA during the period from 2010 to 2012. During this time CSA received continuous bad press coverage. It wasn't easy to find any form of sponsorship. The corporate environment in South Africa is relatively small, and if some of the captains of industry turn on you, it won't be easy. I realised the importance of better communication and a different voice for CSA. The Protea's doctor and team manager, Dr

Moosajee, suggested Altaaf Khazi. At the time, he worked in soccer. It was a good appointment; he used his charm and media connections well. I realised that with CSA under pressure, we cannot have the same CSA staff speaking to the same potential sponsors and media. Marc Jury, the Commercial Manger and Khazi, the Communication Manager, were untainted and well-known in their respective industries. I knew what needed to be done, but at the national federation level, one always has a new crisis.

I explained that we would implement the Nicholson report as far as possible and address the suspended CEO via a disciplinary hearing. Sponsorship remained a problem. Marc Jury worked with the CSA sponsorship at SAIL, an agency that sells sponsorship. We found a friend in Danie van den Berg, the marketing manager at Momentum Insurance. We needed one credible sponsor to come on board for the others to follow. Marc displayed tenacity in our search for sponsorship. He needs to be credited for the Momentum sponsorship. Soon after, he was appointed as the Commercial Manager at CSA.

SASCOC threatened to suspend CSA if it instituted a board with an independent chairperson. We had to postpone the CSA annual meeting and eventually gave in to the SASCOC demands. I lost my cool in a heated debate with the SASCOC chairperson, and it nearly got physical. In retrospect I should have composed myself better. I sometimes reacted with anger and frustration but usually regretted it later. I got better as I gained more experience. Composure is essential, especially when your organisation is under pressure.

We ended up with a more independent board but without a majority and a non-independent chairperson. I had to inform a top independent candidate, Geoff Whyte, that he would not serve on the board due to the change. Geoff is a leading man with great ethics and executive experience. Cricket lost out on his contribution.

The one focus area that we actioned well was informing the staff about our progress; we held regular staff meetings and were honest and transparent with the staff. Sadly, the staff is neglected as a stakeholder group during a crisis. The staff often lied when questioned about where they work. A training service provider once informed me that our staff introduced themselves to other classmates as Standard Bank employees. When an organisation's reputation is publicly attacked, the staff experience trauma.

Late in 2012, media reports claimed that Dr Basson was involved in the chemical warfare programme during the apartheid era. Dr Basson's enemies had leaked the allegations. This was a big shock as he was a fierce fighter for transformation. He denied that he had any offensive involvement and was merely involved in the defence aspect of chemical warfare during the apartheid era government. He asked me if he should resign as acting president. The problem was that it created the impression that he was guilty. He decided to weather the storm and see his term through. He told me that any storm runs out of rain at some stage. He knew there would be hard times ahead but decided to see it through. Ultimately, he would be remembered for his efforts to transform the sport. The chemical warfare allegations did not define him; he achieved much more.

One of my last duties was to attend the ICC board meeting in Dubai. This completed a full circle for me as I now would have followed board meetings on all levels in cricket, from club to the ICC. Dr Basson refused to attend the board meeting and instructed me to go. He was not keen on attending the meeting due to the allegations of his involvement with the apartheid government chemical warfare programme.

When the recruitment process for a permanent position started, I did not apply. I felt the board had already decided to appoint Haroon Lorgat. He was more than qualified for the job as he was in the previous ICC Chief Executive position. There was only one problem; he had a strained relationship with India. Up to eighty percent of our broadcast revenue came from India's incoming tour to SA. India warned us that they would shorten the tour, but we ignored the threats from our biggest trade partner and paid the price. Looking back, we were very naïve to think they would not do so. CSA had around R1 billion in reserves at the time, and maybe we believed we could cushion the blow. These reserves came mainly from lucrative broadcasting deals.

At the time I often felt that many decisions were made behind the scenes rather than during the formal processes. Despite the losses from the Indian tour, CSA experienced a prosperous period till 2017. We came close to winning the World Cup in 2015 but lost in the semi-finals. There was a public outcry when reports surfaced that the team was changed due to political influence. Such reports always divide fans on a racial basis. CSA was eventually seen as a very political organisation. This may have upset many fans and all racial groups. Depending on who you spoke to, CSA must be the only sports organisation criticised for doing too much for transformation and not enough for change.

The Proteas remained highly competitive during this period, and CSA signed lucrative sponsorship deals. The organisation seemed to have recovered well from the bonus scandal. The period was also relatively crisis and scandal-free. The more independent board added necessary skill sets and experience to the organisation, and Lorgat was an experienced operator.

Post 2012, CSA had a new board with 5 of the 12 directors being independent. CSA had stability and signed lucrative sponsorship agreements. In September 2017, the CEO and CSA board parted ways after a breakdown in their relationship. This was related to the Global T20. CSA announced the series and was in an advanced planning stage. Eight private team owners were announced in London, United Kingdom and presented to the world. The tournament was supposed to take place in South Africa. After the CEO's resignation, it was decided not to continue with the series. This ended a period of relative stability with the Proteas being competitive, although they still did not win a World Cup.

Northerns Cricket Union/Titans Cricket 2013 - December 2019 and August 2020

Elise Lombard, the Titans CEO, sadly passed away in 2012. She was a friend and colleague. Furthermore, she was an excellent administrator with Northerns and Titans for 33 years. I applied for the CEO's position at NCU and Titans and was appointed. The organisation was known for its stability and administrative excellence. They had excellent custodians of the game; I admired Vincent Sinovich as a CSA board member with cricket at his heart. He was the president at the time of my appointment. After that, I served under John Wright and Tebogo Siko, both great men. It is much easier to deal with challenges when there is a trusting relationship between the CEO and the president.

Despite the union's stability, we had severe financial challenges, and the company was not a going concern. The company was making significant losses. In the end, you can only increase income and cut costs. We did both successfully, tripling our sponsorship income and reducing costs by 27%. This was a team effort, and I was proud of our accomplishments.

During an international match hosted at our stadium, we received an e-mail with a bomb threat. The receptionist doubled as the ticketing officer and only read the mail around three hours after it was sent. I ran to the Venue Operating Centre and informed the police officer. He phoned his superiors and then told me to make a call if we should evacuate or not. This was a shock as I was not trained to assess bomb threats. I argued that if we evacuated and nothing happened, I could justify this because of a bomb threat. If we don't evacuate and there is an explosion, I would be held accountable as I was aware of the danger. My COO, at the time, Patricia Kambarami, suggested that we consult with Rory Steyn. He was the CSA security advisor at the match. For the second time in my career Rory helped me. He suggested that we don't evacuate and deploy the bomb squad with sniffer dogs. The first suite I entered to look for suspicious items was the AB de Villiers suite. I ran into my daughter, Leandri; I thought to myself I hope we made the right call. Providing leadership under these circumstances is not easy. I am still here to write about it so it worked out fine. All credit to Rory Steyn and Patricia Kambarami for saving the day. I came to trust both to provide sound advice.

The next five years were the most successful of my career as we dominated on and off the field. I focused on upskilling the staff and inspiring them to seek greatness. CSA introduced an incentive scorecard that assesses all aspects of a cricket union. We won the competition five years in a row. We became arrogant as if nothing could go wrong and as if we were perfect. In 2017 we were brought back to earth with a bang.

We had a case of fraud and theft in our financial department. We discovered it quite early on. The lady was still busy with her three-month probation period. Although there was no concrete evidence, the financial manager wanted to avoid appointing her full-time and sighted concerns. The employee alleged racism, and I made the call to employ her full-time. I later realised that the racism claims were just a cover-up and that the financial manager was spot on. Our auditors advised me to inform the board and all staff immediately. This was sound advice, as one is tempted to keep these incidents a secret mostly because you are embarrassed.

We had a serious wake-up call as an administration. When it became known that we appointed a career criminal with a false ID document, her husband phoned me. He informed me that if we involved the police, they would approach the media and bad-mouth the union, including claims of racism. I was appalled by the threat and informed him that we would involve the police. She left our employment and committed theft and fraud at her new employer about five kilometres from the cricket stadium. She was later found guilty and received a jail sentence. We beefed up our appointment process and did a proper criminal screening before making an appointment. We focused on preventative measures; the value of a crisis is that it could improve operations.

The next crisis still sends chills down my spine. Laudium is a predominantly Indian area in the greater Tshwane area. Four development coaches lived in a neat double-story house at the Laudium Cricket Club ground. In 2017, two coaches were murdered, and two were brutally assaulted. I had to appoint four bodyguards for their protection at the hospital. The events shocked all involved. I immediately informed CSA, our board and addressed the staff personally. I was factual and warned against speculation and rumours. This is always a danger in these situations, and I had to warn staff to refrain from gossip and half-truths.

The hardest part was to meet with the families of the murdered staff. We agreed to cover the funeral costs. One of the family members asked to meet with us in private. He insisted that we support the mother of one of the deceased for the rest of her life. He threatened us with adverse media reporting and with ensuring an outcry from the community. I felt this was unfair and opportunistic. We declined. In events with a high level of emotion, be cautious to act from a feeling of sympathy. The family was also keen for Northerns Cricket to take some form of accountability for the murders.

We clarified that we were shocked and saddened by the horrific events but were not accountable for their murders. I was careful with my terminology when engaging with the family to avoid creating expectations. Meeting someone who has lost their son while in your employ is never easy, and it still haunts me. At the time of writing the book, the murders have not been solved.

Advising Zimbabwe Cricket

I visited Zimbabwe for the first time in the 1990s as the coach of the North West Under-19 team. I fell in love with the country and the people. They were warm and welcoming, and I enjoyed my stay in Harare.

In 2018, the International Cricket Council requested that I assist Zimbabwe Cricket. I was interested to understand how they went from being reasonably competitive on the field and having financial reserves in the 1990s to where they are today. They had various financial challenges, mainly due to the economic situation in the country and historical transactions. I was impressed with the tenacity of the staff. They were positive despite their dire circumstances. Sometimes, the challenges are so overwhelming that one cannot make drastic improvements but rather make consequential decisions that may have a negative outcome for various stakeholders. Some challenges need unpopular decisions to have long-term benefits. I advised on income generating opportunities and invited them to visit Titans cricket. They took up the opportunity and were impressed with our commercial programme. Benchmarking or best practices is a powerful management tool that must be utilised.

I was flattered that the ICC requested me to help Zimbabwe Cricket. I believe that I did help them. I was pleased when they invited me back to assist further. I could not do so due to my second secondment to CSA and COVID-19. Zimbabwe Cricket remains a stern reminder of how things can go so wrong and leave you almost on the brink of collapse and how difficult it is to turn the ship around even if the current people are competent and willing.

Guiding Namibia Cricket

I always had a soft spot for Namibia Cricket because they are just the best people in the world. I have become friends with Francois Erasmus, a successful lawyer and businessman who has served cricket with distinction. He invited me and our Cricket Services Manager, Johan Muller, to Windhoek for a strategic session. They had financial challenges, and the team needed to be more competitive. For years the federation was mainly run on the contribution of volunteers. I looked at the people around the table during the strategic session. They were all highly successful and ethical individuals. They just needed some guidance in order to succeed.

My advice was straightforward: appoint a good CEO, coach, and implement a brave strategy, professionalise your cricket operations as far as possible. They appointed Johan Muller from Titans as the CEO and Pierre du Bruin from the University of Pretoria as the coach. I cannot take credit for what followed, but it was amazing how these two gentlemen, with the help of others, turned Namibia Cricket into a fairy tale story. They not only qualified for the World Cup but also for the playoff rounds. Johan Muller implemented many of the things we do at Titans cricket. He was an exceptional CEO and needs to be credited for their progress. In May 2023, they were the highest-ranked Associate team, ranked 13th globally.

Comparing North West Cricket and Northerns Cricket Union

Despite all the negative publicity on governance in cricket, there have been very positive developments between my start at North West 20 years ago and when I joined the Northerns Cricket Union. The Good Governance Code and King reports' development influenced how we operated. We were primarily amateurs at NWC, promoting cricket as best as we could versus the involvement of stronger business-type individuals at NCU. This helps when you need to deal with challenges. I had also grown as a leader. We also had access to better external resources to help us. NCU has always been politically very stable, with leaders serving the game. The three presidents (Sinovich, Wright and Siko) were all fantastic ethical leaders. This sound base is beneficial. I was blessed to work with sound, cricket-loving people at NWC and NCU.

Graham Abrahams chaired the Titans Pty Ltd board on an alternative year basis. He is the best chairperson of a sports board meeting I have ever encountered. He has mastered the art of cutting out waffling by board members and focusing on what is important. Graham has always been my "banker" during my career at Titans. I have tremendous respect for him and the support I have received from him. Very few people have so much knowledge about the sports industry as Graham. In my opinion, SuperSport's involvement with the Titans brought a higher level of professionalism to the organisation.

Comparing Consulting with Zimbabwe and Namibia (Turnaround strategies)

I respect the administrators from both countries. The most significant differences are related to the economic situation within the two countries. Namibia has a small but thriving economy, whilst the Zimbabwean economy has taken a battering for decades. It is also easier for Namibia to tap into South African resources. It is closer, and the culture is the same. Zimbabwe is a full member of the ICC, and Namibia is an associate member. Zimbabwe receives more funding but must compete with all the major cricketing countries.

Second secondment to CSA December 2019 - August 2020

I was travelling back from Cape Town on 7 December 2019 and was waiting at the airport when I received a call from the CSA President. He informed me that the CSA CEO had been suspended and requested me to act as CEO again till June 2020, when he felt all the disciplinary processes would be completed.

Since 2017 the CSA board was under continuous attack by the media. A significant sponsor withdrew their sponsorship, and another insisted that the CSA board resign. CSA management suspended senior managers late in 2019. The pinnacle came when CSA management revoked the accredited journalists who had been criticising CSA. This resulted in a unified attack by all media outlets and an outcry from many South Africans, sighting their hard-earned press freedom. In 2019, the CEO was suspended. England was touring South Africa and was playing the Boxing Day Test on 26 December 2019 at SuperSport Park. My appointment was 19 days prior to the test match, and we did not have a director of cricket, coaches or selectors. The President, Chris Nenzani, wanted to appoint Graham Smith as soon as possible so that the other appointments could be made.

CSA commissioned a forensic audit of their finances. This was a noble intention but did not result in much else than the abuse of credit cards. This was already known. There was an outcry when CSA announced that only a report summary would be released. The report was also delayed. The board must have taken guidance from the independent board members; however, they seemed less successful than the board appointed in 2013. I mention this to illustrate a point that merely having independent board members with good corporate experience and knowledge is not enough to solve challenges. In 2012 there were fewer independent directors. The challenges in 2020 were much bigger than in 2012 and the internal functioning of the operations was not as effective as in 2012. The staff morale was low and they were not in a safe working space.

I was concerned about the low responsiveness of the organisation and implemented tracking mechanisms to speed it up. Staff and management were divided. I did a climate assessment, which included both quantitative and qualitative measures. The result of the evaluation indicated that there was a very low level of psychological safety. Climate assessments are a scientific way of gauging the current staff's mood. I was shocked by the quantitative research results and invited the staff to set up a meeting should they need to. These meetings would take place at my office at the CSA building. One staff member was so scared that she requested to see me off-site. I was further shocked by the qualitative research outcomes. The staff felt unsafe. The management team was divided, and sadly, racial politics was the underlying reason. For the first time in my career, I could not unite our efforts. I received calls from all communities warning me that there is an active coordinated campaign to remove Smith, Boucher and myself from CSA.

I always felt that specific individuals within the organisation wanted Smith, Boucher and myself out of CSA. We also conducted the Fundunzi forensic audit, and I realised that specific senior staff were in trouble and would be charged in disciplinary hearings. They needed political backing from the BLM hype and hoped that any action against them will be seen as anti-transformational. It was the worst period in my career. I later had to testify in disciplinary hearings against my former staff. The damage done during that period would haunt CSA for long after.

The Black Lives Matter campaign and allegations against CSA led to the establishment of the Social Justice Nation Building (SJN) hearings. This was a sad period in the history of CSA, where social media seemed divided by race, debating the severe matter of racism. Some claimed all allegations to be accurate; others regarded the SJN to be a witch hunt. CSA was under continuous attack, and in 2011, there was a request by the media and other commentators for the minister to intervene; they insisted that the CSA board resign. There were claims of a bullying independent board member who unduly influenced payments. Add to this that we had to deal with the COVID-19 epidemic, and you will realise we had the perfect storm.

The board remained under pressure, eventually resigned, and was replaced by an interim committee appointed by the Minister of Art, Sports and Culture, Nathi Mthethwa. The standoff between the interim board and Members' Council led to further negative publicity, with the media primarily supporting the interim board and painting the Members' Council in a negative light.

The interim board proposed a new Memorandum of Incorporation (MOI), with a majority of independent directors and an independent chairperson. This resulted in a standoff between the Members' Council (MC) and the interim board. The Members' Council consists of the union presidents. The Minister of Art, Sports and Culture threatened the Members' Council with withdrawing CSA's recognition as an official federation. Eventually, the MC conceded, and a historic new MOI was adopted. This contradicts the SASCOC constitution, and CSA remained the only federation that has a majority of independent directors with an independent director as chairperson.

The new board was tasked to appoint permanent staff and deal with outstanding labour disputes. They dealt with this relatively successfully, and more stability returned. Unfortunately, the Protea men's team could not secure a title sponsor.

The last decade has seen CSA challenged as an administration on various levels. Their corporate governance has been at the centre of focus. The mere fact that there are more independent directors does not necessarily contribute to effectiveness. It does add to the independence and skillset needed to be successful, but it is essential to ensure that the right people without a toxic agenda are selected.

CSA does have the ability to stabilise after a governance crisis. Regrettably, their dirty laundry is continuously aired in the public domain, but that is true for all sporting codes. This leads to a negative perception that may result in a loss of sponsorship and more importantly, the support from spectators. It highlights the need for a sporting body to have a sound governing structure. By 2022, there was more stability at CSA, and more decisive leadership returned at all levels. They were able to deal with most of the issues they inherited. The lack of sponsorship was a result of the sins of the past.

I also pride myself on trying my best to turn crises around; I admit I was much more successful in 2012 than in 2020. We had a perfect storm of challenges with many toxic people involved. Some organisations need drastic intervention before they can recover and will not be able to self-correct. I believe CSA was in a much better position by 2023 with a functional board and effective administration. I don't take credit for it and many individuals involved after my resignation brought the organisation back to more stable ground and they must be credited for it. I felt that there were individuals who targeted me and by staying on at CSA, I would not be helping the organisation.

Lessons learned from my two secondments to CSA

Both secondments in 2012 and 2019 were on short notice and followed the suspension of the CEO. I was more equipped in 2019/2020 than in 2012. However, the latter presented real toxic challenges and issues driven by raw emotion. The leadership in 2012 was less emotionally reactive and more structured. They were also not bullied into a decision that most of them knew was not the right one.

The saying "we are where we are because of who we are" summarises 2019/2020. I have seldom come across the level of mistrust as during that period. Responsiveness was a significant issue. We announced, with the best intentions, a recovery plan with a timeline, only to see none of the due dates met. People in leadership roles actively worked against each other and used the media to fight on their behalf. Nothing was confidential, and even contracts were leaked to the press. You need to have a certain level of stability for any turnaround strategy to work. There was a toxic environment with significant role players being opportunistic in promoting their own interest to the detriment of CSA.

Learning from others in a crisis

The best advice I can provide in surviving a crisis is to start consulting with as many people as possible as soon as possible, especially if they have gone through a similar situation. Be careful to seek advice from only one person. The more information you can obtain from many people, the better. In cases where you are dealing with a sensitive matter, you need to take care of the confidential nature of the situation.

As a young administrator, I was shy to ask for help and, at times, even embarrassed about it. As I gained more experience, I realised the importance of consulting with others. You will be surprised at how eagerly people will offer you advice. Remember the old hands of the industry. They will provide wisdom.

Strategy and crisis

A short-term tactic can be used to address a crisis. I have done this on occasion. It is essential to assess the impact of the problems on your current strategy. The current strategy may require adjustments. The strategy should always focus on continuing with business and other activities during a crisis. The crisis may be reviewed if the concerns significantly impact the organisation. The impact must be scrutinised to assist the effect.

A crisis plan should not replace a strategy; the tactic may place the strategy on hold and impact the way forward. There should be a dual focus. This may require a new division of tasks and duties, with some staff focusing on the crisis and others on the current strategy. To leave everything and only focus on the problems is not recommended.

Low responsiveness is a big red flag when an organisation struggles to cope. They miss due dates, and many of their processes take a long time. Their response to emails could be faster, and every administrative action takes longer than usual. It is often blamed on crises or inadequate staff. There may be some truth to this, but there are usually indicators that a culture of low responsiveness has developed over time.

In my experience, the organisation experiences it differently from other role players and stakeholders. It is genuinely the analogy of the boiling frog. Improving responsiveness is a vital step in the turnaround strategy. Tracking dashboards must make responsiveness visible, and you need to perform effective consequence management. You may experience resistance to these steps. A culture of dishonesty sometimes partners with low responsiveness. This is a dangerous combination and makes a turnaround strategy difficult.

Summary

While doing research in writing this book, I realised I should have been taught crisis management skills and know-how at the start of my career. It would have come in handy in a twenty-year career aiming to serve a sport I love to the best of my abilities. I have seen the best and worst in cricket administration, and this is also true for how people dealt with the crises. Bad administrations were responsible for most of their problems, and they were good at scoring own goals.

It is also true that unforeseen tragedies and crises will be part and parcel of the sporting environment, and leaders must deal with them on all levels. I have had mixed successes in my career, sometimes due to my shortcomings and sometimes due to the environment that did not allow positive intervention. Toxic, unethical individuals will cause self-inflicted pain to an organisation. When selecting board members, make sure that they have a strong moral compass.

CHAPTER 2

WHAT IS A CRISIS IN SPORT?

Jacques Faul

Introduction

It is important to have a basic understanding of the definitions of a crisis and introduce a brief history of crisis management theory. This chapter mentions various crises related to sports. Crises in events are covered in Chapter 9. The Armstrong and Pistorius case studies underline how serious and devastating a crisis can be.

This chapter aims to categorise crises in sports and highlights examples of South African sports bodies that had to deal with challenges. Lastly, the chapter deals with the most current crises in world sports.

What is a crisis?

Kahperd[1] notes that sports organisations are not immune to crises. A crisis is an event, situation, or occurrence (Stoldt et al.).[2] Seeger et al.[3] indicates the presence of a sense of surprise that catches the organisation off-guard. Once triggered, a series of events disrupt normal organisational operations. The crisis continues until the organisation achieves a near-normal operational state once more.

Coombs[4] echoes the sense of unpredictability associated with a crisis but suggests that a crisis should not represent an unexpected event. Coombs also emphasises negativity and threats to an organisation's ability to perform as characteristics defining a crisis. Seeger and Ulmer[5] suggest a crisis represents devastating events that create urgency, threat and loss for an organisation and its stakeholders. A sports crisis is the arousal of an unexpected hazardous situation in a sports complex such as spectators rushing onto the pitch, throwing explosives, and embroilments of players or fans. There can be various other crises in sport that relate to players, athletes, the event and sponsors including doping scandals, cheating and reputational crises such as the Tiger Woods wife cheating scandal.

History of crisis management theory

Zamoum and Gorpe[6] note that the Chinese Mandarin character for crisis includes "danger" and "opportunity". This is true for sports; many opportunities may arise from a crisis.

Pfaltzgraff[7] argues that as we look back, crises have been a part of the personal, domestic, and international landscape from time immemorial, from the ancient world to the twenty-first century. Thucydides for example, describes a crisis between Athens and Sparta that resulted in the Peloponnesian War (431-404 BC).

Coombs[8] said that the roots of crisis management are in emergency and disaster. Mitroff & Anagnos[9] argue that in contrast to the disciplines of emergency and risk management, which deal primarily with natural disasters, the field of crisis management deals mainly with man-made or human-caused crises. Disaster and crisis do not mean the same thing. Crisis management may occur in disasters, but disasters are more significant in scale and require coordination. Coombs[10] states that a crisis can be embedded in disaster and poor disaster management, resulting in problems for the agencies responsible for dealing with it. Disasters require society and society's network to deal with them, and the collaboration process is emphasised in disaster management.

Zamoum and Gorpe[11] conclude that examples of different types of crises are identifiable throughout human history, even though they may not fully integrate the professional and academic knowledge of crisis management as we know it.

History is also rich with examples where public opinion is not paid attention to, thus resulting in negative consequences. Public opinion, public safety, positive image, and less damage to the inflicted parties have been essential pillars in a crisis. For example, Suleiman the Magnificent, the longest-reigning Sultan of the Ottoman Empire, died during the Battle of Szigetvár. Still, his death was kept a secret to avoid further negative situations. In any interaction, we can see any of these happening – information, persuasion, compromise, and cooperation – reminding us of the function of crisis management stages. Public opinion has been an essential force in history, and we see examples of leaders/organisations that have scanned the public's opinion informally and thus showed respect for the people's opinions.

Milašinoviæ and Kešetoviæ[12] note that the concept of catastrophe can be approached from four central angles: according to source or original root (natural or technological); according to consequences (degree of loss and damage, intensity and length of time); according to course of events (interventions of different actors, response, organisation and community capacities) and according to the degree of risk involved.

Crises in sport

Sport has many moving parts making it susceptible to various crises. Historically, several categories have been identified to group the possible crises. Crises in sports are by no means restricted to the table below.

Table 1 Possible crisis situations in sport

Players; coaches + match officials	Sporting event	Administrative	Pre-event
1. Doping 2. Integrity-related 3. Racism 4. Not performing 5. Player revolt 6. Unacceptable social behaviour	1. Negative fan experience 2. Loss of life or injury to fans 3. Force majeure 4. Racism during the event 5. Non or low attendance at the event 6. Financial loss 7. Infrastructure failing: Power/water 8. Staff/supplier issues	1. Governance-related issues 2. Socially unacceptable behaviour by officials 3. Dishonesty or integrity-related issues 4. Financial issues	1. Facilities not completed or ready for the event 2. Bidding corruption claims 3. Withdrawal of sponsors 4. Labour disputes

Mega sports crises

First terrorist attack

The first terrorist attack in a world sporting event shook the world and changed how mega and major events were hosted.

Shipway, Miles and Gordon[13] note that the 1972 Munich Olympics were marred by a terrorist attack carried out by the Palestinian group "Black September." They kidnapped 11 Israeli athletes and coaches, demanding the release of Palestinian prisoners. The situation escalated, resulting in a failed rescue attempt by German authorities. Tragically, all 11 hostages were killed during the ordeal.

Pakistan 2009

David Becker is a vastly experienced lawyer specialising in the sports sector. He was the former Head of Legal of the International Cricket Council. He has dealt with crises in sports on many levels over many years. He differentiates between a threat of a crisis and an actual crisis.

An example of a threat of a crisis is the threat of a terrorist attack before the 2011 Cricket World Cup final match hosted in India. He recalls the anxiety experienced by all. Thankfully, nothing came of it. Another example is allegations that were made shortly before an international game in England that the game had been fixed.

An example of an actual crisis is the terrorist attack on the Sri Lankan team convoy in Pakistan on 3 March 2009. Becker recalls viewing the incident with horror on television that morning, in which his colleagues (match officials employed by the ICC) were being shot at by 12 gunmen near Gaddafi Stadium in Lahore. The driver of the support vehicle carrying the match officials was killed. Six police officers were killed in the attack and several players and officials were injured. The Sri Lankan team bus reportedly had 38 bullet holes from the prolonged attack.

This was the first attack on a sports team or event since the 1972 Munich Olympics. It shocked the sporting world. FBI Director Robert Mueller flew to Pakistan the day after the attacks. Due to the attack no cricket teams visited Pakistan until May 2015, when Zimbabwe toured Pakistan. In the aftermath of the incident, Becker drafted minimum standard regulations for safety for all ICC members when hosting bilateral tours. However, ICC members refused to adopt the regulations at the time, citing the differing security issues in each country[1]. This remains one of the most significant crises in the world of sport.

Crisis and individual athletes and players

Chapter 9 deals with crises during sporting events; however, crises are not just restricted to events; individual athletes and players can cause crises mainly for themselves and sometimes for the sporting code. Two extreme examples are the Oscar Pistorius case and Lance Armstrong.

Oscar Pistorius

Times Live[14] reports that Oscar Pistorius, known as the "Blade Runner" because of his prosthetic legs, went from public hero to a convicted murderer. The court case was covered in detail and drew global attention. Here is a timeline of how this came about:

1986 November 22 — Oscar Leonard Carl Pistorius was born in Johannesburg. He was born without fibulas and had both legs amputated below the knees before his first birthday.

2003 — Pistorius started sprint training in high school after learning to walk on prosthetic legs.

2004 — Running on carbon-fibre prosthetics, which earned him the nickname "Blade Runner", Pistorius became a paralympic gold medallist when he won the 200m in Athens. This shot him to stardom in South Africa, and the world started noticing.

---

1 At the date of writing, ICC members are encouraged to adopt template minimum safety processes at national level when hosting bilateral matches.

2008 — Pistorius won three gold medals at the Paralympics in Beijing.

2012 — Hailed as a turning point for disabled athletes, Pistorius became the first double amputee to compete at the Olympics, where he reached the 400m semifinals in London.

He won two gold medals at the Paralympics. He is now a world star, attracting lucrative sponsorship deals, including a Nike sponsorship. He became a well-recognised face worldwide.

2013 February 14 — Pistorius kills his girlfriend Reeva Steenkamp, a law graduate and model, when he fires four shots through a locked bathroom door at his Pretoria home on Valentine's Day. The story receives worldwide coverage.

February 15 — Pistorius is charged with murder in a Pretoria court.

2014

12 September 2014 - Judge Thokozile Masipa found Oscar Pistorius guilty of culpable homicide and reckless endangerment with a firearm but not guilty of murder. Sentencing was adjourned until 13 October 2014, when Pistorius received a maximum of five years in prison for culpable homicide. He also got a three-year suspended sentence for reckless endangerment.

21 October 2014 - Pistorius starts his jail sentence - a tragic account of a world star falling from stardom.

December 2015 - The Supreme Court of Appeal overturned the culpable homicide verdict, changing it to murder. On 6 July 2016, Pistorius was sentenced to six years in prison for murder. In November 2017, the sentence was increased to 15 years. Pistorius became eligible for parole in 2023 but was denied in March. Released on 5 January 2024, he served around 11 years of his 15-year sentence.

Sponsors

Pistorius had many sponsors, with Nike being the most prominent. Weir[15] reports that Nike froze its contract with "Blade Runner" Oscar Pistorius after he was charged with murdering his girlfriend, the latest in a series of scandals to hit athletes sponsored by the sportswear giant.

Media reporting

The worldwide media attention and reporting on the case was unprecedented and like nothing seen before.

Impact of crisis

Pistorius's career and life were ruined, and he will struggle to recover. He had several failed attempts to be awarded parole and had to approach the courts to be successful. He was finally released on parole in January 2024.

Lance Armstrong

The Armstrong scandal must be one of the biggest cycling and sports scandals in the world.

ESPN[16] reports that former American road-racing cyclist Lance Armstrong helped promote cycling to global popularity. His seven consecutive Tour de France victories, from 1999 to 2005, and his status as a cancer survivor made him one of the most iconic and revered athletes outside of the professional sports world. The world respected him as a true hero and an inspiration to all fighting cancer.

Armstrong consistently faced doping allegations, particularly after recovering from cancer and winning the Tour de France a few years later.

The following is a timeline of events:

2010: Armstrong makes his 2010 race debut at the Tour Down Under, finishing 25th out of 127. At the Vuelta a Murcia in Europe, he finished in seventh place overall before pulling out of a handful of other races due to bouts with gastroenteritis. After a crash in the Tour de California, he finished second in the Tour of Switzerland and third in the Tour of Luxembourg. In the 2010 Tour De France, which he had said would be his final, he finished in 23rd place. However, Team RadioShack won the team competition thanks to Armstrong's contributions.

At the same time, American cyclist Floyd Landis, who was Armstrong's teammate for two years and won the 2006 Tour De France, admits he used performance-enhancing drugs. In emails to United States and European cycling officials, Landis says he began doping in 2002 – his first year alongside Armstrong, who again denies the allegations against him, saying in May: "It's our word against his word. I like our word. We like our credibility. Floyd lost his credibility a long time ago." Those strong words by Armstrong would come back to bite him.

2011: Armstrong again announced his retirement from competitive cycling in February, at age 39, to focus on his family and his cancer foundation. But the walls obscuring his past use of performance-enhancing drugs are cracking. Two other U.S. Postal team members came forward, acknowledging their PED use and further implicating Armstrong.

2012: Federal prosecutors drop their criminal investigation against Armstrong and the U.S. Postal Service team in February, with no charges filed. However, the United States Anti-Doping Agency accused Armstrong of doping and trafficking drugs in June. In October, the

USADA formally charged him with using, possessing, and trafficking banned substances and recommended a lifetime ban. In choosing not to appeal the findings, Armstrong was stripped of all his achievements from August 1998 onward, including his seven Tour de France titles. Armstrong still publicly denies the use of performance-enhancing drugs.

2013: In a January interview with Oprah Winfrey, Armstrong finally admits to doping during each Tour de France win from 1999 to 2005. The revelation shocked the world and disgraced Armstrong as a sporting hero.

Sponsors

As with Pistorius, Nike ended its contract with Armstrong.

Impact

Armstrong will remain a disgraced sportsman and lost out on millions of dollars in endorsements.

Sporting organisations

Various sporting organisations have been facing challenges, as the table below illustrates.

Table 2 Crises: Sporting Organisations

Organisation	Crisis
Cricket South Africa 2012	Bonus scandal
Cricket South Africa 2019/2020	Revoking of accreditation/BLM/CSA Board and Council dispute
South African Football Association 2023	Allegations of financial mismanagement
South African Rugby Union 2023	Elton Jantjies and Zeenat Simjee affair
South African Athletics 2011	President fired for lying
Tennis South Africa 2015	Bob Hewit sex scandal
SA Netball 2023	Allegations of mismanagement and bullying

It should be stated that not all allegations are facts. However, the negative media reporting and public perception may cause damage to the sporting organisation.

The recent crises in world sport

Calacus[17] reports on the three crises in 2022 relating to sports: FIFA World Cup, LIV golf and IBA (Boxing).

FIFA World Cup Qatar 2022

Calacus notes that not all was well during the FIFA World Cup in Qatar. There were serious rumours about the bidding process. The World Cup was moved to the winter, an unprecedented move that divided the domestic seasons in Europe in two.

The reports suggest 6,500 migrant construction worker deaths with reports of terrible working and living conditions, which has seen the tournament labelled "The World Cup built on modern slavery." Qatar's strict alcohol controls were extended with no alcohol sold at stadia apart from the hospitality sections, with sponsor Budweiser losing out.

FIFA, who has been criticised for its treatment of the LGBTQ+ community in Qatar, threatened teams with sporting sanctions if players wore a rainbow armband with "One Love" on it.

LIV Golf

A new golf competition, LIV Golf, backed by Saudi Arabia's funding, aimed to broaden and widen the appeal of the game. However, LIV Golf has always seemed to be a money-making scheme for its players without the need for the recognition that a sporting competition requires. In the usually conservative sport of golf, introducing a new concept and format is not bad if presented positively. Prominent golfers such as Rory McIlroy and Tiger Woods criticised players joining the tour.

But LIV Golf came in with a bold, aggressive, and some might say arrogant approach that appeared intent on upsetting more than just the status quo. "Sportwashing" has become a term used for countries trying to improve their image.

IBA

Boxing, one of the first sports at the Olympic Games, has been hindered in controversy for a long time, with in-fighting and accusations of corruption causing the sport to fall into a crisis.

The International Olympic Committee (IOC) has stripped the International Boxing Association (IBA) of its rights to organise boxing events at the Paris 2024 Olympic Games, the second consecutive Games it will be excluded from due to ongoing concerns over governance issues.

Financial crisis

Many sporting bodies have experienced financial sustainability challenges. Cantillon[18] states that the UK rugby club, Wasps, owe £2m in unpaid taxes and £35m to bondholders related to the purchase of their stadium in 2014; they have continually made losses. The club have won four Premiership titles and two European Cups. This came on the back of the news that Worcester Rugby Club have been relegated from Premiership, in addition the club lost their entire playing and coaching staff due to the company holding the contracts going into liquidation; the future of the club rests on a takeover. These two famous European rugby clubs are examples of the drastic impact of a financial crisis.

Conclusion

There are many examples of challenges and crises in sports. This trend will continue. A crisis is usually an unexpected event that most likely damages organisations, teams and sporting organisations. A crisis poses both danger and opportunity.

The impact of public opinion during a crisis should not be underestimated. Governance issues and integrity-related behaviour are primarily at the heart of self-inflicted crises for sporting organisations and athletes. Terrorism has been mostly absent in sports since the 1972 Munich massacre. However, it showed its ugly face again in the Pakistan shooting incident during the Sri Lankan cricket tour in 2009. World events present a platform for activist groups to raise their voices, and the impact of this should not be underestimated.

CHAPTER 3

MANAGING CRISES IN SPORT - LESSENS FROM CEOs IN SPORT

Suané Nortje & Ivanke Broodryk

Introduction

Professor Jacques Faul established the CEOs in Sport Association in 2019 to create a platform for senior-level executives in the sports industry to connect, share expertise, and foster professional growth. The association aims to support and promote executive-level administration, recognise contributions at the senior level, contribute to the sports administration field, and provide a communication platform for sports executives. Over the past two years, the association has rapidly expanded, attracting participation from rugby, cricket, soccer, athletics, and golf, as well as professionals like CEOs, managing directors, and directors. The association has proven to be a valuable networking opportunity for sports industry professionals, allowing them to meet and interact with key figures in their field.

In May 2022, the association held its first CEOs in Sports Indaba at Camp Discovery. Sponsored by South African Breweries and Camp Discovery, the conference brought together 40 CEOs from various sports fields to discuss critical topics affecting the sports industry, such as dispute resolution, diversity, conflict management, and stakeholder management.

Building on the success of the first conference, the association held its second event at Sun City Resort in the North West Province, again sponsored by South African Breweries.

The conference focused on two key themes: stadiums and facilities in sports and crisis management in sports. This chapter delves deeper into the latter theme, summarising the content presented by a range of speakers.

Prof. Jacques Faul - 10 interviews: Crises in Sport

At this conference the interviews covered various sports, including five cricket-related interviews, two soccer-related interviews, and three rugby-related interviews, and yielded 20 valuable lessons for crisis management.

The 20 lessons learned from Professor Faul's interviews with individuals who experienced a crisis in their respective fields within the sporting industry are:

1. Surround yourself with a war room of experts you can trust.
2. Put up a brave face. People don't get on a plane with a nervous pilot.
3. Protect yourself from emotional scars.
4. If possible, slow down decision-making.
5. Remember process, procedure, and policy.
6. Don't be forced into drastic decision-making due to pressure.
7. Involve many experts and obtain second opinions.
8. Have clarity on facts, assumptions, opinions, or rumours.
9. Have a well-thought-out action plan.
10. Inform key stakeholders as soon as possible.
11. Don't expect support from people just because you have been supportive.
12. Honor due dates, especially if communicated to the public. Be careful to communicate a specific date (rather than a week or month).
13. Inform/update staff.
14. Establish a clear media protocol; not everybody can speak to the press.
15. Stay calm, and don't overthink.
16. Be careful not to stimulate attention to the crisis.
17. Manage your audience; timing; message, and messenger.
18. Don't forget about your day-to-day business.
19. Debate issues, not people.
20. Mediate disputes or set up a forum to discuss disputes.

Chapter 3: Managing Crises in Sport - Lessens from CEOs in Sport

Dealing with the worst-case scenario

> ## Luxolo September - CAF
>
> Luxolo September is an executive with over 15 years of experience working for top organisations in the sports industry. Currently, he is the Head of Operations and Media Relations at the Confederation of African Football (CAF), where he is responsible for selling media rights in 54 African countries and 50 other countries. He is also the founder of Moonlight and works as a communications advisor, where he closely collaborates with the president of CAF and CAF itself to manage crises and messaging. September has a wealth of international sports industry experience, having worked at organisations such as the Premier Soccer League (PSL), the Federation of International Football Association (FIFA), the Council of Southern Africa Football Associations (COSAFA), and as a consultant for CAF for a decade.
>
> September is a versatile sports industry expert with proficiency in various areas, including project management, commercial and TV rights, operations, eventing, content management, media licensing, reputation management, media relations management, digital media, communications, spokesperson role, and strategy development. In addition to his career in sports administration, he is also an entrepreneur who has founded multiple start-up businesses.

Luxolo's presentation, entitled "Dealing with the worst-case scenario," offered a valuable insight into crisis management. Drawing from his own experience, Luxolo believes that moments of crisis define leadership and that preparation is crucial in handling the worst situations. During the presentation, Luxolo used the tragic stampede at the Yaounde Olembe Stadium during the Africa Cup of Nations soccer game in Cameroon as a case study to illustrate how crises can unfold.

Luxolo highlighted that a crisis can happen to anyone at any time, including the delegates attending the conference. He emphasised that the scale of the crisis may differ, and some may face a difficult situation that could impact their career and organisation. Unfortunately, some may not recover from their most trying times. However, prepared people will be better equipped to handle the worst moments. Luxolo stressed the importance of preparation in crisis management as it can significantly improve the outcome of a crisis.

In January and February of 2022, the AFCON was held in Cameroon and drew over 490 million viewers. The event was broadcasted in around 150 countries, and CAF's digital platforms received over 2 billion visits within two months. However, a tragic event occurred during the AFCON on January 25th, 2022. While Cameroon was playing Comoros in a crucial knockout match, a stadium stampede resulted in the loss of 8 lives. This event is considered the most significant tragedy to ever occur in the Africa Cup of Nations history.

As the game started, Luxolo discovered that thousands of people were still outside the stadium, some with tickets and others without. Despite this, the decision to begin the match was made after a risk assessment deemed it safe. However, misinformation began to spread within a few minutes, causing panic and uncertainty. The initial report stated that 48 people had died, but they were unsure of its accuracy. In such a critical moment, Luxolo realised the importance of clear thinking and effective communication.

Clarity of thought during a crisis involves establishing communication, verifying facts, and finding a reliable gatekeeper to manage information flow. Luxolo provided detailed insight into the first, second and third public actions taken by CAF in managing the crisis. One of the main strategies employed was quick communication, which involved bringing experts on board to advise on the correct statements to release and the following actions. These experts suggested that CAF confirm the number of deaths, send condolence messages, and inform the public of the unconfirmed numbers, among other things. The overarching message was that CAF was aware of and taking steps to address the situation.

The first public action CAF took was a short and straightforward statement acknowledging the incident and stating that they were investigating the situation, working with the government and the local organising committee (LOC), and visiting hospitals to gather information on what had happened.

The second public action was the CAF president visiting patients affected by the tragedy in hospital.

The third public action was the press conference held by CAF. Luxolo explained that a lot of communication and preparation took place before the conference, including deciding who should be present and the conference's tone. Reports and summaries from various departments, including security, safety, police, CAF internal, LOC, and government, were reviewed to ensure all stakeholders were on the same page. The preparation clarified their decision-making process, resulting in a well-coordinated and effective response to the crisis.

Luxolo highlighted the crucial role of preparation, including having a crisis focus group, a crisis communication document, clear communication channels, and clearly defined roles for key personnel.

Luxolo's session ended with reflecting on the lessons learned from the Olembe tragedy. Here are the lessons:

> **Lesson 1**: In the age of information and misinformation, it is crucial to sift through the two quickly.

Lesson 2: Avoid the temptation to be the first to break the news. Instead, focus on preparing for the official position.

Lesson 3: Even under stress and chaos, carefully consider the first words you will issue to the rest of the world. Involve a few people in the decision.

Lesson 4: Get the first statement out as soon as possible. Acknowledge what happened but resist the temptation to provide details. It buys you more time than you think.

Lesson 5: It is essential to have a strong media/communications team to support you, but the ultimate responsibility lies with you. Only go public when you are ready.

Lesson 6: Preparation is critical. Read as much as possible and request reports from safety, security, LOC, and everyone involved in the crisis.

Lesson 7: Decide who will speak and stick to one official line of communication. Only the most appropriate person should face the media.

Lesson 8: Anticipate questions from the press conference and be open to discussing potential questions with your leader.

Lesson 9: Seek advice from someone who has been through a similar situation. They can provide valuable insight and help structure your thinking.

Lesson 10: Be open-minded and listen to advice, but feel free to follow some good advice only.

Lesson 11: Above all, never lie to the media.

Overall, Luxolo's session emphasised the importance of preparation and thoughtful communication in a crisis. Following these lessons, organisations can effectively manage problems and maintain public trust.

James Sutherland - Sandpaper Gate

Prof Faul had an insightful discussion with James Sutherland about a significant crisis he had to deal with as a sport administrator. James Sutherland is a highly experienced practitioner in the field. James, a former first-class Australian cricketer and cricket administrator, had a remarkable career with the cricket union, successfully navigating challenges during his tenure.

He was the Chief Executive Officer of Cricket Australia, when the organisation's major sponsor went into liquidation. Complicating matters further, the sponsor also happened to be their airline sponsor, leaving James with a daunting crisis to tackle. Despite having already booked all the tickets in advance for the season, a fortunate turn of events saw another airline step in to help with flights. However, the financial implications were severe, requiring a complete budget overhaul. James describes this period as harrowing, but he emphasises that overcoming even the most challenging circumstances is possible with a strong product and belief in oneself.

Fortunately, within a few months, Cricket Australia recovered from the setback. Additionally, they found a supportive long-term partner for the game, thanks to their commitment to revisiting the basics and resolving the crisis.

In 2003, another crisis hit Cricket Australia when Shane Warne, one of their star players, tested positive for a masking agent during the World Cup in Potchefstroom, South Africa. James explained how they had to make a difficult decision regarding Shane's participation in the tournament after receiving notification of the positive test result. They didn't want to risk playing him and potentially face penalties if the second test result was positive. James recalls the daunting task of informing the team and addressing the media in a high-pressure press conference.

James emphasises that a crisis encompasses the challenges faced during the crisis and the processes that must be undertaken afterwards. Regarding the Shane Warne incident, the second test result confirmed his code violation, leading to a 12-month ban. James explains their unique situation, where Cricket Australia, as the code's guardian, had to prosecute their star player. Despite the difficulties, Australia won the World Cup, providing a positive outcome after a stressful period for James as an administrator.

Prof Faul acknowledges the daunting nature of press conferences, particularly during times of crisis, and asks James how he handles such situations, referring not only to the specific incidents discussed earlier but also in general. James responds by emphasising the importance of preparation and seeking expert advice. While some may have access to public affairs experts, media managers, or communication support teams, others may not have the resources to access these experts. James recommends taking a moment to reflect, gather different perspectives, and consider the viewpoints of the public, media, and stakeholders involved. He advises against rushing to provide immediate answers and highlights the significance of careful thought and anticipation of the evolving situation.

James recalls one of his top media advisor's two sayings: "Don't break into jail" and "Treat every question with more respect than the last one". These phrases remind him not to say something in a press conference that would exacerbate problems and to approach each question respectfully, even if they seem repetitive. Administrators can navigate these situations effectively by staying calm, adhering to a plan, and taking things step by step.

In 2004, following the tragic tsunami in Sri Lanka, James cited how sport can serve as a force for good. Cricket brought together diverse communities by organising a charity cricket match at the Melbourne Cricket Ground, raising $16 million for World Vision. This event showcased the power of sports to make a positive impact.

In their conversation, Prof Faul delved into the subsequent crises James had to confront, which involved terrorist threats and attacks. The gravity of these incidents cannot be understated, as they posed a potential threat to lives, thereby placing a significant responsibility on administrators like James to ensure the safety and well-being of their staff and players.

James acknowledged the difficulty of making decisions regarding touring countries prone to terrorist threats. In such situations, administrators are not dealing with concrete facts but rather with the unpredictable nature of threats and the potential for incidents to occur. However, their objective is to act in the sport's best interest, which entails sending teams to different parts of the world to entertain the public. This is part of the reciprocal agreement where those countries also visit Australia to play cricket. However, they must carefully consider the possibility of threats and uncertainties.

To illustrate the challenges faced, James recounted an incident involving one of his senior managers who happened to be in Mumbai for a meeting during the Champions League. Unfortunately, the manager found himself trapped in the Taj Mahal Hotel, which was seized by terrorists in 2008. Following the instruction to lock himself in his room, he soon discovered that the terrorists had set the hotel on fire. The situation grew increasingly dire as the roof of his room began to cave in due to the fire raging on the floor above. In a desperate attempt to escape, he had no choice but to leave his room, braving multiple gunshots as he fled. Miraculously, he managed to survive by jumping out of a window, albeit at the cost of dropping his phone, leaving James unable to contact him and unaware of his well-being.

James emphasised the dual responsibility of an administrator—to uphold the interests of the business while ensuring the safety of the employees, whether they are players, support staff, or management. This duty extends beyond the realm of competition and encompasses a genuine concern for the welfare of those involved in the organisation.

The pinnacle of crises that James had to confront in his career was the ball-tampering incident at Newlands, which profoundly impacted Australian cricket, a team dominating the sport. James vividly remembers how difficult this crisis was and how the role of an administrator had become even more demanding compared to when he first joined Cricket Australia in 2001. The digital age amplifies the challenges, with news spreading rapidly, social media erupting, and many opinions being voiced. Even individuals in positions of authority, including politicians, are buffeted by the waves of public opinion and social media reactions.

Reflecting on 2018 and the ball-tampering incident, James acknowledges its seriousness and the disappointment felt by the country, Cricket Australia, and the cricketing community. However, he believes the global explosion and response to the incident were disproportionate. Timing played a significant role, as the incident occurred during the third day of play in South Africa.

When the crisis emerged, James found himself in Australia, navigating the situation from a considerable distance and managing the challenges of different time zones. The immediate response involved stripping the captain and vice-captain of their leadership positions. Simultaneously, they had to anticipate how the situation would unfold in the coming days and proactively manage potential issues. While the crisis was rapidly spreading in the media, James also had to consider the importance of following established processes and ensuring natural justice.

Recognising the need for a thorough investigation, James swiftly dispatched the head of integrity to South Africa to interview the players and coaches and ascertain the facts surrounding the incident. James set a 48-hour deadline for uncovering the truth, as he and the board of directors needed to make crucial decisions about the team's composition for the upcoming test match and determine the appropriate disciplinary actions.

People will inevitably form their judgments regarding the severity of the punishments handed down to the players involved. The two senior players received two-year bans, while the younger players faced one-year and nine-month bans. James suggests that the players might have received more lenient penalties if they had been forthcoming with the truth.

In James's view, the most significant offence occurred when the players held a press conference on the night of the incident and deliberately lied about what had transpired. This act tarnished the reputation of the game and Cricket Australia, prompting a widespread examination of the team's culture and behaviour.

The incident provided an opportunity to witness the diverse responses of individuals and observe how leaders conducted themselves during challenging times. It also highlighted who stood by the team and demonstrated loyalty in personal relationships, within the organisation, among stakeholders, and in commercial relationships.

Prof Faul concluded the session by distilling the key takeaways from the discussion. Firstly, he emphasised the importance of adhering to established processes and not succumbing to the pressures of social media, which often push for rash and unnecessary decisions. Secondly, he underscored the significance of maintaining composure, acknowledging that remaining calm during crises is challenging but vital. Thirdly, he stressed the value of seeking expert advice. As leaders, it is easy to believe that we must have all the answers, but leveraging the expertise of those around us is essential. Lastly, Prof Faul encouraged everyone to consider how they conduct themselves during turmoil, which speaks volumes about their character and leadership.

In addition, James shared a final piece of wisdom: he advised against giving too much weight to the noise generated by a minority, particularly on social media. Instead, he urged listeners to pay attention to the thoughts and opinions of the majority, who typically seek justice and truth in such situations. By prioritising the perspectives of the majority, a clearer understanding of the path forward can be gained.

Professor Jacques Faul - Tiger Woods case study

Professor Jacques Faul also delivered a case study on Tiger Woods. The study began with contextual information about Tiger Woods, widely regarded as one of the greatest golfers in history. With 70 PGA tournament victories and a prominent position among the world's best golfers, Woods had also secured endorsement deals with renowned brands, including Nike, marking the most significant endorsement in professional sports history at the time. However, everything changed following a car accident in November 2009 that opened the floodgates for tabloid revelations of Woods' extramarital affairs.

The scandal unfolded as follows:

> On November 23, 2009, the story broke in the National Enquirer, alleging that Tiger Woods had an affair with Rachel Uchitel.

> On November 27, Woods was involved in a car accident while attempting to leave his home in the early morning hours. He was subsequently hospitalised.

> On November 29, Woods made a statement regarding the situation as a private matter and expressed his desire to keep it that way.

> From December 1 to December 8, eight women claimed to be Woods' mistresses. This number increased to 11 mistresses over the next few weeks.

> On December 9, Gatorade announced they are discontinuing their sponsorship deal with Tiger Focus.

> On December 10, Tag Heuer removed all in-store ads featuring Tiger Woods.

> On December 11, Woods announced an indefinite leave from professional golf, and more of his sponsors subsequently severed ties with him.

The timeline continued into January 2010 when Woods checked into a behavioural rehab centre. In February, he publicly apologised on national television at the PGA Tour headquarters. By March, Woods announced his return to the Masters tournament, and on April 11, 2010, he achieved a tie for fourth place. It was in April 2019 that Woods secured his first major title since the scandal.

Professor Faul's session addressed the question, "Why did Nike continue sponsoring Tiger?"

According to Prof Faul, Nike's spokeswoman, Marian Sylla, explained that the sponsorship remained unchanged because Woods continued to be the world's best golfer, and they respected his performance in the sport. Nike's decision was based on whether Woods' personal choices and actions affected his performance, which is the aspect they sponsored him for. In contrast, Nike withdrew their sponsorship of Lance Armstrong when it was revealed that the cyclist had engaged in cheating that directly impacted the integrity of his performance.

During his discussion, Prof Faul highlighted several vital insights extracted from the Tiger Woods incident:

Nike's support for Tiger Woods was grounded in logical and reasonable arguments. They found justification to continue sponsoring him based on his exceptional skills as the world's best golfer.

Many sponsors terminated their partnerships with Woods without providing explicit reasons, indicating the scandal's significant impact on their association with him.

No evidence or literature suggests that Nike faced negative consequences for maintaining their sponsorship of Woods. Their decision had no discernible adverse effects on their brand or reputation.

Tiger Woods regained public support over time, and his comeback victory is an iconic moment in sports history. This demonstrates the public's capacity to forgive and move forward.

Woods played a crucial role in rebuilding his public image by openly admitting his wrongdoing and taking responsibility for his actions. His willingness to confront the situation directly contributed to restoring public trust.

The prevailing external mindset and societal acceptance during that period may have contributed to a more forgiving public perception of Woods. The framework of social acceptance at the time likely shaped the public's response to his actions.

Cheating in one's sport is unacceptable and unlikely to be forgiven easily. The incident serves as a reminder that integrity and fair play are highly valued in sports, and transgressions tend to be met with severe consequences.

Overall, the Tiger Woods case offers valuable insights into the dynamics of public perception, forgiveness, and the role of sponsorship in the face of a scandal.

CHAPTER 4

LEADING THROUGH A CRISIS

Jacques Faul

Introduction

It is widely held that sporting organisations fail due to a lack of leadership and good governance. Sport is a socially constructed phenomenon and means different things to different people. Sport has become a significant global industry. Hollander[19] notes that sport has three segments: participation, production, and promotion. Sport is a truly global industry that has the power to unite probably a whole country. It is so powerful that it can influence the psyche of a nation and stimulate either pain or pleasure by just winning or losing a sports match. It is important to note that a high level of emotion is involved.

Every industry requires good leaders; sport is no different. Good leaders provide direction and inspire people; most of all, leadership is action rather than position. Sports leadership is in the public domain, and their actions are more closely scrutinised than in other industries. The analogy of a man on a stage with his every move being watched by the crowd is a fair comparison. However, in sport, the leaders on an administrative and governance level are only some of the actors. It is the players and athletes who are the real stars.

Characteristics of great sports leaders

For two decades, I have been blessed to have worked with great and not-so-good sports leaders. Every person has their strengths and weaknesses, and like me, are not perfect. I always felt that leaders with a serving attitude made for better sports leadership. People with good value systems help prevent major crises, specifically self-inflicted situations. They speak up when something is wrong. I have respect for someone like Barry Skjoldhammer, who stood up against CSA during the bonus scandal in 2011.

During the CSA crisis in 2020-2022, strong leadership was required to save the federation. Many individuals that were tasked to do so did not receive the recognition they deserve.

Leadership during crisis management

Leaders should note that crises share six characteristics: rarity, significance, high impact, ambiguousness, urgency and high stakes. A crisis creates a period of discontinuity or a situation where the organisation's core values are threatened, requiring critical decision-making. In addition, there is a destabilising effect on the organisation and its stakeholders.

Koehn[20] states that real leaders are forged in crisis, concluding that courageous leaders are not born; their ability to help others triumph over adversity is not written into their genetic code, but they are shaped as leaders during a crisis. During an emergency, leadership is most needed. Think of a leader as someone standing on a stage with their followers looking at them; they see her every move. The business icon, Johann Rupert, once said "nobody wants to get on a plane with a nervous pilot". A leader needs to provide direction and guidance during a crisis. Many South African sporting bodies have been embroiled in crises, and their poor leadership only increased the negative impact of the crisis. In many cases, the leadership is directly responsible for the crisis, but in other cases, they do not have the experience and skill to deal with it.

There is a proven methodology for dealing with a crisis that, in a broad overview of leadership duties, includes:

1. Get everybody involved to calm down as much as possible.
2. Analyse and assess the factual evidence of the crisis.
3. Obtain the best expert advice possible.
4. Appoint a crisis team.
5. Draft a response plan.
6. Communicate with stakeholders proactively.
7. Action your plan, review and adjust.
8. Learn from the crisis.

A crisis management template for sport is included at the end of this book.

Brand and communication

Sports leaders should not seek the limelight and attention; this should be reserved for athletes and players. However, sports leaders are public figures and will have their own brands, especially if they are ex-players or athletes. They, along with the team, are the face of the sports organisation. In an era of active social media, it is essential to note that the leader's brand will be scrutinised daily.

Teams and sports organisations are brands, as are sponsors; the latter will not associate with sports brands that do not reflect their values. Sports leaders' communication abilities are vital as they operate in the public domain; they must address crowds, meetings and the media. They should be strongly encouraged to receive formal training to help them master this skill.

During a crisis, the leader stands out even more as the face of the organisation. Good communication skills are vital. There is a danger in being forced into admitting certain things or reacting in a popular way rather than clinically addressing the issues. I have witnessed leaders under pressure trying to anticipate what message will calm the storm, just to be confronted with a more significant storm because procedures and rules were not followed. An emotional response is never recommended. This does not mean the leader should not show empathy.

Toxic leadership

Robbins et al.[21] states that toxic leadership is a pattern of repeated, deliberate, destructive behaviour and mistreatment of subordinates. Further to this, it influences the victim's health and productivity. It creates a fearful environment. It is tough to deal with this as the leader intimidates the subordinates, and they fear repercussions. Nonperformers may lay claims of toxic leadership as a survival strategy.

The Indian Express[22] news article published on 9 July 2021 reports: "ICC (International Cricket Council) CEO Manu Sawhney resigns amid inquiry over conduct". It is alleged that Sawhney's "authoritarian style of functioning" is far removed from the inclusive approach of Richardson and has not gone down well with the employees. He has resigned pending an enquiry. The article further suggests that he had an abrasive attitude towards his colleagues. These allegations were taken so seriously that the ICC investigated his behaviour. Similar claims were made against a high-ranking Cricket South Africa official involving the unfair dismissal of Clive Eksteen in 2020.

Leaders, including sports leaders, are influential, and processes must be established to track and address such behaviour. Anonymous staff questionnaires will be of great value. Mentorship programmes for young leaders are encouraged. Everyone needs to buy into a code of conduct based on respect. This includes the leaders of a sporting organisation.

I believe too many toxic individuals were involved in 2020 during my second stint at CSA. This made it almost impossible to implement a turnaround strategy.

Fractal crisis theory

Leaders should be mindful to include staff on all levels when designing the response to a crisis. Topper & Lagadec[23] state that Fractal Crisis Theory teaches us that crises happen on all scales. Further, the built-in invariants imply that leaders and decision-makers will be impacted by effects the same as those closer to the situation. It would be a big mistake to take the decision power away from those closest to the ground, being in the best position to evaluate their needs, and giving it to people far from ground level and supposedly less impacted by the crisis.

What is important is the conflict between how decisions circulate and how information flows. There are more effective approaches than a complete top-down or bottom-up approach. An inclusive approach is strongly suggested, with early consultation recommended. It will allow buy-in to a recovery plan.

Strategic leadership

Leadership's primary function is to provide strategic direction during a crisis. I was acting CEO at CSA during the COVID-19 pandemic. There was a high level of uncertainty. The CEO of Boland, James Fortuin, came up with scenario planning as the basis for our strategic planning. We prepared mitigation strategies based on scenarios. As the scenarios became real, we knew which steps to implement.

Shipway[24] et al. state that there may be strategic and conflicting objectives for the sport following a significant crisis. There will likely be a series of strategic goals for sporting role players. Strategic objectives include to (1) minimise loss, (2) provide a quick and appropriate response, (3) ensure rapid recovery, (4) adopt a proactive approach, (5) ensure risk reduction, and (6) ensure recovery to be less vulnerable.

In the aftermath of a sport-related crisis or disaster, typical response activities might also include (1) evacuation of the stadium/event venue, (2) search and rescue, (3) ensuring the security of the affected sports venue or event, (4) provision of relief (be that health, shelter, security, food or water), (5) activation of distribution systems and (6) communications management. In South Africa, this may be coordinated by disaster management authorities.

The objectives of a sport-related crisis management plan may include (1) to achieve maximum survival or injury limitation; (2) to start bringing order to a state of chaos; (3) to provide relief; (4) to inform the public via suitable channels of communication; (5) to ensure that essential services are restored if affected; (6) to encourage self-help amongst sport fans and affected communities; (7) to begin the process of facilitating an investigation into the incident; (8) to protect and maintain the reputation of the affected sports event or venue and organisation; and (9) return to normality as soon as possible.

Shipway et al. conclude that the main aim would be to lay a solid foundation for recovery and ensure that the event and venue recover in the aftermath of the crisis or disaster. Conflicting and competing objectives could depend on the different role players. These objectives and critical priorities will vary between the national and regional governing bodies.

Strategic partners and alliances

Ali Bacher is a world-famous ex-international cricketer and administrator. He is credited for uniting cricket in South Africa in the early nineties. Ali recalls meeting Steve Tshwete, an ANC stalwart, in the Eastern Cape. He formed a close relationship with Tshwete that led to South Africa being welcomed back into world cricket. He states that Steve Tshwete saved him when the transition to democracy was difficult. Bacher highlights the need to have strategic partners and powerful alliances. This is true for your daily effectiveness but can be called on during a crisis. It is essential to have sound relationships with influential people. Bacher notes that as a young administrator, he made significant decisions without consulting with anyone. As he became more experienced, he realised the advantages of consulting and collective decision-making.

Bacher remembers the Hansie Cronje match-fixing scandal and how shocked he was about it. The fact that he had access to powerful government officials helped steer the way. The saga came at a cost for him and his relationship with Hansie's father. Ali Bacher recalled that he always had a good relationship with Hansie's father, Ewie Cronje. Ewie was a legendary Free State cricket player and administrator. Bacher recalls that without fail, Ewie would phone him on his birthday. After the Hansie scandal broke, Ewie stopped phoning him on his birthday. He realised that there was a breakdown in their relationship. He regrets not talking to Hansie after the incident. However, he reached out to his father before he died. Despite the scandal, Hansie Cronje remains a well-loved figure in South Africa.

I know members of the Cronje family and witnessed first-hand how first, the scandal and, later, his death caused them tremendous sorrow. Ewie Cronje was a legendary cricket player and administrator with a passion for serving.

Building a relationship with your superiors

It may sound like common sense, but not everyone understands the importance of having a sound trust relationship with your superiors. I have witnessed CEOs surviving a crisis or surviving longer just because they had a good relationship with their superiors based on trust and transparency. A sound relationship with your superiors will come in handy during a crisis.

I am not advocating that you should not be assertive or allow board members or other superiors to be involved in operations; rather be aware that you need to establish a trusting relationship with your superiors.

Surround yourself with people you can trust

The saying goes, "friends in need are friends indeed". However, it is not always possible to determine who are real friends. I interviewed a CEO who successfully navigated a sporting organisation through a significant crisis. The CEO notes, "I had a war room of good people whom I could trust and who could steer the ship. These individuals formed part of the war room. It gives me great comfort to know that they have my back".

Furthermore, it is essential to involve experienced experts. I have seen leaders fall into the trap of thinking they are solely responsible for developing a crisis plan. Consult widely and seek more than one opinion. Unfortunately, there will always be opportunistic people who seek personal gain from the circumstances and will tailor their advice to achieve this.

Don't show emotion

A senior sports leader noted that during a crisis, he would have to have an almost "out of body experience", putting up a brave face so staff can see that the people in charge are not falling apart. It was emotionally draining and caused a lot of trauma, but there was also the realisation that you cannot stop and must go on. This is sound advice that many leaders can implement during a crisis. It is the same principle that the general will wear a red jacket in battle so that the soldiers don't see when he is wounded.

I overreacted as a young leader, reasoning that it would create urgency among my staff. Instead, I created panic. I have improved over the years; however, I sometimes still behave this way. If the leader is deflated and does not inspire hope, it is a failure in leadership. Maintaining this level of composure is challenging, and you should seek people you can trust who will allow you to vent your emotions. Further to this, you need to take time out, even if it is for just one day.

Leadership and governance

Becker[25] states that most crises in sport can be attributed to a lack of leadership and governance. A European-based CEO whose club faced significant challenges agrees, saying the lesson learnt from this is that governance is essential. Today the club is more focused on governance, and as a result, they are ten times stronger. Don't waste a good crisis; accept what is happening.

I can recall how someone like Vincent Sinovich, a CSA board member in 2012, had the conviction to challenge the rest of the board on certain matters. He was always well-prepared and was never one to follow others blindly. Board members like him are worth gold.

The leadership is, like all involved, custodians of the governance in the organisation. Governance promotes transparency, accountability, and adherence to procedures. During a crisis, panic may result in making rushed decisions, disregarding the governance requirements.

Pressure from the media

The media only reports on the information known to them. For various reasons, some information will not be known to them. The media may also sensationalise certain aspects of a story. Sports are covered extensively in the media, and dirty laundry is always a good story. The press may pressure leaders to respond in a certain way or create urgency with them. Leaders may be pressured to act swiftly without considering all the facts.

I have witnessed a reporter write that "surely the board needs to meet and discuss the matter". I then received calls from board members to call a board meeting. I replied that we had a meeting scheduled in a month, but they insisted it was urgent. I sensed the pressure came from the media report. The press is not always wrong, but one should be careful not to let the media influence decisions to stop adverse reporting.

Leadership mistakes during a crisis in sport

I have witnessed and made a few of the following leadership mistakes during a sporting crisis:

1   **Absent and not visible**

    Leaders need to be present and visible during a time of crisis. They need to be seen to deal with urgent matters actively.

2   **Trying to solve everything yourself**

    Especially during a major crisis, you are going to need help. Embrace the contributions of others.

3   **Being bullied**

    Leaders are sometimes vulnerable during a crisis, and opportunistic bullies may use the opportunity to further their agenda. Leaders get harassed into decisions they know are incorrect just to avoid conflict with bullies. This seldom leads to anything good.

4   **Not communicating**

    Communication is vital during a crisis, and leaders must communicate often and effectively. This includes communication with key stakeholders.

5   **Not verifying information**

    Leaders make crucial decisions based on assumptions and unverified information. This may have drastic consequences. It is also embarrassing when assumptions turn out to be incorrect.

6. *Overreacting*

This is a common mistake; leaders overact, turning a minor incident into a significant crisis. The inability to assess the magnitude of the problem may lead to a total overreaction.

7. *Not acting or providing direction*

The opposite of overreacting is not acting and providing leadership in a crisis. Leaders are forged during challenging times.

8. *Calling too many meetings*

Too many meetings during a crisis can be counter-productive and lead to overthinking and wasted time. Decide on a meeting schedule and stick to it. Determine a timeline to deal with the issues. You cannot call a meeting every time a decision has to be made. Group issues to be discussed at set meetings.

9. *Not allowing management to deal with specific challenges*

Some senior managers and sporting boards jump too early, not allowing managers to deal with challenges. This results in managers never developing problem-solving skills.

10. *Reflect on the crisis*

Some leaders neglect to honestly reflect on how they have dealt with the situation and never learn from it or are so defensive that they miss out on the opportunity to improve.

11. *Announcing a plan and timeline and not honouring it*

If there is uncertainty about the feasibility of a due date, don't communicate a specific date. You will be held to that date. Instead, use responses such as "we hope to conclude this in the next seven to eight months if nothing unforeseen happens".

Conclusion

Leadership is vital during a crisis; leaders should be visible and provide strategic guidance. They must inspire followers and show composure. Effective communication is critical to success. The recovery plan requires structure and input from all levels. Surround yourself with experts you can trust.

Don't be bullied into rushed decisions or commitments. Governance is always a key focus point. Learn from the crisis and reflect on how you and the organisation dealt with it. There will be other crises in future, and the lessons learnt will equip you to handle them better.

CHAPTER 5

STAKEHOLDER MANAGEMENT DURING A CRISIS

Jacques Faul

Introduction

The value of effective stakeholder engagement during a crisis is underestimated, and so is the importance of having sound stakeholder practices in place all the time. This relationship will come in handy during a time of crisis.

Defining stakeholder management

Edward Freeman, in the now classic text, Strategic Management: A Stakeholder Approach,[26] defined a stakeholder as "any group or individual who can affect or is affected by the achievement of the organisation's objectives". Typical definitions of "stakeholder" from the public and non-profit sector literature include several variants, such as "all parties who will be affected by or will affect (the organisation's) strategy" or "a person, group or organisation that can place a claim on the organisation's attention, resources, or output, or is affected by that output"[27] and "people or small groups with the power to respond to, negotiate with, and change the strategic future of the organisation".[28]

Brenner[29] defines stakeholders as people who "are or which could impact or be impacted by the firm/organisation". Donaldson and Preston[30] define stakeholders as "persons or groups with legitimate interests in procedural and substantive aspects of corporate activity". Sport has many diverse stakeholders, including the following but depending on the sport, not limited to the table below:

Table 3: Possible Sports Stakeholders

Participants	Events	Facilities	Other
Players	National Federation	City Council	Media
Players Associations	Fans	Suppliers	Other sporting codes
Players' wives, girlfriends and family	Security	Police	Opponents
	Vendors	Traffic Authority	Administrators
	Hospitality suppliers		
Ex-players	Police		
Match officials	Traffic Authority		

Stakeholder – King IV: Principle 16[31]

The King IV report notes the responsibility of an organisation in Principle 16 as follows: "In the execution of its governance role and responsibilities, the governing body should adopt a stakeholder-inclusive approach that balances the needs, interests and expectations of material stakeholders in the best interest of the organisation over time".

Understanding stakeholder management

To effectively manage stakeholders, it is essential to have a basic understanding of stakeholder theory and, more importantly, the approaches to stakeholder theory. Further to this understanding are stakeholders' power and interests and the mapping of stakeholders.

Approaches to stakeholder theory

There are three approaches to stakeholder theory: the normative approach, the descriptive/empirical approach, and the instrumental approach. It will be of value to grasp these concepts. As with communication management, stakeholder management is the steering wheel and not the spare wheel of the organisation. The mere fact that a sporting organisation manages its stakeholders effectively will most likely prevent specific crises. It will be helpful during a problem as you will have a relationship with stakeholders based on trust and transparency.

Normative approach

The normative approach categorises moral guidelines that dictate how firms should treat stakeholders. There have been many examples of society questioning the ethical guidelines sporting organisations follow. This includes the treatment of women in sport, racial discrimination and claims of corruption. Business ethics has incorporated stakeholder theory as an ethical theory to deal with the alternative of only maximising shareholder returns. One of the prominent arguments of this approach is that firms should attend to the claims of all their stakeholders, not only those of their shareholders. Nevertheless, a focus is often placed on the relative importance of ethical obligations to the different stakeholder groups.

This normative approach relates to the organisation's purpose and how it should be responsible for processes, institutions, and society. This approach to stakeholder theory has been used to support Kantian capitalism, fairness, community concepts of the common good, critical theory, and integrative social constructs.[32] This resonates well with the purpose of recreational sport that is for public benefit.

Descriptive/empirical approach

The second approach is the descriptive/empirical approach, which focuses on the genuine behaviours of firms. It aims to describe and explain how firms interact with stakeholders. Scholarly work on this approach has shown that firms proactively address the anxieties of stakeholders perceived to be critical to the firm's well-being because of their potential to satisfy urgent organisational needs. Henceforth, in terms of the descriptive and empirical approaches, firms consider some stakeholder groups to be more critical than others.

It is common knowledge that India is important to all other cricket-playing countries. They will be the biggest trade partner for cricket-playing countries. While traditional economic analysis focuses on shareholders, when the word *stakeholder* becomes part of an organisation's culture, managers can be assessed to determine whether they create value for all stakeholders. India is not a shareholder in other cricket-playing countries but has more economic influence than their shareholders. If the value is designed for all stakeholders, many of the normative concerns of stakeholder theory will be incorporated into the descriptive/empirical approaches to stakeholder theory.[33]

Instrumental approach

The third approach is the instrumental approach. The instrumental process forms part of the positive perspectives. The instrumental policy to stakeholder theory describes what will happen if firms behave in a certain way.[34] It provides a framework for examining the relationships between stakeholder management—which comprises processes, structures, and practices related to the firm's stakeholders—and corporate objectives such as profitability and growth.[35]

This approach to stakeholder theory foresees that those firms that can relate to their stakeholders based on mutual trust and cooperation will gain a competitive advantage over firms that do otherwise.[36] Loss of sponsorships in cricket, player revolt and continuous attacks by the media are stakeholder relationships that could sink a sporting organisation. Clarkson[37] argues that the survival and performance of a firm are functions of the ability of its managers to create sufficient wealth, value, or satisfaction for all its primary stakeholder groups without favouring one group at the expense of another. In this sense, the claims of all legitimate stakeholders are of intrinsic value, and no set of claims is assumed to dominate the rest (for example, see Jones & Wicks[38]).

The instrumental approach houses economic premises but does not address conflicts between social and economic imperatives. The normative approach could address these conflicts.[39,40] Major sporting events are a powerful lobbying platform for environmental and civil rights activists; ignoring these groups as event stakeholders may be catastrophic.

This instrumental stakeholder management theory focuses on the contract (i.e. a metaphor for the relationships between the firm and its various stakeholder groups). The firm will gain a competitive advantage if it can develop relationships with its stakeholders based on mutual trust and cooperation. Implicit in this theory is the notion that the problems of opportunism and a lack of confidence and collaboration are real problems in firm/stakeholder relations, such that instrumental conclusions are appropriate.

A stakeholder strategy and philosophy for a sporting organisation

Every sporting organisation should have a clear stakeholder strategy and philosophy on how to deal with their stakeholders. They should have the relevant resources in place to do so. They should measure key relationships and mitigate possible breaks in relationships. A relationship matrix must be presented to the sporting boards.

The organisation should engage with stakeholders to determine the current relationship status and actively manage the relationship. If it is true that you cannot control what you cannot measure, then stakeholder relationships must be measured and reported on.

Important stakeholders to be considered

The captains of industry as stakeholders

South Africa's business community is relatively small. In 2022, during the bonus scandal at CSA, the federation lost almost all its sponsors. I met with as many captains of the industry as possible and explained our strategy. It made it possible for sponsorships to flow.

Lobbying groups and activists

Lobbying and activist groups may use the international platform of major or mega events to drive their cause. This may result in embarrassment for the organisers and the hosting countries. Human rights and environmental issues may be highlighted. Proper scanning and mapping must be done to anticipate and mitigate the possible negative effects of these groups.

The media as a stakeholder group

A sporting organisation should have a structured professional relationship with all media outlets. Making an enemy out of the media is a crucial mistake. Revoking five journalists' media accreditation in 2019 was a major mistake on CSA's part and it united the media against CSA. The media will not stop writing negative articles just because you stop engaging with them.

It may vary from organisation to organisation, but the media remains a significant stakeholder and should be treated with respect. The media, especially on national and international level, is not a PR company and will most likely be keen to report negative stories. There will always be some tension between a sporting organisation and the media.

Players' associations

I was a CEO of North West Cricket in 2003, just as the South African Players Association was formed. They have done a lot of good work for players and cricket over the years. Tony Irish, a founding member, and the current CEO, Andrew Breetzke, are outstanding and credible administrators.

A sporting trade union must not be treated like a normal trade union. They are much more powerful than that. The players differ from normal employees and are much more difficult to replace. In 2019, CSA had a public dispute, and the sentiment of the public and media was squarely with the players' trade union, the South African Cricketers' Association (SACA).

In my personal dealings with SACA, I have been impressed by their professionalism. The criticism levelled at them during the SJN was unfounded and professionally handled by Breetzke at the hearings. He followed my advice and appeared in person. He testified brilliantly. Players and players' associations will always be powerful stakeholders and should be engaged with early and often.

Ex-players and officials as stakeholders during a crisis

During a crisis, ex-players and administrators will most likely have strong opinions. The media will report on it. This stakeholder group is mainly ignored. However, their influence in creating perceptions should not be overlooked. Ideally, they should be managed actively as a stakeholder group but may be a more relevant group during a crisis.

During the CSA crisis relating to BLM, many ex-players spoke out in the media. They painted a picture of cricket being institutionally racist. Other sporting codes had ex-players mentioning isolating incidents, but not as many as the ex-cricket players.

Ex-administrators still involved in the system or still commentating on the federation can be equally damaging. Especially if they have scores to settle, it could be problematic; they may also be keen to use the media to drive their toxic agenda. The media and public may also view them as credible.

This is a difficult stakeholder group to manage, however, you ignore them at your peril. Recognition for their contribution, courteousness and respect may help keep them positive. Some people leave the organisation bitter and twisted and that is difficult to manage.

Mapping stakeholder power and interest

Sporting organisations have many stakeholders. They have different levels of power and interest related to the organisation. Categorising stakeholders according to the level of power they have over the organisation and to their interest in the organisation, is called mapping.

It is important to map stakeholders according to their power and interest to determine the level of engagement. The organisation needs to understand who are key stakeholders and who merely needs monitoring. Mendelow's power interest matrix is a management tool used to map stakeholders.

Each stakeholder is mapped in one of the four quadrants depending on their level of power and interest and are engaged accordingly. Due to a change in the external or internal environment the level of power or interest may change and a stakeholder may become more or less prominent.

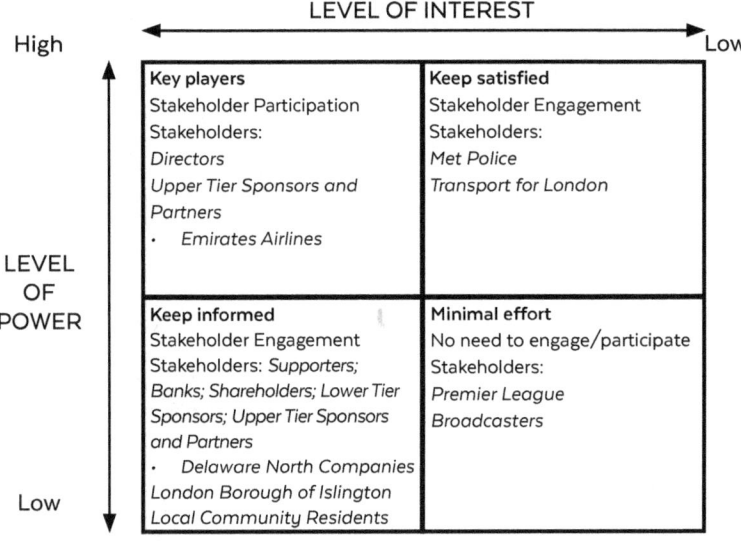

Figure 1: Mendelow's power/interest matrix[41]

Scanning and mapping of stakeholders during a crisis

Mendelow's power interest matrix only deals with the power and interest of a stakeholder. However, legitimacy and urgency must also be considered when assessing a stakeholder.

There is a strong argument for scanning and mapping stakeholders during a significant crisis. A crisis may change the mapping of a stakeholder as there may be a sudden increase in power and/or interest.

Scanning will help identify stakeholders, and mapping will rank them according to interest and power. This will help structure engagement and engagement strategies. It will also direct interaction with stakeholders that are key in normalising and mitigating.

Stakeholders and events

According to Sarkaria[42] communication and decision-making must be evident during a crisis. Pre-planning plays a vital role in assigning different roles allocated to team members. Information should flow both ways and needs to be factual and precise. Similarly, decision-making should be inclusive and transparent for proper outcomes.

Essential questions to determine your stakeholder engagement

The following should guide you in your engagement strategy with stakeholders:

Quality indicators: what will constitute a good engagement? What are you trying to achieve, what is the purpose of the meeting? You must almost reverse engineer the process to make sure that you achieve your goals.

Format and design of engagement: how will you engage? This may include in-person meetings, e-mails or digital platforms.

The organiser of the meetings or engagements will be able to determine the sequence of stakeholders to meet and who should attend the meeting, i.e. the audience. Successful engagements should be structured and planned carefully and you should have a clear understanding of the desired outcome.

Important considerations

Buy into a stakeholder philosophy and have clarity on your approach.

Engage with key stakeholders early and often; this is very important to establish a trust relationship. Be honest and transparent. Stakeholder management must be structured and considered to be an important function for the organisation.

Report on and review your current stakeholder relationships. A dashboard will be sufficient to indicate if the relationship is red (not good), amber (some issues), or green (good) and to provide a list of issues. There needs to be accountability for stakeholder management.

Conclusion

Stakeholder management is important for all organisations and that includes sporting organisations. If you have a good, trusting relationship with your stakeholders it will help to weather the storm during a crisis.

Scanning and mapping stakeholders on a regular basis is vital as the landscape changes all the time.

CHAPTER 6

CRISIS COMMUNICATION

Johan van Zyl, Luke Alfred & Jacques Faul

Introduction

Communication during a crisis is of vital importance. In most cases, the organisation's reputation will be threatened, or sound communication is needed to direct stakeholders and normalise circumstances as soon as possible. Johan van Zyl worked at the North-West University's Communication Department and has first-hand experience in dealing with an attack on the university's reputation by the media. Luke Alfred is most likely the most senior and experienced journalist reporting on sport.

In this chapter I provide a personal context on my lessons learned, especially during my two stints at Cricket South Africa. I suggest a strategy focusing on positioning the organisation under the radar for a specific time to avoid attracting more negative responses. My insights are primarily based on mistakes made by sporting organisations.

Johan van Zyl: Develop an effective communication plan during a crisis

In today's world, crises are a common occurrence that can happen in any organisation or society. They can arise from various factors, such as natural disasters, accidents, scandals, or pandemics. While preventing a crisis is impossible, what matters most is how it is managed and communicated to the affected parties. Effective crisis communication is essential to mitigate the negative impact of a crisis and maintain trust and confidence in the organisation or society.

This chapter will explore the importance of effective crisis communication, the critical elements of a crisis communication plan, and the best communication practices during a crisis. It will also examine case studies of successful and unsuccessful crisis communication and the role of social media in crisis communication. Lastly, this chapter will conclude with recommendations for organisations and individuals on effectively preparing for and managing a crisis.

The Importance of effective crisis communication

crisis communication is communicating with stakeholders during a crisis to inform them of the situation, guidance on how to respond and reassure them that the situation is being handled. The Joint Commission Centre for Transforming Healthcare's 2017 report on improving patient and worker safety, highlights the importance of effective communication in crises. It states that effective crisis communication is essential because it can help to:

1. Mitigate the negative impact of the crisis: When a crisis occurs, the priority is to minimise the damage to the affected parties, including employees, customers, shareholders, and the general public. Effective crisis communication can help mitigate the crisis's negative impact by providing timely and accurate information and guidance on responding.

2. Maintain trust and confidence: During a crisis, stakeholders can become anxious and lose faith in the organisation or society's ability to handle the situation. Effective crisis communication can help to maintain trust and confidence by being transparent, honest, and empathetic in the messaging.

3. Protect reputation: Crises can damage an organisation or society's reputation and brand. Effective crisis communication can help to protect reputation by managing the narrative, correcting misinformation, and demonstrating a commitment to resolving the crisis.

4. Provide opportunities for improvement: After a crisis, there is an opportunity for an organisation or society to learn from the experience and improve its crisis management processes. Effective crisis communication can provide insights into what went well and what needs improvement.

Critical elements of a crisis communication plan

an organisation or society needs a crisis communication plan to communicate effectively during a crisis. A crisis communication plan is a comprehensive document that outlines the procedures, roles, and responsibilities for communicating during an emergency. According to Mitroff and Anagnos,[43] the following are the critical elements of a crisis communication plan:

1. Crisis communication team: A crisis communication team manages the crisis communication process. It should include representatives from all key departments, such as public relations, legal, human resources, and management.

2. Communication channels: The crisis communication plan should identify the communication channels to be used during a crisis, such as social media, email, phone, or press releases. It should also specify the timing and frequency of updates.

3. Messaging: The messaging should be consistent, transparent, and empathetic. It should provide accurate information about the crisis, including the cause, impact, and actions being taken to resolve it.

4. Stakeholder identification: The crisis communication plan should identify all stakeholders who must be informed of the crisis, including employees, customers, shareholders, media, and government agencies. It should also specify the messaging for each stakeholder group.

5. Spokesperson(s): The crisis communication plan should identify the spokesperson(s) who will represent the organisation or society during the crisis. They should be trained and experienced in crisis communication and have the authority to speak on behalf of the organisation or community.

6. Crisis simulation: The crisis communication plan should include a crisis simulation exercise to test the plan's effectiveness and identify areas for improvement.

Communicating during a crisis

Effective communication can significantly affect how the problem is managed and its impact on stakeholders. Seeger, Reynolds and Day,[44] highlight the following as best practices for communicating during a crisis:

1. Be transparent and honest: During a crisis, stakeholders seek accurate and truthful information about the situation. It's essential to be transparent about what is happening and provide updates regularly.

2. Show empathy: Crises can be emotional and stressful for stakeholders. It's essential to show compassion and understanding for their concerns and feelings.

3. Act quickly: During a crisis, time is of the essence. Acting swiftly to provide accurate and timely information to stakeholders is essential.

4. Use simple language: Stakeholders may be overwhelmed with information during a crisis. It's essential to use simple language that is easy to understand.

5. Coordinate messaging: During a crisis, messaging should be coordinated across all communication channels to ensure consistency and accuracy.

6. Address rumours and misinformation: During a crisis, rumours and misinformation can spread quickly. It's essential to address them promptly and correct any misinformation.

7. Provide guidance: Stakeholders may need guidance on how to respond during a crisis. It's essential to provide clear and concise advice on what to do.

8. Monitor social media: Social media can be a powerful communication tool during a crisis. It's essential to monitor social media channels to identify and address any concerns or questions from stakeholders.

Case studies of successful and unsuccessful crisis communication

Case studies of successful and unsuccessful crisis communication can provide valuable insights into what works and what doesn't work during a crisis. The following are some examples of successful and unsuccessful crisis communication:

1. *Successful: Johnson & Johnson's Tylenol Crisis Management*

    In 1982, seven people died after taking cyanide-laced Tylenol capsules. Johnson & Johnson responded quickly and transparently by recalling all Tylenol products and working with law enforcement to investigate the tampering. The company also informed the media, offered a $100,000 reward for information, and introduced tamper-proof packaging. As a result of their swift and effective crisis communication, Johnson & Johnson regained trust and confidence in their product.

2. *Unsuccessful: United Airlines Passenger Dragging Incident*

    In 2017, a video surfaced of a United Airlines passenger being forcibly dragged off an overbooked flight. United Airlines initially issued a statement defending their actions and blaming the passenger. The company faced a significant backlash on social media and lost millions of dollars in stock value. United Airlines' crisis communication was seen as insensitive and lacking empathy for the passenger's situation.

The role of social media in crisis communication

social media has become a powerful tool for communicating during a crisis. It provides a platform for organisations and societies to reach a large audience and provide real-time updates quickly. However, social media can also be a double-edged sword, as misinformation and rumours can spread rapidly. The following case study is discussed in more detail as the author of this chapter experienced the incident first-hand. It demonstrates how social media can be used to communicate to the masses, defuse a crisis, restore reputation, and even how to use this medium to benefit and gain support from a problem.

From 2010 to 2017, the author of this chapter, Johan van Zyl, was employed by the North-West University (NWU) in South Africa as its media liaison officer. In 2014, a group of students at the Potchefstroom campus of the North-West University in South Africa, was photographed and video-recorded performing a greeting ritual at their residence, similar to the controversial Adolf Hitler Nazi salute. The "greeting" was recorded and shared on social media, triggering a series of reports by various media outlets, including the Beeld newspaper. Although the students performed the ritual or "greeting" allegedly oblivious of the similarity to the controversial Nazi salute, the university still decided to temporarily suspend selected students, pending the outcome of an internal investigation.

Students' thoughtless use of social media landed the university in hot water, but the same social media platforms later benefited the institution during the salute scandal. Twitter and Facebook played a significant role in spreading the so-called scandal and the images of the students' actions from the particular newspaper's side, generating public outrage and condemnation. In return, the university launched a massive social media campaign where the institution's response to the incident was also shared and discussed on social media. This tactic generated much support as to how the university handled the matter. Social media provided a platform for the university to respond to the incident and communicate its actions and decisions to the public. This helped to manage the public's expectations and maintain transparency in the investigation and disciplinary process.

In many instances during the publishing of the articles, employees, students, and members of the public accused the newspaper of biased, hostile, and reckless reporting. The NWU engaged social media to reach the masses, correcting the alleged biases by sharing alternative viewpoints and more accurate information. Their support grew to the extent that it later outnumbered the print run and readership of the newspaper by far. Additionally, social media provided a platform for individuals to fact-check the news, and the media organisation was held accountable for their reporting due to complaints to the Press Ombudsman.

The following are some best practices for using social media during a crisis:

1. Monitor social media: During a crisis, it's essential to monitor social media channels to identify any concerns or questions from stakeholders. It's also necessary to address any misinformation or rumours promptly.

2. Use social media to provide updates: Social media can be a powerful tool for real-time updates. It's essential to use social media to keep stakeholders informed of the situation and provide guidance on how to respond.

3. Be transparent and honest: During a crisis, it's essential to be transparent and honest about what is happening. Social media provides a platform to be transparent and provide updates regularly.

4. Engage with stakeholders: Social media provides an opportunity to engage with stakeholders and address any concerns or questions they may have. It's essential to respond promptly and show empathy for their concerns.

5. Coordinate messaging: During a crisis, messaging should be coordinated across all communication channels, including social media, to ensure consistency and accuracy.

6. Use social media to correct misinformation: Social media can be used to correct misinformation and rumours that may be circulating about the crisis. It's essential to address misinformation promptly to prevent it from spreading.

7. Resources: Social media can provide resources for stakeholders, such as hotline numbers, websites, and other helpful information.

Cultural considerations in crisis communication

Crisis communication is not a one-size-fits-all approach. Different cultures may have different expectations and perceptions of crisis communication. It's essential to understand cultural considerations when communicating during a crisis. The following are some examples of cultural references in crisis communication:

1. Language: Language can be a significant barrier in crisis communication. Communicating in the local language is essential to ensure the message is understood.
2. Values: Different cultures may have different values that affect how they perceive and respond to a crisis. It's essential to understand these values and adapt messaging accordingly.
3. Communication style: Different cultures may have different communication styles, such as direct or indirect communication. Understanding the culture's communication style and adapting messaging is essential.
4. Religion: Religion can significantly influence how stakeholders respond to a crisis. Understanding the culture's religious beliefs and adapting messaging is essential.
5. Government involvement: In some cultures, the government may play a more significant role in crisis communication. It's essential to understand the part of the government and adapt messaging accordingly.

Pick your fights on social media

social media has become a vital part of the marketing strategy for companies of all sizes. It allows them to reach a wider audience, build brand awareness, and engage with customers. However, increased social media usage has also become a platform for conflicts, arguments, and heated debates. It is important for companies to know how and when to pick their fights on social media.

Firstly, companies need to understand the importance of a social media policy. A social media policy outlines the do's and don'ts of using social media for the company. It ensures all employees are on the same page when representing the company on social media. The policy should also include guidelines on handling conflicts and negative comments on social media.

Secondly, companies need to understand that only some conflicts on social media are worth engaging in. Before getting involved in a debate or argument, ask yourself if it's worth the time and effort. Does the issue at hand align with the company's values and goals? Will getting involved in the conflict have a positive impact on the company? If the answer is no, it's better to steer clear of the conflict and save your energy for another battle.

Thirdly, pick your battles wisely. Companies should be selective about the issues they engage in on social media. Some conflicts are necessary and demand the company's attention, such as issues related to the company's products, services, or reputation. In such cases, it's essential to address the problem and take action to resolve it. On the other hand, some conflicts may not be relevant to the company, and it's best to stay out of them.

Fourthly, it's essential to approach conflicts on social media with a level head. It's easy to get carried away in the heat of the moment and say things that the company may regret later. Take a moment to step back, gather your thoughts, and respond calmly and professionally. Being respectful and considerate in your interactions with customers on social media is essential.

Lastly, understand the power of social media. Social media can be an excellent tool for building brand awareness and engaging customers. However, it can also be a platform for negative comments and criticism. Monitoring social media regularly and responding to negative comments promptly and appropriately is essential. Companies should also use social media to showcase their values, mission, and customer commitment.

In conclusion, effective crisis communication is critical for managing a crisis and minimising its impact on stakeholders. It requires transparency, empathy, and a coordinated approach across all communication channels. Understanding cultural considerations and using social media can also improve crisis communication. By following best practices and learning from successful and unsuccessful case studies, organisations can effectively communicate during crises and regain trust and confidence in their brand.

Luke Alfred, a journalist's perspective

Crisis management is one of those over-subscribed fields many people purport to know a great deal about. There are agencies, "experts", consultants, companies and charlatans. Most look good, charge much and say little. Your great aunt Hester in Polokwane, is often more intelligent, cunning, and worldly. Phone her in a time of crisis and ask her advice. You'll save yourself from a bomb.

What follows doesn't pretend to be definitive, but here are some thoughts on the subtle and under-appreciated art of crisis management, which will (hopefully) provide food for thought. They could even save you money and prove useful. At the very least, they might even hold your attention until you read to the end and encourage you to chuckle occasionally as you read.

First, some philosophy: It is important to remember that one man's crisis is another man's ordinary day at work. Let's be clear here. If a listed company, famous for its ethical stance on re-cycling is suddenly found to have dumped toxic waste in the sea, it's undoubtedly a crisis. If it is proven beyond a shred of doubt that the chief executive of a listed company is found guilty of insider trading, it's a crisis; we can all agree on that.

What is loosely and complacently termed "a crisis" sometimes appears to be a crisis. Sometimes, the working relationship between the media and a company, federation or institution is poor. Something small and relatively insignificant (a drunk-driving incident featuring a high-profile person or executive) can appear like a crisis. Clue: This probably isn't a crisis. Remember, we're in the age of crisis. There's a crisis around every corner, over the subsequent rise, beyond the next bend. Be prudent; be calm. Ask yourself unemotionally: "Is this a crisis?"

To be facetious, the very notion of crisis is in crisis. Sometimes, the best remedy to a crisis is to sleep on the crisis—to do nothing at all, in other words. If the issue still appears like a legitimate crisis in the morning, then assume you have a legitimate crisis. After that, you can act in various intelligent and responsible ways (we will come to this in a moment) to mitigate the crisis.

The second thing worth unpacking is how we understand—how we conceptualise, in other words—the notion of crisis. Most people subscribe to what might be called "The Weather Notion of Crisis." What do I mean by this? I mean that most people see a crisis as blowing up from nowhere. The crisis is like a bad storm, a sudden downpour, a thunderstorm (with hail) on an otherwise sunny day. This is an unhelpful definition of crisis. It is an unhelpful definition of crisis because it locates the crisis externally, out there, and gives the impression that a crisis is arbitrary and unfair. I prefer to think of a crisis (if it is a crisis, remember) as something that may occasionally happen in the overall communication landscape or environment. It is not an external event but part of your communication world.

What do I mean by this? A crisis is managed better or worse within a pre-existing communication environment. In suitable communication environments, essential people on one side of the fence engage frequently (hopefully meaningfully) with the media and the people on the other side of the wall. This can take several forms. It can take the form of media breakfasts. It can take the form of off-the-record briefings. The media, whether print, social, or other examples of electronic media like television, are human. They like to be liked. They want to feel important and be taken seriously. Know them by name. Charm them if need be. Spread your message in focused ways to carefully chosen individuals. Build your brand and your authority that way. Too much media engagement in contemporary South Africa with non-news worthy information will not be of much value. Media releases must be more specific and scattergun, and the release will land in a spam folder. This is a waste of your time.

Furthermore, it won't hold you in good stead when the proverbial pawpaw hits the fan. A crisis might not cease to be a crisis if it happens in the context of fundamentally good relationships with the media, but it might be lessened or softened if the connection is strong. Like other relationships, the relationship with the media relies to a certain extent on good faith; without good faith, you are lost in a crisis. This is why I wrote earlier that crises (plural) happen in a larger landscape or ecosystem. They might not necessarily be made better if that larger ecosystem is healthy, but they will certainly be made worse if it is unhealthy.

This happened in the latter stages of Thabang Moroe's fractious and destructive period as chief executive of Cricket South Africa a couple of years ago. So bad was CSA's relationship with the media in the latter stages of Moroe's term of office that we had a kind of rolling crisis. The straw that broke his (and his cronies') back was, on the face of it, insignificant: some high-profile journalists had their accreditation revoked.

Although significant, this might not have caused such a kerfuffle under ordinary circumstances. But so fraught—and riven with suspicion and mutual distrust—was the relationship between Moroe and CSA and the media that the outpouring of criticism and anger proved too much for embattled CSA, and they lost all credibility. They couldn't "manage the message" because they had lost the media's trust long ago. A relatively small and petty act sunk them. And it dropped them because it demonstrated simply and dramatically how unaccountable CSA was, something the media had been saying for months but was struggling to prove in a way that captured the public's attention.

Another point: don't fight the media; it will only lead to heartache. If you like, you can neglect the press, dealing with them courteously only when you have to, but don't initiate an active fight with them. Yes, the media are fickle; there are poor journalists and losers in the press; both statements are factual. But they always have airtime or blank space or emptiness in some digital or analogue form to fill; that's the reality. You can actively see to it that your organisation or federation or chief executive is not the person to provide them with scandal or crisis because the media are always looking to fill space, and the structure of the medium is such that the successful operation never makes the news, but the botched operation does. That's just the way it is.

If a crisis does happen and everyone agrees it is a crisis, how best to behave? First, speculation thrives in a vacuum, so get out there and manage the message. You can call a press conference or get on the phone with newspaper editors explaining your side of the story. Take a journalist to breakfast. You can take out adverts as a last resort, although this is often costly and provides precious little bang for your buck.

The phrase used above, "your side of the story", is important. People see the world through different lenses and filters. People see even the same event differently. A Makazole Mapimpi try for the Springboks might be seen by disaffected township youth watching in a shebeen or tavern as a statement for black pride. An *oom* sitting in his *voorkamer* in Klerksdorp might see it as the defining moment in a narrow victory over the All Blacks. Interpretation is everything. And we live in a legally, commercially and ethically complicated world. If there is another side to the story, and that's your side, make sure you get out and tell that story clearly and widely in times of crisis.

Another rule of thumb in a crisis is not to panic. This is easier said than done. Newspaper journalists are phoning you for comments; social media is awash with speculation. Your great cousin Hendrina Doormaker is in contact, telling you she's seen something on the television news. Are you part of a rhino horn smuggling ring? It's very easy to panic. Try not to. Keep your message simple and consistent once you've got your head around "not panicking". Stress what you can say and neglect what you cannot say (or tell the media there are specific questions you will not take). You can even go so far as to say, "This is our side of the story", and will remain so until further notice or when additional facts become available.

Banging away at your side of the story (hopefully, there is one) has the advantage of humanising the debate. Fronting up to people in the media, rather than hiding behind secretaries and underlings, also shows a human face. If (see earlier in this essay) you already have a pre-existing relationship with the media of some worth, this shouldn't be too difficult.

If your communications department has been spamming the media with six irrelevant press releases a day, some about under-9A football in Richard's Bay (if you are the SA Football Association), they don't particularly care for you anyway. In that case, you have an uphill battle. Don't start treating the media with respect because you or your organisation is on the firing line, and you suddenly need them to start treating you with respect.

Finally, remember that we live in South Africa, which we all love and want to see prosper. South Africa is a very odd place. It is even a hilarious place at times. Things change quickly here. Some people have long memories, but most people don't. Not panicking can also involve sticking to your guns over a week or two as the storm blows out. This isn't comfortable. It isn't pleasant. But crisis management sometimes boils down to nothing more than sticking to your story. That means sticking to your account, saying precisely the same things (sometimes in slightly different ways) repeatedly. If you stick to your story long or often enough, you will tire the media out. You might even bore them. If they are bored, they will go on to another story.

If compelled to act, you can always pull the *Oom* Cyril move and call for an investigation. Or an inquiry. Or a panel. You can take up excessive time detailing who will be on this panel, its ambit, how it will be funded, and when it will start. This will take up time. If you do it thoroughly enough, you will bore the media so much that they will forget about the crisis. Why? Probably because this is South Africa. In South Africa, another concern is always just around the corner. That's your crisis management: buying enough time until the next problem appears.

The media are overworked and underpaid. They, themselves, are in crisis. If you want to be cynical, lack a moral compass and don't play by the rules of any game, do what I've just suggested. Remember, this is South Africa, where every day is a crisis.

Jacques Faul: Sometimes it is better to go into hiding for a little while

I have experienced a very intense vocal response in the media during a crisis and a more minimalistic subtle response during a crisis. The circumstances will most likely determine the response. Both need to be considered before deciding on a strategy. The long-term impact of the strategy needs to be considered. The possibility that your response may fuel adverse reactions to your media engagements must be considered.

What is the right approach?

Whenever the sport organisation's reputation is threatened, it is tempting to increase its presence in the media. This is mainly seen as a strategy to defend their reputation and tell their side of the story. In my experience, this can go wrong and attract even more negativity. CSA congratulated the Springboks on winning the World Cup in 2019. The specific post by CSA was attacked in most of the comments posted by the public. The comments painted a picture of a dysfunctional organisation.

I don't suggest that an organisation should not respond to the media. There is wisdom in not providing a story with more airtime than it would have if you had not answered. Michael Owen Smith, the CSA strategic media advisor, was a great source of wisdom to me during my time at CSA. He anticipated well when a story would die down. In 2020, CSA started to ignore his sound advice, with devastating consequences.

The Black Lives Matter crisis resulted in claims of racism against most mainstream sports. Cricket was maybe the most under attack, and understandably, the organisation wanted to be seen to take these allegations seriously. We were very vocal in the media and announced the Social Justice and Nation Building hearings. There were allegations of racism against rugby; to be fair, they were less intense than the allegations against cricket. They acknowledged that there is work to be done and displayed a "RADAR" banner at matches—an acronym for Rugby Against Discrimination and Racism. In my opinion, rugby did just enough to respond to the crisis, whereby cricket overreacted. In the following three years, rugby secured lucrative sponsorship deals whilst cricket struggled to secure a sponsorship for the men's team. I know that CSA's intention was noble, and they sincerely wanted to address racism within the organisation. I deal with this matter further in chapter 13.

Northerns Cricket Union (NCU) were implicated in the BLM and SJN saga; however, they followed the approach of minimum media engagement on the allegations. Titans and NCU retained their sponsors and signed new ones during this time. We communicated frequently with our stakeholders on matters related to the crisis. Like rugby, we did just enough to show we are taking the allegations seriously. The timing of our media engagements was vital. We engaged when the hearings cleared us and we could announce the steps we would take to ensure we addressed racism. I must acknowledge that dealing with this on a regional rather than a national level is easier.

The danger of not responding to the media and not addressing the issue

Problems do not go away just because you ignore them or if you chose a strategy not to respond publicly to them. There is always the danger that the media will accuse you of trying to sweep the issue under the carpet. Organisations prefer to deal with their issues privately, not in the public domain. However, due to the very nature of sport, it will most likely be reported in the media.

CSA cannot be faulted for their attempts to deal with racism in sport and their sincere willingness to provide a platform. The fact that the crisis came after revoking five journalists' accreditation did not help. In my opinion, revoking the accreditations remains CSA's biggest mistake.

Punishing the media because they report negatively on you should not be a consideration; ignoring the press is not an intelligent approach. I have learnt that even if you ignore the media, they will still write about the issues.

Lay low for a while!

A strategy to be considered if your sporting organisation is under severe attack from the public and media is to minimise your response so as not to attract negativity. Aiming to generate a positive image of your organisation during an attack on your reputation may lead to arguments from the media trying to prove you wrong and continuously referring to the crisis. It is a matter of timing. Slowly stimulating positive reporting as the fires seem to die down rather than an aggressive, offensive approach at the height of the crisis, may be a consideration.

I don't believe there is a single approach that would always be effective, but rather choosing what method will work for the specific circumstances. I have experienced how an aggressive approach was not successful and led to even more damage to our reputation. Organisations must consider a strategy that mitigates the adverse effects most effectively.

World Cups – Major events

The Springbok rugby team won four world cups at the time of writing this book. It united the country and filled many South Africans with pride and joy. They received a hero's welcome at the airport, followed by open bus parades. This is not the case for all teams returning from a world cup event. Fans will be devastated and disappointed and most likely voice their dissatisfaction on social media. The written and electronic media may also be brutal in their assessment of the team's world cup efforts. This is very relevant for soccer, rugby, athletics and cricket as these codes have a big following.

The federations need to have a clear communication plan and strategy after these events and the players need to buy into it. Being over-defensive or justifying why the campaign was a success (even if the team did not win the title) will only stimulate a counter debate and fuel already angry fans. Stating that you do not care about the outcry on social media should be avoided. There could be a potential negative effect on a sporting brand, if not dealt with effectively. It is strongly recommended that a formal structured communication plan is designed and implemented on the team's return.

Conclusion

Effective crisis communication is critical for managing a crisis and minimising its impact on stakeholders. Crisis communication is not a one-size-fits-all approach. It is essential to apply the most effective communication strategy most likely to yield you the best results in mitigating damage to your reputation. It is vital to have continuous good public and media relationships. This will come in handy during a time of crisis. There needs to be a clear plan to communicate during the crisis. Carefully analyse and understand the power of social media. Social media can be a tool for building brand awareness and engaging customers. However, it can also be a platform for negative comments and criticism.

The timing of your reputation rebuilding efforts is vital. Carefully consider the long-term effect of your strategic approach. It may cause significant damage in the long run.

CHAPTER 7

GOVERNANCE IN SPORT

Rian Cloete

Introduction

The various governance structures that exist in sport at different levels, such as international governing bodies [Federation Internationale de Football Association (FIFA), World Rugby, International Cricket Council (ICC), World Athletics, World Netball] and national sport federations [South African Football Association (SAFA), South African Rugby Union (SARU), Cricket South Africa (CSA), Athletics South Africa (ASA), Netball South Africa (NSA)] will be explored. Their roles and responsibilities are examined against the specific challenges they face that impact the governance in sport. This includes corruption, doping, ethical dilemmas, financial management, decision-making processes, and balancing interests among stakeholders.

Overall, this chapter on governance in sport aims to enlighten the reader about the fundamental principles, challenges, and best practices in sport governance, empowering them to contribute to developing and improving governance in South African sports.

Definition of governance in sport

there is no exact definition of "corporate governance". It can, however, be defined as a system whereby companies and other entities are directed and controlled. Governance in sport refers to the system, processes, and structures which manage, regulate and direct a sport's governing bodies. It involves establishing and enforcing policies, rules, and procedures that guide the conduct and operation of sports at various levels, including international federations, national sport federations, and local sport organisations or clubs. Corporate governance systems must be adopted to benefit all stakeholders in sport.

Importance and values of good governance in sport

governance in sport plays a crucial role in ensuring the proper functioning and development of a particular sporting code. Good corporate governance makes business sense because well-managed and transparent sporting bodies attract and retain sponsorships. This ensures the continued financial sustainability of the sporting body and gives stakeholders reassurance that the sport is managed correctly. But good governance is about more than rules and regulations. It is a mindset. It is about the governing body's ethical culture and people's behaviour.

Transparency, accountability and responsibility

Effective governance in sport ensures transparency, accountability, responsibility, fairness, integrity, and the protection of the rights and welfare of athletes and stakeholders. It promotes transparency in decision-making processes, financial management, and the overall management of governing bodies in sport. It ensures that stakeholders have access to information which enables them to make informed decisions. This empowers stakeholders to hold governing bodies accountable for their actions, promoting trust and confidence in the sport. Governing bodies in sport must assume responsibility for the assets and actions of the sporting body and must be willing to take corrective actions.

Sustainability

Good governance facilitates sustainable sport development by implementing long-term financial strategies, promoting grassroots participation, and creating opportunities for talent development in the community. It involves resource management, strategic planning, and financial stability to support the growth and longevity of the sport.

Inclusivity and diversity

Good governance in sport promotes inclusivity and diversity by creating equal opportunities for participation and representation. It encourages the involvement of underrepresented groups, such as women, minorities, and individuals with disabilities, in decision-making processes and leadership positions on the board of governing bodies.

Corporate governance in South Africa

Most governing bodies[2][45] in professional sport are run by incorporated entities such as private companies. Unfortunately, most of these governing bodies have a poor corporate governance record.[46] Corruption, fraud, bribery, nepotism, mismanagement and other integrity-related scandals have tainted the image of sport and sport keeps hitting the headlines for all the wrong reasons in South Africa.[47] This necessitated governing bodies to implement corporate governance principles and practices. It is important to note that all sporting bodies should comply with corporate governance, even if they operate through unincorporated entities such as voluntary associations.[48,49]

The King IV™ Report on Corporate Governance

The first King Report on Corporate Governance (King I) was released in 1994 by the Institute of Directors in response to a growing concern over corporate failures in South Africa. The purpose

---

2   King IV defines a "governing body" as the structure that has primary accountability for the governance and performance of the organisation and in respect of a company, it is the board of directors.

of King I was to promote the highest standards of corporate governance.[50] The King II report was finalised in March 2002 and emphasised accountability, responsibility, and transparency.[51] The King III report[52] followed in 2009 and was replaced with the King IV report on 1 November 2016.

The King IV™ Report on Corporate Governance[53] is a comprehensive document that provides guidelines for good governance practices. The legal status of King IV is that of a set of voluntary principles and leading practices. In South Africa, a hybrid system of corporate governance has developed over time. Some practices of good governance have been legislated (for example, in the Companies Act, 71 of 2008) in parallel with the voluntary King Code of Governance. The law prevails if there is a conflict between legislation and the King Code. Company directors have always demanded accountability, transparency, and fiduciary duties under the common law and the Companies Act. Common law fiduciary duties include, for example, a duty to act in the company's best interest, exercise reasonable care, skill, and diligence, act in good faith, and avoid a conflict of interest.

King IV builds on its predecessors' positioning of sound corporate governance as an essential element of good corporate citizenship, with a clear emphasis on transparency. Good corporate governance is integral to society and has accountability towards all stakeholders.[54] With the introduction of an '*apply and explain*' regime, King IV asks governing bodies to be transparent in applying their corporate governance practices by 'applying' the principles and 'explaining' how they are being affected.[55] King IV outlines the following 17 principles that are fundamental to good governance:[56]

Table 4 King IV: Principles

Principle 1	The governing body should lead ethically and effectively.
Principle 2	The governing body should govern the ethics of the organisation in a way that supports the establishment of an ethical culture.
Principle 3	The governing body should ensure that the organisation is and is seen to be a responsible corporate citizen.
Principle 4	The governing body should appreciate that the organisation's core purpose, its risks and opportunities, strategy, business model, performance and sustainable development are all inseparable elements of the value creation process.
Principle 5	The governing body should ensure that reports issued by the organisation enable stakeholders to make informed assessments of the organisation's performance and its short, medium, and long-term prospects.
Principle 6	The governing body should serve as the focal point and custodian of corporate governance in the organisation.
Principle 7	The governing body should comprise the appropriate balance of knowledge, skills, experience, diversity, and independence to discharge its governance role and responsibilities objectively and effectively.

Principle 8	The governing body should ensure that its delegation arrangements within its structures promote independent judgement and assist with balancing power and effectively discharging duties.
Principle 9	The governing body should ensure that the evaluation of its own performance and that of its committees, its chair, and its individual members support continued improvement in its performance and effectiveness.
Principle 10	The governing body should ensure that the appointment of, and delegation to, management contribute to role clarity and the effective exercise of authority and responsibilities.
Principle 11	The governing body should govern risk to support the organisation in setting and achieving strategic objectives.
Principle 12	The governing body should govern technology and information to support the organisation in setting and achieving its strategic objectives.
Principle 13	The governing body should govern compliance with applicable laws and adopted, non-binding rules, codes and standards in a way that supports the organisation's efforts in being ethical and a good corporate citizen.
Principle 14	The governing body should ensure that the organisation remunerates fairly, responsibly, and transparently to promote achieving strategic objectives and positive outcomes in the short, medium and long-term.
Principle 15	The governing body should ensure that assurance services and functions enable an effective control environment and that these support the integrity of information for internal decision-making and the organisation's external reports.
Principle 16	In the execution of its governance role and responsibilities, the governing body should adopt a stakeholder-inclusive approach that balances stakeholders' needs, interests, and expectations in the organisation's best interests over time.
Principle 17	The governing body of an institutional investor organisation should ensure that the organisation practises responsible investment to promote good governance and creates value by the companies in which it invests.

These principles aim to guide governing bodies in achieving effective, responsible, and ethical governance practices that benefit all stakeholders and contribute not only to the long-term success of the governing body, but also to the sport and its athletes.

Sports governing bodies

1. *National sports federations*

    National sports federations (such as SAFA, SARU, CSA, ASA, and NSA) serve as the governing and regulatory bodies for specific sports within a country. National sports federations play a crucial role in governance within their respective countries' sporting landscapes and are affiliated with the South African Sports Confederation and Olympic Committee (SASCOC).[57] SASCOC is South Africa's national multi-coded sporting body responsible for the preparation, presentation, and performance of teams to all multi-coded events, namely the Olympic Games, Paralympic Games, Commonwealth Games, World Games, All Africa Games, Olympic Youth Games, Commonwealth Youth Games and Zone VI Games. SASCOC is also responsible for awarding National Protea Colours to athletes/officials who have met the criteria for representing South Africa in different sporting codes and arenas and endorsing the applications for bidding and hosting international events.

Currently national federations face management and governance challenges unheard of in the past. Public scrutiny is more intense than ever before, and funding for sport is under increasing pressure. Therefore, national federations must ensure they operate as effectively and efficiently as possible. National federations must be held accountable for their internal governance and administration. To oversee the federation's operations, federations must establish proper governance structures, including boards and committees. Federations should develop strategic plans, manage finances, implement policies, and ensure compliance with legal and ethical standards. Federations must establish and enforce rules, regulations, technical standards and policies to govern the sport nationally. These rules and regulations must be aligned with the rules and regulations of the international federation. Federations are also responsible for organising and managing national-level competitions, championships, and other events within their sport.[58] They handle event planning, logistics, venue arrangements, officiating, and ensuring compliance with relevant regulations.

Sports federations play a vital role in stakeholder management. They engage with various stakeholders, including athletes, coaches, officials, clubs, sponsors, and government entities. National federations promote the interests of their sport and its stakeholders at national and provincial levels. They represent their sport in discussions and negotiations with government bodies[59] (Department of Sports, Arts and Culture), SASCOC and funding agencies (National Lotteries Commission)[60] to seek support and resources to advance the sport's development and create an enabling environment for athletes and participants.

National sports federations are also responsible for selecting and managing national teams and athletes for international competitions. They establish criteria and processes for athlete selection, manage team logistics, and provide support services for athletes. National federations represent their country's interests in international sports federations (such as FIFA, World Rugby, World Athletics and World Netball) and facilitate athlete representation in decision-making processes.

2. *International sports federations*

International sports federations (such as FIFA, World Rugby, ICC, World Athletics, and World Netball) are international non-governmental organisations responsible for the integrity of their sport on the international level. International sports federations are responsible for managing the world's various sporting codes. They monitor the everyday administration of their sport and coordinate efforts with national sports federations (SAFA, SARU, CSA, ASA, NSA) from various countries. They establish national sports federations' recognition and membership criteria and guide their governance and administration. National federations must abide by the decisions of the international federation.[61] International federations represent their sports internationally and maintain relationships with other international organisations, such as the International Olympic Committee (IOC).

International federations organise and oversee international competitions, such as the Olympic Games, World Cups, World Championships and Continental Championships. They establish qualification criteria, coordinate event schedules, and manage the overall organisation of these events. International sports federations are also responsible for the rules and regulations for their respective sports and must ensure fair play and integrity.

Overall, international sports federations act as the governing bodies for their respective sports, ensuring their growth, development, and global representation. They undertake a wide range of responsibilities to regulate, promote, and advance their sport at the international level.

Influence of global sporting events on governance

Global sporting events have a significant influence on governance in various ways. Some of the critical aspects of how international sporting events have an impact on governance are:

1. ***Increased scrutiny and accountability***

    Global sporting events, such as the Olympic Games or FIFA World Cup, attract substantial media attention and public scrutiny.[62] As a result, sports organisations hosting these events face increased pressure to uphold governance standards, transparency, and accountability. The spotlight on governance practices during major events often leads to enhanced scrutiny and measures to protect fundamental human rights. The controversy surrounding the 2022 Qatar World Cup about the country's alleged human rights violations, specifically migrant worker rights, women's rights and the rights of the LGBTQ-community, became the most prominent issue and demanded reforms from western countries.

2. ***Infrastructure development and governance reforms***

    Hosting major sporting events (such as the 2010 FIFA World Cup in South Africa) requires significant investment in infrastructure, including stadiums, transportation systems, and accommodation facilities.[63] This infrastructure development goes hand in hand with governance reforms, as host countries or cities must comply with specific governance standards and human rights. FIFA has been accused of failing its human rights responsibilities by refusing to compensate migrant workers for abuses while preparing and delivering the 2022 Qatar World Cup.

3. ***Legacy and sustainability***

    Mega sporting events, such as the Olympic Games and FIFA World Cup, impact host cities and countries in the long-term. The financial impact of hosting these events can be devastating. Governance considerations are therefore crucial in legacy planning, which involves establishing governance structures (such as legacy committees) that facilitate the effective management of legacy funds and the repurposing of event infrastructure, stadiums, and resources.

4. ***Policy and regulatory reforms***

    Hosting global sporting events often necessitates introducing or revising legislation, policies, and regulations. Adopting the Safety at Sports and Recreational Events, Act 2 of 2010 directly resulted in hosting the 2010 FIFA World Cup in South Africa. Other reforms may encompass human rights such as gender equality, freedom of expression, right to education and the right to non-discrimination based on race, ethnicity, religion, and disability. Global sporting events catalyse policy changes as host countries or cities align their governance practices with international standards and expectations. For instance, FIFA has implemented a robust anti-discrimination framework, acting against racism, sexism, and other forms of discrimination in football.

5. ***Broadcasting rights and commercialisation***

    Global sporting events attract substantial broadcasting rights deals, sponsorship agreements, and commercial interests. Managing these revenue streams and the associated contracts require robust governance mechanisms to ensure transparency, fairness, and the avoidance of conflicts of interest. The broadcasting rights for the 2023 FIFA Women's World Cup Australia & New Zealand were valued between $1m - $10m, compared to the $100m - $200m paid for the men's 2022 FIFA World Cup. FIFA considers this morally and legally unfair.

6. ***International reputation***

    Hosting global sporting events can significantly impact a nation's or organisation's international perception and reputation. Effective governance is critical in managing the event's organisation, delivery, and legacy to ensure a positive and credible image. It requires transparency, integrity, and adherence to ethical principles, which can contribute to building trust and attracting future events, investments, and partnerships. The 2022 FIFA World Cup in Qatar was overshadowed by corruption and bribery allegations, which tarnished the reputation of FIFA and Qatar.

In summary, global sporting events profoundly influence governance by driving reforms, enhancing accountability, fostering collaboration, and shaping the policies and practices of sports governing bodies. The requirements and demands of hosting such events necessitate effective governance to ensure successful delivery and leave a lasting positive impact.

Ethical issues and challenges in sports governance

Ethical issues and challenges in sports governance encompass a range of complex and multifaceted concerns that can arise in the management and administration of sports governing bodies. Here are some key ethical issues and challenges:

1. **Corruption and bribery**

    The Prevention and Combating of Corrupt Activities Act 12 of 2004, is the primary legislation governing corruption prevention in South Africa. Corruption can be defined as the abuse of entrusted power for private gain. Sports governing bodies worldwide have faced challenges related to corruption, bribery, and financial irregularities. These include issues such as secret commissions, embezzlement, kickbacks, and the misuse of funds. Effective governance must address these issues through robust financial controls, transparency, and accountability mechanisms. Governing bodies should have an effective internal audit system. An audit committee consisting of a majority of independent directors with a financial background should be established to ensure compliance with the King IV principles.

2. **Match-fixing and betting**

    Any person who undermines the integrity of any sporting event is guilty of a criminal offence in terms of section 15 of the Prevention and Combating of Corrupt Activities Act. This includes any form of match-fixing or spot-fixing. Illegal betting poses a significant ethical challenge, undermines the integrity and fairness of competitions, erodes public trust, and has financial implications. Effective governance must include preventive measures, strict regulations, and education programmes to combat match-fixing and protect the integrity of sport.[64] Governing bodies must establish an anti-corruption unit to monitor and investigate match-fixing offences.

3. **Conflict of interest**

    Governing bodies and board members have a fiduciary duty to act in good faith and must always act in the best interest of the federation. Conflict of interest occurs when individuals in positions of power or influence have personal or financial interests that may compromise their objectivity or decision-making. This can include situations where administrators, officials, or board members have affiliations with commercial entities, sponsors, suppliers, or agents that may influence their actions. Robust governance frameworks should address and manage conflicts of interest to ensure fair and impartial decision-making.

4. ***Emerging sports technologies***

    Rapid technological advancements, such as wearable devices, performance-enhancing equipment, and data analytics, raise ethical questions in sports governance. Issues include using prohibited technologies, data privacy concerns, and the potential for unfair advantages. In 2009 the Fédération Internationale de Natation (FINA) banned the LZR Racer swimsuit after 23 out of the 25 swimming records at the 2008 Beijing Olympics were broken by athletes wearing the Speedo LZR Racer swimsuit. In 2020 World Athletics banned the Nike Vaporfly running shoe after the Kenyan runner Eliud Kipchoge became the first person to run a marathon distance in under two hours. The governing bodies are responsible for navigating these challenges by establishing clear guidelines, monitoring technologies, and ensuring a level playing field.

5. ***Athlete exploitation and abuse***

    Protecting athletes' rights and well-being is a critical ethical responsibility in sports governance. Physical and emotional abuse, harassment, discrimination, and inadequate support systems can arise. Strong governance should prioritise athlete welfare, enforce strict codes of conduct, and provide safe reporting mechanisms such as whistleblowing to address and prevent athlete exploitation.

6. ***Drug Use and anti-doping***

    The South African Government is a signatory to the World Anti-Doping Code and formally recognised the World Anti-Doping Agency's (WADA) role through the Copenhagen Declaration of Anti-Doping in Sport (2003). WADA provides the framework of the Anti-Doping Rules of the South African Institute for Drug-Free Sport (SAIDS) that governs the conditions under which sport is played in South Africa. SAIDS is a public entity established by an Act of Parliament, Act 14 of 1997.

SAIDS's core focus is to tackle doping in sport and ensure clean and fair competition. Anti-doping governance faces challenges in using performance-enhancing substances, testing procedures, sanctions, and the evolving landscape of doping practices. SAIDS collaborates with other national anti-doping agencies worldwide to achieve international harmonisation and improvement of standards and practices in anti-doping. Governing bodies are responsible for complying with the WADA Code and SAIDS's anti-doping rules through effective governance and rigorous anti-doping measures and education of athletes.

Addressing these ethical issues and challenges requires a comprehensive approach that includes robust governance frameworks, transparent policies, ethical codes of conduct, education and awareness programmes, and mechanisms for reporting and investigating misconduct. It requires the commitment and collaboration of stakeholders, including the sport's governing bodies, athletes, officials, and regulatory bodies, to uphold the sport's ethical values and integrity.

CHAPTER 8

COMPLIANCE AND RISK MANAGEMENT

Janie Marais

Introduction

All organisations are exposed to risks which are often difficult to pre-empt and identify, with failure that could lead to costly lessons. In my experience as a compliance officer in sport, who started at a stadium with few to no compliance systems, I soon realised the importance of two things. Firstly, the importance of a compliance and risk framework, and secondly, the relationships with and between various stakeholders. Building a compliance department from scratch was in no way an easy task that happened overnight, and the entire process had its challenges. Time, patience and consistency was the key to the success.

One would think to comply is merely a checkbox exercise by reading a regulatory act, policy or procedure and then applying it. But with anything involving people, an organisation's compliance becomes as strong as the individuals responsible for implementing the compliance requirements. For an organisation to take risks in compliance holds no additional benefit as compliance is not an option but a requirement. Non-compliance is often ignored, and the argument is "it will never happen to us", but what if it does? Failure to comply could see a CEO, managing directors and board members faced with prosecution and fines, as it only takes one percent (1%) of negligence to prove non-compliance. In today's world, where technology allows people to connect in a blink of an eye, public pressure has grown too, and breaches of the rules threaten major damage for companies' image and reputation. The media and social media can intensify this effect, as can the public.

Compliance matters are synonymous with unethical behaviours such as governance issues, fraud, discrimination and sexual harassment. Stadiums run further risks linked to non-compliance, such as loss of sponsorship, reputational damage, cancelling of events and stadium closure. Most scandals result from a disregard of external and internal compliance. Therefore, understanding the interrelationship between governance, risk and compliance is crucial. Compliance awareness should be created continuously where key stakeholders are adequately trained and guided on compliance issues and preventative measures are taken due to effective risk management.

Compliance in sport and risk appetite and tolerance

Compliance in a stadium refers to adhering to laws, regulations, policies and guidelines related to safety, security and other aspects of stadium operations. This ranges from compliance with local building codes, fire safety regulations to health and safety requirements for spectators and staff. Stadiums may also need to comply with event-specific regulations related to crowd management, alcohol sales, tickets and privacy laws. Sport, like any other industry, is obliged to comply with various regulations, from the code governing bodies' clothing and equipment regulations to various regulatory laws of the country. The Safety at Sports and Recreational Events Act 2 of 2010 (SASREA), for instance, provides guidelines that ensure conformity to include broader interests of sports federations, unions and bodies. Compliance is vital in hosting events.

Although stadiums could agree to a larger risk appetite when accepting risks involving new operational ventures and opportunities, a zero-tolerance to non-compliance is advised, with a low-risk appetite associated with compliance risks. Tolerance of risk does, however, mean that an organisation understands and acknowledges that it cannot always be fully compliant. Risk appetite and risk tolerance relate to an organisation's willingness to invest in the controls associated with compliance management. To ensure that the residual risk is handled within the organisation's risk appetite for core or high-risk compliance requirements, greater controls will be required. It is understandable that an organisation can often only establish and maintain a reasonable compliance framework and that non-compliance results from human intervention. It is, therefore, important for organisations to ensure measures, risk appetite and tolerance are established to ensure processes and controls are running at an acceptable level of assurance.[65]

Regulatory compliance vs corporate compliance

The compliance framework consists of rules, regulations and practices and involves two types, namely corporate and regulatory compliance. Corporate compliance involves policies and procedures developed by internal and external stakeholders; whereas external regulations influence regulatory compliance. The two types of compliance hold various similarities, with the difference being whether internal or external regulations influenced them. Understanding the difference between external and internal compliance is key since these could influence the framework for managing compliance risks which helps to manage legal and regulatory risks and operational and reputational risks. Building a compliance culture that supports good governance and ethical behaviour, along with understanding international, national, regional or local regulations, is therefore crucial, with all stakeholders understanding the importance of compliance and taking the responsibility to maintain it. In the long run, maintaining a compliance-healthy organisation would secure a competitive advantage and increased investor opportunities as it would promote stakeholder trust relationships due to a good reputation.

King IV and compliance

King IV is a set of guidelines developed in 2016 by the Institute of Directors in South Africa (IDSA). It guides the principles of compliance with corporate governance that organisations must follow. King IV emphasises the importance of compliance with laws, regulations and standards and views compliance as an opportunity to promote good governance. King IV warns against viewing compliance as an isolated function within the organisation and suggests that responsibility should rather be shared collectively by all stakeholders. The report encourages a compliance culture embedded throughout the organisation, from the board to the front-line staff.

Imagine the house below is a company. Corporate governance is the roof, also referred to as the "tone at the top", and sets the direction, objectives and road map for the future. For the board to make the right decisions, information is needed, which comes from the pillars of policies and procedures, which flow through the different departments and levels within the organisation, and then back to the top.

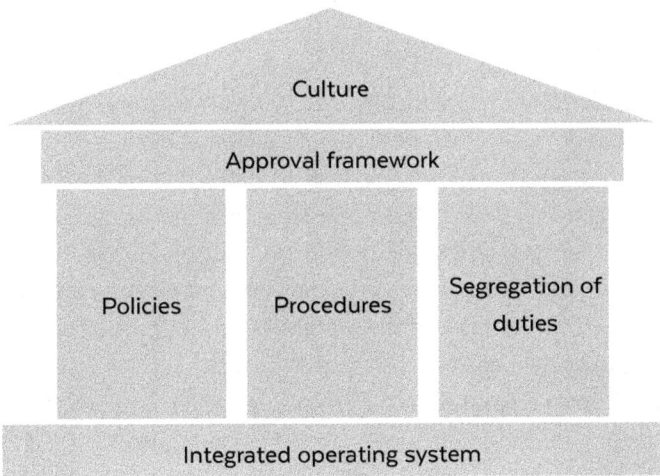

Figure 2: Corporate Governance

Let us look at a case where governance caused an entire board to resign. In 2020, after a series of events that placed the governing body of South African cricket in the media for nothing but bad news, the board of Cricket South Africa resigned one day before the then Minister of Sport, Mr Nathi Mthethwa, would intervene in the organisation's saga. His involvement would lead to the potential suspension of South African cricket from the International Cricket Council, which, according to its constitution, forbids the interference of national governments in its member nations.[66] The board can delegate responsibility to design, implement and monitor the risk management plan. With a board that does not comply with its governance requirements, it is unlikely that compliance could be implemented at lower operational levels. Risk management and the governance framework of the organisation include the compliance function as a critical component. Given the importance of the legal framework in which sports organisations function, compliance provides the ground rules for key stakeholders. It mitigates the risks of non-compliance and its related consequences, such as fines, liability and reputational harm. By understanding good governance, organisations can continuously identify and mitigate risks before damage is done. The likelihood of non-compliance is significantly reduced if an organisation's governance, compliance strategy, and culture work together.

Something that needs to be understood is that non-compliance could lead to the obvious consequences stated already. Still, it snowballs to underlying issues that further impact its stakeholders, such as job losses, a toxic working environment and a breakdown in employer-employee trust relationships. In the case of Cricket South Africa, after investigations were launched into various matters, an interim board was appointed in 2020, and its CEO and some of its executive members were released from their duties. If the "tone at the top" is murky, the rest of the structure becomes messy.

Compliance and risk management in sport

In a previous section of this chapter, I mentioned the two most important things I learned. The importance of a compliance and risk framework and the relationship with key stakeholders. As with any organisation, stadiums are always faced with certain types of risks. The good news, however, is that regulatory compliance is probably one of the risk types that is the most controllable and preventable. What I also realised is that compliance cannot fail itself, however, people can. For reasons they do not understand, people see the need or simply act on a regulatory or legislative obligation. Non-compliance often results from people who forget to act or just decide not to act or leave the process for too long, resulting in non-compliance, sometimes leading to costly penalties. Another issue often results from the inability to pre-empt risks or report non-compliance, resulting in a so-called "surprise factor". This makes it difficult to implement mitigating strategies to avoid the consequences of non-compliance. It is therefore crucial to foster a compliance and risk-focused culture and to create a psychologically safe environment for open discussion around compliance issues and how to resolve them.

Furthermore, allocating responsibilities to relevant individuals is key to successful compliance management. Dealing with people made me realise that compliance is not naturally accepted as a key aspect of everyday business. Have you ever heard the saying "if you fail to plan, you plan to fail"? This is the exact reason why a risk management programme should be put in place. This can be done in four phases.[67]

1. The first is to compile a **compliance universe**. It is important to know what exactly you need to comply with. This can be done by looking at compliance obligations, such as acts, regulations, by-laws, etc., which could apply to your organisation. Input should be requested from relevant employees as they could provide valuable information in

identifying applicable compliance obligations. Regulatory approvals and licencing should also be documented (Refer to Table 5: Compliance Universe).

2. The second phase is a **compliance risk assessment** to create a risk profile. Once the compliance universe is compiled, the requirements are categorised as 1) **core** (licencing required to operate), 2) **topical** (no licence required but still has a high impact on the organisation through penalties) or 3) **secondary** (impact of non-compliance is less severe and is not core to the organisation, however applicable). Compliance obligations are then assessed and prioritised based on impact (seriousness) and likelihood (probability) rating risk scales. Depending on the organisation's risk appetite, materiality levels determine when matters are to be escalated to key stakeholders such as governing bodies or regulators.

3. The third phase involves compiling the **compliance risk management plan**, which includes the core and high risk obligations. Regulatory provision is analysed, associated obligations and risks are identified, risk drivers (root causes) for non-compliance and its consequences are listed, control measures are established, and suggested controls are determined. Responsible individuals are identified, and timeframes for actions to be completed or controls to be implemented are indicated (See Table 6: Compliance Risk Management Plan).

4. The final phase involves **risk monitoring** used to evaluate and report back on compliance matters. It is used to ensure the effectiveness of implemented controls and report to applicable stakeholders. Furthermore, this phase determines whether responsible people are performing the tasks that were allocated to them to ensure compliance. It also allows for reviewing the reliability of the compliance system.

Table 5: Compliance Universe

Law Library Category	Regulatory Provision	Interpretation	Compliance Obligation	Risk Level	Impact	Applicable sections	Penalty
Framework legislation	Constitution of the Republic of South Africa	Chapter 2: Bill of Rights It outlines the fundamental rights and freedoms that are protected and guaranteed to all individuals in South Africa. These rights include equality, human dignity, life, freedom of expression, freedom of religion, and various socio-economic rights. The chapter also emphasises the importance of promoting and respecting these rights in South African society.	Yes	Medium	The organisation must ensure that all individuals are treated fairly and equally.	Chapter 2	Reputational
Legislation	Employment Equity Act No.55 of 1998	The Employment Equity Act aims to foster inclusive workplaces and advance equal opportunities for all individuals, contributing to a more equitable and diverse South African labour market.	Yes	Medium	EPG scorecard, EE reports	All	Fines, imprisonment up to 3 years
Legislation	Hazardous Substances Act, No 15 of 1973	This Act was promulgated to control substances that may cause injury, ill-health or death because of their toxic, corrosive, irritant, strongly sensitising or explosive nature. The Hazardous Substances Act also provides for matters concerning the division of such substances or products into groups in relation to the degree of danger, the prohibition and control of the importation, manufacture, sale, use, operation, application and disposal of such substances.	Yes	Low	Liability as an employer for a hazardous substance-related act or omission.	Section 16	Fines, imprisonment up to 2 years
Legislation	SASREA Act, No. 2 of 2010	The Act provides for measures to safeguard the physical well-being and safety of persons and property at events, assign accountability of event role-players, provide prohibitions, risk categorisation, the establishment of measures to deal with safety and security, accreditation, control of access, and applicable certificates.	Yes	High	Liability as venue host for any non-compliance-related act or omission	Sections 4, 6, 7, 8, 10, 11, 12, 13, 17, 18, 19, 20, 21, 22, 23, 24, 25	Fines, imprisonment up to 20 years
Legislation	National Environmental Management Act: Waste Act	This Act regulates waste management to protect health and the environment by providing reasonable measures for preventing pollution and ecological degradation and securing ecologically sustainable development. Additionally, it covers institutional systems, planning issues, national norms and standards for controlling waste management, and particular waste management practices. It includes provisions for the national waste information system, contaminated land restoration, and the licensing and regulation of waste management activities. The topic of compliance and enforcement is also covered.	Yes	Low	Management of waste	Section 15,1 6,17,18,21,22 ,24,25,26,2 7,28,29,30, 31,32	Fines, imprisonment up to 5 years

Chapter 8: Compliance and Risk Management

Table 6: Compliance risk management plan (CRMP)

Item		Risk factors		Risk rating			Control environment		Compliance monitoring and reporting plan			Frequency of monitoring						
	Interpretation	Risk drivers	Consequences	Impact	Likelihood	Risk rating (high, medium, low)	Relevant existing controls	Suggested additional controls	Responsible parties	Monitoring person	Monitor method	Ad hoc	Daily	Weekly	Monthly	Quarterly	Bi-annual	Annually
Regulatory provision																		
SASREA Act, No. 2 of 2010, Section 7(2)	A local authority may issue a grading certificate	No grading certificate issued	Closure of the stadium. Reputational Damage, Fines	3	A		Application in process	System to flag upcoming due dates	Stadium Management	CEO	Reporting							x
OSH – Fire Extinguishers Inspect, maintain, and test all portable fire extinguishers in the workplace. [29 CFR 1910.157(e)(1)]. Visually inspect portable extinguishers or hoses monthly. [29 CFR 1910.157(e)(2)].	Fire extinguishers are to be inspected on a monthly basis, and maintenance is done annually. Retention of documents in terms of equipment purchases and maintenance performed is required.	Inspections were not done. Documents not retained.	Damage to facilities. Loss of equipment and documentation. Accidents and incidents. Reputational damage/fines/imprisonment	5	D		Appointments in place. Training up to date.	Ongoing training.	Compliance Officer	CEO	Training plan and attendance of training performed reported to COO. Feedback at the meetings on training.				x			

83

Non-compliance in sport

As discussed, there are different kinds of non-compliance and types of risks. Compliance is everywhere and applicable to all. If done right, an event will run smoothly. Non-compliance in sport has other related risks than the already mentioned consequences of reputational damage, financial loss and imprisonment.

1. In 2016, a former South African football boss was banned by FIFA's ethics committee for a match-fixing scandal involving the national team in 2010. Kirsten Nematandi was banned for five years.[68]

2. The FIFA corruption scandal in 2015 involved seven FIFA executives who received enormous bribes over two decades. A focus was placed on the accusations that the bribery was connected to the awarding of hosting rights for the 2018 and 2022 World Cups. The executives were arrested and jailed.[69]

3. In the 2019 African Cup of Nations (AFCON), the Confederation of African Football (CAF) stripped Cameroon of hosting rights for the AFCON due to concerns over the country's readiness to host the tournament and its ability to comply with CAF's regulations. The security of spectators and other key stakeholders could not be confirmed after an escalation in violence throughout the country which involved English-speaking separatists and government forces. Morocco subsequently hosted the tournament.[70]

4. The 1986 Commonwealth Games were scheduled to be held in Edinburgh, Scotland. Concerns over costs and the country's compliance with financial regulations, along with its political decision not to apply economic sanctions to South Africa and its apartheid administration, resulting in a white-only event, led to event organisers being faced with the possibility of a cancelled event. Although Edinburgh refused to cancel the event, it experienced a great loss of financial income from cancelled broadcast and advertising revenue. These games will always be remembered as "the Boycott Games".[71]

These examples demonstrate that non-compliance can have significant consequences, including cancelling major events. Event organisers need to prioritise compliance and implement effective governance structures and processes to ensure compliance with relevant regulations and standards to avoid the cancellation of events.

Conclusion

Even though it is impossible for an organisation to always be completely compliant, it is easy to meet regulatory compliance. It starts with the tone at the top, but the importance lies in managing the middle. There must be agreement that compliance is the responsibility of an entire organisation. Employee cooperation is crucial; therefore, a compliance and risk-focused culture can be built through ongoing training on compliance matters such as company policies and procedures and the allocation of roles and responsibilities to relevant individuals. Employees can often provide critical information to assist in the prevention of non-compliance. The goal of compliance management is not to police and reprimand people but to identify, assess, implement and monitor risks and to provide assurance to key stakeholders in the organisation. The importance lies in keeping track of changing laws and regulations, identifying potential regulatory risks and implementing and monitoring the controls to ensure compliance. Audits and inspections should be seen as part of the process of building a compliant organisation. Furthermore, relationships with the regulator are important to build a reputation as a transparent and cooperative organisation. Lastly, stadiums face several risks, and the compliance environment is forever changing. Still, once a system is in place and processes are followed, stadiums will benefit from providing a safe, secure and compliant ground for all stakeholders to enjoy our sports.

CHAPTER 9

THE CRISIS MANAGEMENT OF SPORTING EVENTS

Jacques Faul

Introduction

Sporting events are usually well-reported in the media. If it is scandalous, it will attract even more attention. Event organisers have a legal duty of care, which must be taken seriously. Sadly, we have seen stadium disasters over some time. Event organisers must equip themselves to manage possible challenges proactively; they should know how to deal with them when they occur.

It is essential to look at disasters that have happened in the past. Learning from experienced practitioners will be of great value to all. Significant events attract big crowds, and this increases the risk profile. South Africa has unique infrastructural challenges that require contingency plans. This chapter also provides practical advice to anticipate and proactively mitigate risks.

Crisis related to events

Crises related to events may present some of the biggest challenges. They are usually unexpected, and there is little time to react. The potential for reputational damage is always great. The loss of life is traumatic for anybody associated with an event.

Frosdic[72] states that the crisis factors in sport include inappropriate structure of sports complexes and overlooking the values and trends of spectators. Additionally, Taylor,[73] in his studies on sports incidents, mentions the following factors: lack of sufficient planning for spectators' comfort; insufficient knowledge about crisis management; lack of special training for the police forces; socioeconomic problems of spectators; simple facility management issues including locked doors, improper re-entering of a facility; and most likely poor design, construction and signage. Other factors include rowdy crowds and rioting.

David Becker is a well-known lawyer and event specialist and advises many clients within the sports and events industry. During a music festival in Cape Town, Becker had to advise his client when the DJ collapsed onstage and died in the medical tent. The organisers felt pressurised to put out a statement. He wisely advised that the deceased's family needed to be informed first. The sequence of engagement is vital when it comes to stakeholders. I deal with this in the chapter on stakeholder management.

Becker has a three-point approach to dealing with a crisis. First, the legal consideration, including, among other things, a duty of care. Secondly, commercial considerations, and thirdly, public relations. This is an excellent framework that I strongly recommend.

Tarlow[74] states that when a risk has occurred during an event, it is no longer a risk but a crisis. The sports event risk manager becomes a crisis manager who will determine the state of the sporting crisis and put a plan into place. Tarlow indicates that there is a diverse range of potential crises that could occur at an International Sporting Event (ISE) including fire, active shooter, act of terrorism, a bomb leading to crowd panic, an attack on a sports figure by a fan or a riot at the ISE or International Sporting Venue (ISV) or in the host community by either fans or locals.

Even before mitigating an incident, Tarlow[75] argues that international sports events/international sports venue professionals must consider various factors. These might include how many people are at the event or whether there is one or multiple venues for the event; or what the demographics of the attendees are. Is there significant media presence surrounding the event, how frequently is the stadium/arena used, and are there external factors outside the stadium that might be problematic, such as changing weather conditions or traffic congestion?

Anant Sarkaria is an experienced stadium and event manager and has worked at the Indian Premier League and SA20 cricket tournaments. He is an engineer by trade and an Oxford graduate. He states that crises in sporting events are real-time and must be dealt with immediately with the best resources. Most crises might need precedence or a Standard Operating Procedure (SOP) to follow, thus requiring experience and resourcefulness from the leadership and the team handling the event.

The most crucial aspect that immediately comes to mind is safety. During any crisis, the safety of spectators, staff, players and officials should be paramount and take precedence over all other matters. Once safety has been secured, all other aspects can be taken care of afterwards.

According to Sarkaria, in most circumstances, crises can be divided into two groups:

1. Crises with infrastructure or spectators
2. Crises which might affect the sport or game itself

In either case, the response differs, and immediate decisions need to be taken to assure safety for all and, after that, the safe and successful execution of the game and the event.

Most crises can be unique and may require presence of mind and tactful thinking to resolve matters. Under such circumstances, experience plays a vital role in the response and the outcome.

From a leadership perspective, it is essential that the information you get is disseminated clearly and that decisions are inclusive. Despite decisions being inclusive, senior leadership should take charge and responsibility for communicating these decisions responsibly and clearly to all stakeholders.

Hugo Kemp[76] has been the stadium manager for Loftus Versfeld since 1998. He is one of the most experienced and respected stadium managers in South Africa. The stadium hosts rugby, soccer and concerts. The stadium also hosted the FIFA Soccer World Cup in 2010. The stadium is a historic landmark in Pretoria and has been operational since 1938. South Africa is a country with infrastructure challenges. This includes power and water supply. These two critical resources are vital for a stadium hosting events. Waste management has become a problem for the stadium as the municipality struggles to deliver this service for various reasons. Loftus often hosts events exceeding 50 000 attendees.

Kemp concluded that it requires more planning than ever; you need a backup plan for a backup plan. Over the years, he has forged good relationships with the city authorities and ward councillors. This has come in handy during a crisis. He mentioned that there has been an increase in staff turnover in the city and building relationships has become more challenging.

He recalls that the stadium had its power or water cut off during events. Electricity supply can be resumed via generators. However, generators also break down. Water trucks are a substitute for water supplies from the council. Both are expensive options. The stadium has boreholes and is working on a project to store water in tanks. Kemp concludes that a stadium needs to invest in its capacity to address water and electricity supply. The stadium has outsourced waste management to a private company.

Hosting events at SuperSport Park

SuperSport Park is a multi-use stadium that caters for cricket events, concerts, and running events. It is essential to have a multi-use stadium to sustain income. The stadium was initially designed to host cricket matches only and no other events. However, we have devised ways to host other events such as concerts and religious events. Protecting the playing surface is very important, especially the pitch area.

There is a real risk that concerts and running events will damage the surface, making it unusable for cricket matches. The stadium was built in 1986 and requires significant maintenance. It was also built on a dolomite area, which presents challenges. In the last decade, we have made a concerted effort to benchmark stadiums worldwide and introduce best practices at the park.

Stadium/event disasters

A stadium disaster is usually characterised by loss of life. The following is a timeline of major stadium disasters. The Boston bombings were not a stadium event. Chapter 2 covers other crises in sport.

Le Mans 1955

A racing car in the Grand Prix careered into a grandstand and killed 82 spectators in Le Mans, France, on June 11, 1955.

Lima Peru 1964

In 1964, 340 soccer fans were killed and 500 injured during the riot that followed an unpopular ruling by a referee in a Peru vs. Argentina soccer match in Lima, Peru, on May 24.

Glasgow 1971

Sixty-six fans were killed in a crush at the Glasgow Rangers home stadium in Glasgow, Scotland, on January 2, 1971, after soccer fans tried to leave. They chaotically encountered fans attempting to re-enter the stadium after hearing that a late goal had been scored.

Columbia 1980

Several bullring bleachers collapsed, leaving 222 spectators dead in Sincelejo, Columbia, on January 20, 1980.

Lenin Stadium Moscow 1982

Three hundred and forty soccer fans died at the Lenin Stadium in Moscow, U.S.S.R on October 20, 1982, when exiting soccer fans collided with returning fans after scoring a late goal. The fans were crowded into one particular section of the stadium by the police.

Bradford City Stadium Fire 1985

The Bradford City Stadium fire happened during a third-division football match on 11 May 1985. The fire killed 56 football supporters and injured over 250 people.

The Heysel Stadium Disaster: Brussels, Belgium 1985

The Heysel Stadium disaster occurred in Brussels, Belgium, on 29 May 1985 during the European Cup Final between Juventus (Italy) and Liverpool (England). Thirty-nine people, primarily Italian

Juventus fans, were killed following the collapse of a wall while trying to escape from Liverpool fans. A further 600 supporters were injured.

Nepal 1988

In Katmandu, Nepal, on March 12, 1988, eighty soccer fans seeking cover during a hailstorm at Nepal's national stadium were crushed to death in a stampede because the stadium doors had been locked.

The Hillsborough Disaster in Sheffield, England, 1989

The Hillsborough disaster on 15 April 1989 in Sheffield, England, left a profound physical, psychological, and emotional impact on safety at sports stadiums in the UK. The human crush at the FA Cup semi-final game between Liverpool and Nottingham Forest resulted in 96 fatalities and over 750 injuries in the worst disaster in British sporting history.

National Stadium in Guatemala City 1998

Eighty-four fans were killed, and 147 were injured when soccer fans stampeded before a 1998 World Cup. The cup qualifying match between Guatemala and Costa Rica was held at the Mateo Flores National Stadium in Guatemala City, Guatemala, on October 16, 1996.

Ellis Park Disaster 2001

Bowley et al[77] note that on April 11, 2001, approximately 80,000 spectators tried to cram into Ellis Park Stadium, Johannesburg, South Africa, a venue with a capacity for around 60,000 people, for a premier league soccer match between the two most popular teams in Johannesburg. Less than 4,000 tickets had been presold. The ensuing crush disaster, in which 43 spectators were killed, has been the subject of a judicial enquiry. The events at Ellis Park were the first of three African soccer stadium disasters that killed around 170 people in the space of one month.

Seven fans were killed and 51 seriously injured at the end of April 2001 in a stampede at a match in the Democratic Republic of Congo after police used tear gas to control rioting fans. In May 2001, at least 120 people died in a crush at a match in the Ghanaian capital of Accra.

With the massive global interest in soccer, this report serves as a reminder of the potential problems of the gatherings of large partisan crowds.

Boston Marathon 2013

The Boston Marathon bombing took place on 15 April 2013. Three hundred people were injured in a terrorist attack by two Kyrgyz brothers. This created chaos during the race, and runners needed to be rerouted.

Crowd management in sport

According to Shipway et al.,[78] the potential for disaster is always present whenever more significant spectators come together to watch a major sports event. Risks might arise due to factors such as crowd behaviour and when groups of sports fans adopt a crowd mentality. It is acknowledged that collective resilience among members of the public is a vital part of safety and security.

Crowd behaviour in emergencies and disasters falls into two categories: those assuming a default psychological vulnerability and those emphasising psychosocial resilience. Shipway et al.[79] argue that the former identifies crowds as a source of psychological weakness and excludes any possibility that they could contribute positively to coping with danger, whilst the latter emphasises the potential positive influences offered by crowd membership. Literature on mass panic assumes that the crowd becomes a conduit for dysfunctional and irrational behaviour.

The London and Manchester bombings in the UK suggest that such events allowed people to identify with others as part of the crowd, which enabled them to cope practically and emotionally with the inherent dangers they faced. In the sporting context, behaviours are perhaps influenced not by mass panic and irrationality but are contingent on social norms in sports and fan identities.

Anti-social behaviour is a broader challenge for international sports events and venues regarding crowd control. Spectator-related conflict can occur inside and outside the venue, including ticket scalping, littering, loitering, traffic congestion, crowd control in open areas and public thoroughfares around the venue, public intoxication before the event and underage drinking or terrorist activity.

Sports event organisers and venue managers need to assess a variety of factors and ask questions on the venue layout, such as the size of the stadium, how the seats are arranged, what the noise levels at the venue are, how emotionally charged the particular fixture is; are there specific characteristics of the crowd demographic that the police should be aware of; is the game a single match or part of a more extensive series of events; what are the alcohol policies at the venue; what are the levels of security staff training; and how well venue security staff interacts with other emergency services at the venue?

Crisis scenario planning

I was blessed to obtain a certificate in Executive Event Management from the Sydney University of Technology and Sports Knowledge Australia. During the course, we sat in on a planning session for the City-to-Surf, a running event in Sydney. This is an annual running event from the centre of the city to the beach. During the planning session, the committee discussed various potential crisis scenarios and how to deal with them. I suggest that event organisers dedicate time to do this.

Who makes the call during an event?

During an international match at SuperSport Park, I was called upon to make a decision to evacuate or not after receiving a bomb threat. The Venue Operating Centre is supposed to make calls related to safety. It did not happen that day! Various other decisions are required during events, and there needs to be clarity on who can do so. I have also been guilty of making a decision without consulting with the stadium manager, who has made a different decision. This is potentially embarrassing and unprofessional.

Knowledge of project management

A sporting event is a project. Good project management knowledge will help manage possible challenges proactively and structure the organisers' efforts. The Project Management Body of Knowledge provides guidance. Training in event management will benefit organisations. It will be a mistake to underestimate the complexity of hosting events, especially if you have no experience in hosting events or hosting significantly big events.

Checklist and feedback meeting

It is best practice to develop checklists to plan for events. Furthermore, feedback meetings are essential to learn from past events and to continuously improve. This should be ever-expanding, with lists being updated with feedback. Good event organisers anticipate well; this comes from experience. Organisers who are new to hosting events must rely heavily on checklists and feedback.

This will also aid with succession and training of new staff. A Standard Operating Procedure (SOP) must be developed and documented. It should then be reviewed and updated regularly.

Pre-event day and event day physical inspection

There is tremendous value in a physical inspection of the venue before and during the event. Some platforms are big, and will require more than one person for the inspection. It provides excellent insights into fan experiences and people waiting for toilets and food.

The inspection also allows you to identify risk areas. Don't remain stuck in the venue operating centre for the entire event without having a walk around. There are many moving parts the day before the event, and you will be surprised by how many unauthorised activities and advertising are done. It is wise to record your findings either by document or phone.

Use of technology

New technology, such as face recognition and improved visual monitoring, will help with safety and crowd control. Event and stadium managers must continuously scan for new technology that will help prevent incidents and disasters.

Stadiums must budget for new technology annually and upgrade systems regularly. Some technology products may be unaffordable, but you must aim to upgrade technology regularly. Early detection of unwanted crowd behaviour may save you considerable embarrassment, but you will need sufficient cameras.

Automated access control is improving continuously and may enhance both the stadium experience as well as the safety of spectators.

Cultivate compliance

Compliance management is discussed in chapter 7. A compliance mindset cannot be reserved for event day but should be actively pursued by the stadiums and event organisers daily. This will mitigate risks and liability. It is strongly recommended that a culture of compliance and safety be entrenched within the company culture. This must include resources to monitor and implement compliance. It should not be seen as an ad hoc function for a manager but should be a priority activity. The manager must report to the audit and risk committee. The board or management committee must oversee this function.

Lead time management

After two decades in the industry, I am still amazed at how much still needs to be done on event day and the day before. The event project plan must have precise due dates. Time management is of the essence. Some unexpected crises are difficult to avoid, but the challenges related to bad planning must be minimal.

There needs to be more communication, coordination and consequence management to regulate lead time mishaps, and senior management needs to develop rules and regulations to make this effective.

Conclusion

There is a historical record of stadium disasters that sadly resulted in loss of life. There needs to be continuously innovative solutions to address challenges related to infrastructure. Always focusing on improving the event must be a part of the company's DNA. This includes learning from experienced practitioners and anticipating possible challenges.

Better management practices, including lead time management, will minimise challenges that could have been avoided by proper planning.

Sound project management knowledge is vital to minimise risks associated with hosting sporting events. The same goes for the effective use of new technology. The threat of terrorism remains relevant, and the impact of a terrorist attack during a sporting event must always be considered a priority threat.

A culture of safety and compliance cannot be switched on for an event but should be cultivated within the organisation on a daily basis. The history of disasters and your duty of care should be a stern reminder of how to approach the hosting of events and its associated risks.

CHAPTER 10

MENTAL WELLNESS

Monique de Klerk

Introduction

Crisis management is a skill where an individual must change their perspective about the situation to protect their soul.[80] A crisis refers to any abrupt or unforeseen situation which causes an individual or group of individuals to experience psychological distress, which refers to a state of emotional turmoil which makes coping with daily activities difficult.[81, 82, 83] In the context of sport, a crisis might refer to a life-threatening injury, an injury ending an individual's career or not being chosen for the team. The nature of a crisis can be seen as an unexpected event which is unpredictable, having a significant impact on coping with daily activities and responsibilities and where support and mitigation are deemed necessary.[84, 85, 86, 87, 88, 89, 90] When the physical and psychological safety of an individual facing a crisis is not handled with care, then the soul starts trembling, leading to an individual experiencing trauma.[91] Therefore, a crisis can be seen as a precursor for trauma. Untreated trauma can present in a fluctuation of emotional responses, re-experiencing of the event, a decrease in functional relationships, as well as physical symptoms such as headaches, nausea and many more.[92] Although the main principle of a crisis is breaking down the coping abilities of an individual, every crisis should however be seen as an opportunity to bring about positive change.[93] Hence the importance of effective crisis management to prevent experiencing trauma, is therefore deemed as an urgent psychological intervention with the purpose to restore one's soul.[94]

There are different types of traumas, including small t trauma, Big T trauma, and complex trauma.[95, 96] Small t trauma occurs when an individual feels hopeless and unable to cope but it does not threaten the individual's life. Small t's might include divorce, conflict, bullying, and financial difficulties, amongst other things.[97] A Big T trauma is seen as a significant event that causes an individual to feel powerless and out of control.[98] Examples include natural disasters, vehicle accidents, sexual assault, physical injury and so forth.[99] Complex trauma refers to exposure to multiple events and can be deemed as severe and pervasive, including abuse and profound neglect.[100] It is essential to keep in mind that everyone has their own perception of a situation and that trauma is different for each individual, based on how the brain and body deal with various threats.[101]

Before the soul can be protected, one must first and foremost understand the core mechanism of the soul, and this is the human brain and the neurological process involved when a crisis or trauma is experienced.

The brain is wired for survival, and when an individual experiences a crisis, the brain experiences definite neurological changes.[102] Most individuals want to avoid any threats to function in a state of equilibrium, and for that predictability is fundamental. When an individual is faced with predictable situations, he/she can organise, plan, solve problems and regulate their emotions with ease.[103] These functions form part of the person's executive functioning where the prefrontal cortex (PFC) is at work.[104] When an individual is faced with an unpredictable situation, such as a crisis, the brain's ability to execute these functions is compromised as the individual's brain and body is flooded with adrenaline.[105] Due to these changes, the blood flow to the amygdala, the emotion centre of the brain located in the limbic system, increases.[106] This can be seen as our alarm system to keep us from danger.

The increased blood flow to the amygdala and the simultaneous decrease in blood flow to the PFC, lead to memories of an event being fragmented, meaning, that due to the enormous emotional impact of a crisis, an individual may struggle to manage the situation effectively because of how our five senses experience the crisis.[107] Memories can be divided into two broad categories, firstly explicit (conscious) memories which represent the terror of the event, and secondly, implicit (unconscious) memories.[108] Explicit memories include semantic memory, which can be seen as the memory of general knowledge and facts, concepts and names, and episodic memory which refers to the autobiographical memory of an event, including what, who and where.[109] Implicit memory includes emotional memory, which refers to the emotional experiences that an individual goes through during an event, and procedural memory which refers to the way in which an individual performs tasks in a habitual manner.[110] When an individual is faced with a crisis, he/she may find it difficult to remember details about the crisis or experience overwhelming emotions which can influence their daily functioning.[111] A crisis therefore activates the fight/freeze/flight response, the survival mode, which is the body's reaction to protect itself against danger.[112] When the threat is not dealt with properly and the emotions not managed appropriately, an individual might be triggered unnecessarily by other events where the brain misinterprets sensory input which keeps the limbic system (fight/freeze/flight response) activated.[113] Therefore, a false alarm is created to keep an individual safe, even when the threat or danger has subsided. The false alarm influences an individual's cognitive abilities to regulate responses, make proper decisions, solve problems effectively and prevents an individual from being in a fight/freeze/flight response.[114]

What to expect when you are faced with a crisis

According to literature, being faced with a crisis can lead to various physiological responses and symptoms, such as:[115]

- Shortness of breath/rapid breathing
- Increased heart rate
- Tense muscles

- Elevated blood pressure
- Physical pain
- Feeling bloated
- Gut discomfort
- Spasms in the oesophagus
- Nausea
- Sweaty palms
- Increased body temperature

Over-activation of alarm system

When the body's alarm system keeps activated for prolonged periods of time without dealing with the crisis and accompanying emotions, the following might be experienced:[116, 117, 118, 119]

- Being tired despite a good night's rest
- Showing signs of fatigue or exhaustion
- Not sleeping or eating well
- Body aches
- Feeling nauseous
- Feeling emotionally numb
- Feeling out of control
- Feeling irritable and angry
- Feeling hopeless
- Feeling confused or disorientated
- Feeling negative and depressed
- Feeling anxious or panicky (even in the absence of a trigger)
- Showing destructive behaviour such as substance abuse, risk-taking behaviour and more
- Not able to concentrate
- Having difficulty remembering
- Being scared
- Thoughts about hurting oneself or others
- Experiencing thoughts that do not make sense

- Experiencing suicidal thoughts or a suicidal attempt
- Being quiet and withdrawn
- Feeling disconnected even when being part of a group
- Being aggressive
- Suddenly not performing well in different activities

Therefore, when faced with a crisis, an individual will experience a physiological and psychological response, which makes protecting the soul more challenging. It is vital to know how to manage these responses in a healthy way to limit unnecessary activation of the brain's alarm system and to optimise the functioning of the PFC.

Protecting your soul through crisis management

The following model serves as a guideline on how an individual can manage a crisis in a practical manner.

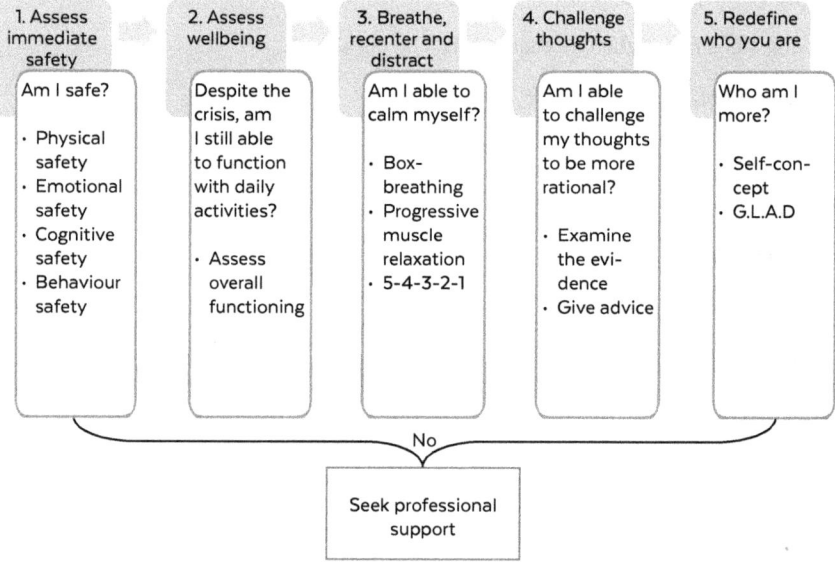

Figure 3: Model on practical guidelines for managing a crisis

Back to basics

The goal of this model is to firstly empower an individual in crisis to be able to move from a state of alertness (emotional centre in the brain) to feeling calmer and being able to cope more effectively with the crisis (PFC).

The model consists of five steps which include: 1) assess immediate safety; 2) assess well-being; 3) breathe, recentre and distract; 4) challenge thoughts; and 5) redefine who you are. Each step consists of a question which the individual needs to answer affirmatively to be able to move to the next step. If the individual is, however, not able to answer the question affirmatively, it is strongly advised to seek professional guidance. It preferable to complete each step with the support of someone the individual trusts. Support is thus deemed as the essence of this model. The literature emphasises the importance of social support during a crisis.[120][121] When an individual feels safe to confide in someone they trust, it is easier for them to be physically safe and able to calm themselves and challenge any unwanted thoughts.

Support

When an individual finds themselves in the crossfire of a crisis, one often leans on social structures with the hope that someone will provide guidance in reducing the stress and helping to cope.[122] Evidence shows that effective support can aid in recovery, longevity, and psychological adjustment.[123] Scientific literature proposed that active engagement, positive reframing, addressing the negatives, practical support and helpful downplaying of the situation can serve as effective support to help an individual to deal with a crisis.[124] Another study revealed that higher, positive levels of support can be linked to lower levels of stress.[125]

Research furthermore indicates that perceived social support plays a significant role in fighting against symptoms of depression, anxiety, and post-traumatic stress disorder after exposure to a crisis.[126] Hence, sufficient information supports the importance of having social support during difficult times, but the question remains: *How can I talk to someone?*

According to Dialectic Behaviour Therapy (DBT), interpersonal effectiveness provides practical assistance on how an individual can voice their needs and communicate more effectively with their social support system.[127] Two of these practical techniques include the D.E.A.R.M.A.N. and G.I.V.E. acronyms.[128] The D.E.A.R.M.A.N. technique enables an individual to communicate his or her needs and refers to:[129]

- *Describe* motivates the individual to communicate facts about a certain situation to get the other individual on the same page.
- *Express* enables the individual to clearly explain their feelings to prevent misinterpretation.
- *Assert* indicates the individual's ability to directly state what he/she wants.
- *Reinforce* denotes to the individual's ability to respond well to a positive outcome during a conversation. This might include thanking the other individual for listening.
- *Mindful* enables the individual to be mindful of the current conversation, without being side-tracked by irrelevant discussions.
- *Appear* confident when expressing needs.

- **Negotiate** with the other individual to see how the person can respectfully get his/her needs met.

The next technique includes the acronym G.I.V.E. which helps the individual to foster positive relationships by focusing on the needs of others.[130]

- **Gentle** shows an individual how to be kind in relationships by not judging or attacking someone.
- **Interested** motivates an individual to listen to someone with interest and focus.
- **Validate** enables the individual to acknowledge the other person's thoughts and feelings and to respect different views.
- **Easy** refers to having an easy attitude by being kind-hearted and caring.

Research indicates that the above-mentioned techniques should be easy to implement if the support structures are flexible in their thinking, realistic, respectful, showing warmth and empathy, sincere, and trustworthy.[131, 132]

Step 1: Assess immediate safety

The first and most important step of the model is to assess whether any immediate threats are involved. There are four areas whereby the individual's safety should be assessed, including physical safety; emotional safety; cognitive safety and behaviour safety.[133, 134]

Physical safety involves checking if there is any threat to an individual's physical safety. If this is the case, the individual should be referred to professional services such as the ambulance services or police services to ensure that the individual is physically safe and free from being a danger to him-/herself and others.[135] Emotional safety refers to assessing whether an individual experiences a stable mood and sense of being in control of their emotions, despite the crisis.[136] When noticeable signs of negativity, anxiety, sadness, hopelessness, disconnect, or hysteria are being experienced, it is best to seek professional help.[137]

Cognitive safety refers to being able to show logical reasoning and being able to make decisions.[138] When an individual struggles with irrational thoughts, intrusive images, difficulty remembering and concentrating, or preoccupation with death or destruction it is best to seek help from a professional.[139, 140] Behavioural safety focuses on appropriate and effective behaviour.[141] When outbursts, risk-taking behaviour, destructive behaviour, or maladaptive coping occur, it is advised to seek help from a professional.[142]

Focusing on these four areas of assessing an individual's immediate safety, will serve as guidance in answering the question: *Am I safe*? If the individual can answer in the affirmative, he/she can proceed to step 2, if not, it is advised to seek professional assistance.

Step 2: Assess well-being

It is essential to be aware of one's overall functioning to be able to assess when a crisis has taken its toll.[143] According to Carl Rogers, the fully functioning person has high life satisfaction, positive thoughts, and low anxiety.[144] When in crisis, an individual presents with the opposite image of being fully functioning. Hence, a test has been developed to assess an individual's well-being to evaluate the level of functioning. Thus, step 2 of this model entails assessing an individual's well-being by focusing on the following components:[145]

- Appearance and self-care: Is the individual able to continue practicing basic self-care functions, such as keeping body and hair clean, brushing teeth, dressing appropriately and more?

- Orientation: Is the individual able to show sound orientation in terms of time, date, and physical location?

- Insight and judgement: Is the individual able to show insight on how the crisis is impacting him/her and think about possible solutions for what they are busy facing?

- Level of consciousness: Is the individual vigilant and alert, or asleep, or confused?

- Eating, sleeping and libido: Is eating, sleeping and sexual activity healthy, or has the individual experienced any increase or decrease in their eating and sleeping patterns and libidinal functioning?

- Mood: Does the individual experience the occasional ups and downs, or does the individual struggle with a low mood with more downs than ups, or feel more anxious/agitated than usual?

- Thoughts: Are the individual's thoughts balanced between negative and positive content, or are their thoughts predominantly negative, troublesome, and evasive?

- Behaviour: Does the individual display behaviour that is healthy, or unhealthy and different to their normal behaviour?

- Social relationships: Does the individual have positive and good quality relationships, or does he/she show the need to isolate themselves and want to be alone?

- Suicidality and homicide: Does the individual feel that, despite the crisis, their life is worth living, or does the individual get intrusive ideas about ending their own life or the life of someone they know?

If the first part of all the questions could be answered in the affirmative, the individual will be able to positively answer the question: *Despite the crisis, am I still able to perform daily activities?* And will therefore be able to proceed to step 3. If not, and at any given time there is concern about the well-being of the individual, professional assistance is recommended.

Step 3: Breathe, recentre and distract

Breathe

After establishing that an individual has the necessary support, that they are not in any physical or psychological danger, and that they are still able to function despite the crisis event, the individual will now be able to start focusing on how to ground him/herself. This can be done by activating the relaxation response. The relaxation response was developed by Dr Herbert Benson in the 1970s. He found that it allows an individual to calm the nervous system and to feel more relaxed and in control of one's emotions.[146] The relaxation technique can have a big impact on reducing the heart rate, levels of cortisol and improving the immune system.[147] One technique that can be used is box breathing, which works as follows:[148]

- Sit or lie down without being distracted by any discomfort. When sitting, the individual must ensure that their feet are firmly on the ground.
- One hand must be placed on the individual's stomach and the other hand on their chest. When performing this technique, both hands should rise as the individual's chest and stomach inflates.
- Take a deep breath in through the nose for 4 seconds.
- Hold the breath for 4 seconds.
- Exhale for 4 seconds.
- Hold breath for 4 seconds. This sequence refers to one box.
- The individual can repeat a box 3-5 times.

This breathing exercise will help the individual to slow down their breathing and therefore decrease their stress level.[149]

Recentre

Progressive Muscle Relaxation (PMR) was developed by Dr Edmund Jacobson in the early 1920s and can be helpful in various conditions, especially to combat stress and anxiety.[150] It consists of two processes where the individual firstly becomes aware of tension in the muscles, and secondly, releasing the tension and becoming aware of what a relaxed muscle feels like.[151]

PMR can be practiced as follows:[152]

- Begin by finding a comfortable position by either sitting or lying down in a location where interruption is limited.
- Allow attention to focus only on the body.

- If the mind starts wandering, bring it back to the muscle that was focused on.
- Take a deep breath through nose, hold for a few seconds, and exhale slowly. Again, while breathing, notice the stomach rising and lungs filling with air.
- During exhale, imagine the tension in the body being released and flowing out of the body. Inhale and exhale. Feel the body becoming more relaxed.
- Remember to keep breathing.

Now one starts

- Tighten the muscles in the forehead by raising the eyebrows as high as possible. Hold for about five seconds and then abruptly relax, feeling the tension disappear.
- Pause for about 10 seconds.
- Now smile widely, feeling the mouth and cheeks tense. Hold for about 5 seconds, and release, appreciating the softness in the face.
- Pause for about 10 seconds.
- Next, tighten the eye muscles by squinting the eyelids tightly shut. Hold for about 5 seconds, and release.
- Pause for about 10 seconds.
- Gently pull the head back as if to look at the ceiling. Hold for about 5 seconds, and release, feeling the tension melting away.
- Pause for about 10 seconds.
- Now feel the weight of the relaxed head and neck sink.
- Breathe in and out. In and out. Let go of all the stress. Breathe in and out.
- Now, tightly, but without straining, clench the fists and hold this position for about 5 seconds, and release.
- Pause for about 10 seconds.
- Now, flex the biceps. Feel that build-up of tension. Visualise that muscle tightening. Hold for about 5 seconds and release, enjoying that feeling of limpness.
- Breath in and out.
- Now tighten the triceps by extending the arms out and locking the elbows. Hold for about 5 seconds, and release.
- Pause for about 10 seconds.
- Now lift the shoulders up as if they could touch the ears. Hold for about 5 seconds, and quickly release, feeling their heaviness.

- Pause for about 10 seconds.
- Tense upper back by pulling shoulders back trying to make the shoulder blades touch. Hold for about 5 seconds, and release.
- Pause for about 10 seconds.
- Tighten the chest by taking a deep breath, hold for about 5 seconds, and exhale, blowing out all the tension.
- Now tighten the muscles in the stomach by sucking in. Hold for about 5 seconds, and release.
- Pause for about 10 seconds.
- Gently arch lower back. Hold for about 5 seconds and relax.
- Pause for about 10 seconds.
- Feel the limpness in the upper body letting go of the tension and stress, hold for about 5 seconds, and relax.
- Tighten the buttocks. Hold for about 5 seconds and release, imagine the hips falling loose.
- Pause for about 10 seconds.
- Tighten the thighs by pressing knees together. Hold for about 5 seconds and release.
- Pause for about 10 seconds.
- Now flex the feet, pulling the toes and feeling the tension in the calves. Hold for about 5 seconds, and relax, feel the weight of the legs sinking down.
- Pause for about 10 seconds.
- Curl the toes under tensing the feet. Hold for about 5 seconds and release.
- Pause for about 10 seconds.
- Now imagine a wave of relaxation slowly spreading through the body beginning at the head and going all the way down to the feet.
- Feel the relaxed body. Breathe in and out, in and out, and in and out.

Distract

Being able to distract oneself during a crisis when feelings are overwhelming, serves as an essential tool.[153] A technique that can be used for distraction, is the 5-4-3-2-1 grounding technique, which focuses on the individual's five senses, and can be practiced as follows:[154]

- Take a deep breath in and out – repeat a couple of times.
- Focus on **5** things that you can **see** (e.g. birds, trees, watch etc.).

- Focus on **4** things that you can **feel or touch** (e.g. the chair that you are sitting on, your hair in your neck etc.).
- Focus on **3** things you can **hear** (e.g. cars passing by, people talking, the clock ticking etc.).
- Focus on **2** things you can **smell** (e.g. the air, flowers, rain etc.).
- Focus on **1** thing you can **taste** (e.g. mints, coffee etc.).
- Take a deep breath in and out.

When an individual feels that he/she can answer the question: *Am I able to calm myself?* in the affirmative, the person is able to calm and recentre themselves and thus ready to proceed to step 4. If not, and the individual feels overwhelmed by all the emotions they experience, please seek professional services.

Step 4: Challenge thoughts

Examining the evidence

When faced with a crisis, negative thoughts might flood an individual's thinking which contribute to feeling overwhelmed.[155] Examining one's thoughts serves as a practical exercise that allows the individual to objectively evaluate whether the current negative thought is a fact or just a thought.[156] The following steps allow a person to examine the evidence for their thoughts:[157]

- Identify the difficult situation that caused the thoughts (trigger) and briefly describe what happened.
- What emotion are you feeling? Describe how intense the emotion is on a scale of 1-10.
- Identify what is happening in your mind. What are you thinking about the situation/yourself/others that are negative.
- Look at the facts that support your thought. What serves as evidence of this thought being absolutely true?
- Focus on facts that do not support your thoughts or provide evidence contrary to what you are thinking about the situation, yourself, or others.
- Develop an alternative mindset by focusing on all the evidence for and against your thoughts. Think about a more balanced, realistic way of thinking about the situation, yourself, or others.
- Rerate what you are feeling on a scale of 1-10.

Being able to distance oneself from negative thoughts and evaluating whether the thought is a fact, or just a thought, empowers an individual to feel more in control of the situation, and therefore decreases the impact of the emotion one is experiencing.

Give advice

Another way of challenging negative thoughts is to guide oneself the same way you would guide your loved ones when they are faced with a difficult situation.[158] This can be done by asking yourself: If _____ (friend, family member, colleague) were in this situation and had this thought, what advice would I give them?[159]

It is found that it is much easier to give advice and compassion to someone one cares about, rather than giving it to oneself. Individuals going through a crisis are motivated to take their own advice and follow it as best they can.[160]

When an individual can answer the question: *Am I able to challenge my thoughts to be more rational?* affirmatively, they are ready to proceed to step 5. If not, and the individual's thoughts are too irrational and evasive, please seek professional guidance.

Step 5: Redefine your role

The final step of this model motivates an individual to look at themselves focusing on the future, and not just on the here and now or past events from the crisis. This step will enable an individual to answer the question, *who am I more?*

The knowledge one has about one's individuality, capability, attributes, qualities and deficiencies, values, and beliefs, can be defined as one's self-concept.[161] Hence, self-concept is how an individual sees him-/herself as an individual. Self-concept is formed early in life and influences an individual's behaviour and actions.[162] There are various parts of the self-concept which is worth defining to be able to focus on who one is, for example other than a sportsman or sportswoman. The individual needs to think about how they would describe the value of each of the following aspects and what they would like it to be in the future:[163]

- Physical self-concept: Refers to an individual's view of their physical health, appearance, physical skill, and sexuality. How would you like to see your overall physical health in the future?

- Moral self-concept: Reflects an individual's satisfaction with their own behaviour and control over their impulses. How would you like to see your behaviour in the future?

- Personal self-concept: Provides information on an individual's sense of adequacy in various aspects in their life. What do you value most in life and what can you do to achieve it?

- Family self-concept: Indicates an individual's relationship with family and close associates. How would you like to see your relationships with your family in the future?

- Social self-concept: Refers to how an individual sees themselves in relation to their peers and friends. How would you like to see your relationships with your friends in the future?

- Academic/work self-concept: Reflects how an individual perceives him-/herself in work and school settings. Other than sport, what would you like to achieve in an academic or work setting one day?

One of the ways in which an individual can determine how they see themselves, is to use the G.L.A.D. technique. To be more aware of what one values in life, try reflecting on the following once a week:[164]

- **G**: one thing you feel grateful for.
- **L**: one thing you learned about yourself or in general.
- **A**: one thing you have achieved, regardless of how big or small.
- **D**: one thing that made you feel delighted.

Using this model will give an individual the ability to protect their soul by focusing on its core, which is the brain. Using these steps will help an individual to get from the brain's emotional centre (amygdala) to the cognitive centre (PFC) to enable him/her to manage their emotions more effectively and solve problems more efficiently, but to also have compassion on themselves and get to know themselves better through each step.

CHAPTER 11

LEGAL CONSIDERATIONS DURING A CRISIS IN SPORT

Bertie Grobler & Rian Cloete

Introduction

South Africa has a vibrant sports culture with several sports organisations and governing bodies. When a crisis arises, it is essential to respond promptly and effectively. The following are some crucial points to bear in mind about crisis management in sport from a South African legal standpoint:

1. Sports organisations have contractual agreements that define their rights and obligations. When a crisis occurs, evaluating these contracts to determine the legal implications and potential remedies is critical. This may include examining issues such as contract breaches, termination clauses, or liability for damages.

2. Most sports have governing bodies that establish rules and regulations governing the behaviour of participants and organisations. In a crisis, assessing whether any regulations have been violated and what disciplinary actions or sanctions may apply is essential. Understanding and using the relevant regulations are crucial to ensure fairness and maintain the sport's integrity.

3. Sports organisations in South Africa must comply with various legislative and regulative requirements and obligations. Ensuring compliance with these legal requirements during a crisis is essential to minimise legal risks and potential liability.

4. Sports crisis management often involves intense media scrutiny and public attention. South African sports organisations should have effective media and public relations strategies to manage the public perception of the crisis.

5. Crises may lead to legal disputes or conflicts. South Africa has a well-established legal system that provides various avenues for dispute resolution, including negotiation, mediation, arbitration, or litigation. Understanding the appropriate legal recourse and engaging in effective dispute-resolution mechanisms can help resolve conflicts arising from a sports crisis.

Sports organisations in South Africa should have comprehensive insurance coverage and risk management strategies in place to mitigate potential financial losses and legal liabilities.

This may include coverage for professional indemnity, public liability, and event cancellation insurance. Sports organisations should ensure proper insurance and risk management processes to mitigate financial risks associated with a crisis.

Managing a crisis in the South African sports industry requires a multi-faceted approach considering several legal aspects. Sports organisations must ensure they have robust contract management, regulatory compliance, media and public relations, dispute resolution, insurance and risk management, and legal advisory processes to mitigate the risks associated with the planning and execution of sporting events.

Legal compliance in event planning and execution

From an event planning perspective, compliance with regulatory and legislative obligations is the most important consideration in the planning, management and execution of any event attended by spectators. Unfortunately, every now and then, sports stadiums around the world make media headlines because of one or other tragedy in the hosting of an event. Often, the tragedy stems from structural issues with the venue. In most cases, however, crowd behaviour and crowd control and management problems are at the root of the crisis.

South African legal position pre-2010

On 11 April 2001, spectators poured into Ellis Park Stadium in Johannesburg for the famous Soweto derby football match between Kaizer Chiefs and Orlando Pirates. Due to the overwhelming number of fans, organisers struggled to manage the crowd, resulting in a stampede and the death of 43 spectators. This tragedy became known as the Ellis Park Stadium disaster - South African history's most severe sporting tragedy.

The South African Government appointed the Judicial Commission of Inquiry into the disaster. In his final report on the Ellis Park disaster, Judge Bernard Ngoepe attributed the incident to a combination of factors: overcrowding, an untimely announcement that the stadium was packed, the use of teargas, and unruly spectator behaviour and the absence of cooperation between various stakeholders. According to his report, several other issues led to the tragedy, such as poor match attendance forecasting—and failure to learn from past experiences. Also, the unclear identification of roles and responsibilities and lack of overall command of the joint operation centre; failure to adhere to FIFA and SAFA guidelines; selling of tickets at the venue with unreserved seating; there was corruption among security personnel; dereliction of duty on the part of certain security officials; inadequate public address system; and finally, the Public Order Policing Unit's failure to react promptly and effectively. At this time, no legalisation was in place to govern the planning and execution of events.

Until today, some legal commentators still believe that the CEO of Ellis Park Stadium should have been charged with contravening section 16 of the South African Occupational Health and

Safety Act of 1993. The Commission of Inquiry recommended the introduction of specialist legislation to regulate safety at high-risk mass events.

South African legal position post-2010

The South African government subsequently established a team to draft the legislation, which was finally enacted as the Safety at Sports and Recreation Events Act, 2 of 2010 (SASREA). SASREA aims to ensure the safety and security of participants, spectators, and officials at sports and recreational events. The Act establishes legal compliance requirements for venues, event organisers, governing bodies, and event sponsors hosting such events to minimise risks and tragedies.

If the venue lacks proper controls and safety measures, all coordinating parties involved, including organisers, sponsors, venue operators, and owners, could jointly and severally be liable for damages and legal claims. Joint and several liability is a form of liability used in civil cases where two or more parties may be liable for damages. In such cases the injured party may seek payment of the entire judgment from any of the parties who are said to be jointly and severally liable. In other words, if a defendant does not have enough money or assets to pay an equal share of the award, the other defendants must make up the difference.

Although the SASREA provides for various duties and obligations on each of the entities, in the event of a disaster and injury to individuals, those injured parties may choose to sue any of the commodities as envisaged by SASREA; whether there was fault on the part of that party or not. For instance, if an injury occurred because of inadequate emergency gates, whilst that may be the venue owner's obligation, the injured may hold the controlling body or the event organiser liable. Those parties cannot deny responsibility because emergency gates were the venue owner's responsibility, as the SASREA has placed a burden on all the entities to ensure safety and accountability at events.

SASREA provides a framework for ensuring the safety and security of participants and spectators at sports and recreational events. Under this Act, several essential venue compliance requirements must be met to ensure the safety of all those involved.

To deal with the consequences of a crisis, it is essential to understand the legislative requirements imposed on parties involved in the planning and execution of events as envisaged in SASREA. Below is a summary of some legal obligations imposed on role-players to comply with SASREA.

Venue authority

From 31 October 2010, all stadiums and venues with a capacity of 2000 or more spectators are required to apply for existing stadium safety and event risk grading certificates (referred to as "safety certificates") according to section 8 of SASREA. This certificate confirms that the venue meets the safety and security standards in the Act. The platform must comply with various requirements to obtain this certificate, including infrastructure, medical facilities, safety, and security. These safety certificates must be applied for on an annual basis.

Controlling body, event organiser and stadium owner or venue authority

The following obligations are placed on the controlling body, event organiser and stadium owner or venue authority:

1. Take all necessary steps to ensure the safety and security of all individuals present at an event at a stadium, venue, or along a route, including their property.
2. Appoint a stadium or venue safety officer to ensure compliance with the Act and take the necessary steps for safety and security.
3. Assist the event safety and security planning committee in developing, reviewing, and amending the written safety and security plan.
4. Ensure the safety and security plan is implemented as the Act requires.
5. Assist and cooperate with the National Commissioner and authorised member, event safety and security planning committee, venue operations centre commander, and all safety and security role-players referred to in the Act.
6. Comply with all relevant legislation applicable to hosting an event at a stadium, venue, or along a route or their respective precincts.

Comply fully with any other duty or responsibility imposed in terms of any other provision of the Act.

National commissioner, authorised member, and SAPS

The following duties are placed on the national commissioner, authorised member, and SAPS:

1. Establish and coordinate the event safety and security planning committee, appoint members, and chair meetings. The event safety and security planning committee must develop and implement measures to improve the safety and security of all attendees, their property and any other individuals at an event hosted at a stadium, venue, or along a route and their respective precincts.
2. Consult with controlling bodies, event organisers, and stadium/venue owners in developing, reviewing, and amending event safety and security plans. Develop internal written operational SAPS responsibilities under the Act.
3. Appoint a venue operation centre commander, of at least Captain rank, for venue operations at an event in a stadium, venue, or along a route.

4. Ensure that local authorities inspect stadiums, venues, routes, or precincts before events to ensure compliance with the Act.
5. Issue, alter, amend, or withdraw high-risk event certificates. Issue, change, amend, or withdraw prohibition notices. Issue and withdraw spectator exclusion orders.
6. Act according to the provisions of the Act at all times. Always act according to the requirements of event safety and security plans. Advise Minister on safety and security related to hosting events at stadiums, venues, routes, or precincts.
7. Direct controlling bodies, event organisers, and stadium/venue owners to apply for high-risk safety certificates within 30 days of designation. Ensure that no unauthorised advertising and ticket/merchandise sales occur in exclusion zones.
8. Establish the Venue Operations Centre according to regulations set by the Minister for Safety and Security. Ensure high-risk safety certificate applications comply with regulations regarding timeframes and requirements.
9. Ensure proper security measures and deployments are in place at events according to regulations set by the Minister for Safety and Security. Ensure sufficient public liability insurance coverage is in place at events as per regulations set by the Minister for Safety and Security.

State Security Services

The SAPS may request the State Security Services to provide reasonable and necessary assistance and support services as per the event safety and security plan outlined in the Act.

Sponsors

Any individual or entity with a significant financial interest in the organisation of an event at a stadium, venue, or along a route, such as an event sponsor or the event's rights holder, must provide reasonable cooperation and support to enhance safety and security at the event when directed or requested to do so under the Act; always comply with the Act's provisions and adhere to the safety and security plan requirements outlined in the Act throughout the event.

Security Service Provider, which includes a Security Business and a Security Officer

When requested or directed by this Act, the provider must cooperate and provide support to enhance safety and security at an event at a stadium, venue, or along a route and at their respective precincts. Comply with the Act and other applicable legislation. Follow the safety and security event plan drafted by the Act and make sure that security officers, if deployed, comply with all relevant legislation applicable to the private security service industry.

Medical personnel

Medical personnel must provide cooperation and support to enhance safety and security at events, as directed or requested under the Act. They must comply with the Act (SASREA), the Health Act, and the Health Professions Act and operate within the event's safety and security plan. They must ensure that the necessary medical services, facilities, equipment, and personnel are present at the event, as specified in the Minister for Safety and Security regulations. Medical practitioners must hold a valid medical qualification recognised by the Health Professions Council of South Africa and be registered with the Council.

Metro police and traffic police

the metro and traffic police must comply with specific requirements. Firstly, they must cooperate and provide the necessary support to improve event safety and security when directed or requested under the Act. They should follow all provisions of the Act and other applicable legislation and act in accordance with the safety and security event plan. They must ensure that any traffic management protocols are enforced and implemented according to the event safety and security plan.

Stewards or marshals

Stewards or marshals must provide their cooperation and support to improve the event's safety and security when directed or requested under the Act. They must comply with the Act's event safety and security plan. While managing spectators, by performing tasks such as ushering, guiding, and providing event support services, they are not allowed to offer security services unless qualified under the Private Security Industry Regulation Act 2001. They should only do so under the direction of the controlling body, event organiser, or the stadium/venue owner.

Disaster management centre, emergency services, and essential services personnel

these personnel must cooperate and provide the necessary support to enhance event safety and security when directed or requested under the Act. They must comply with the relevant provisions of the Disaster Management Act 2002, including following safety and security and disaster management plans specified in the Act. They must ensure that the minimum emergency and disaster management services, facilities, equipment, and personnel categories are deployed at the event, as specified in the Disaster Management Act 2002.

Case Law

Structural issues with the venue

The Inquest Court for the District of Cape Town issued the first official interpretation of the practical operation of the SASREA and how liability can be attributed under this legislation.

This inquest stemmed from a tragic incident on 7 November 2012 during a Linkin Park concert held at Cape Town Stadium—the concert was organised under the auspices of the SASREA.

During the event, a temporary structure advertising the Lucozade brand, constructed using scaffolding, collapsed due to strong winds. The event organiser, Glaxo Smith Kline, had erected this structure and had enlisted the services of Hirt & Carter, a company specialising in media and advertising campaign design, to conceptualise and manage the project. Hirt & Carter appointed Bothma Signs, aware that the latter needed an expert in scaffolding to design the banner wrapped around the frame. Bothma Signs then subcontracted Vertex, a supplier of custom scaffolding solutions, to assist with the construction.

The magistrate was tasked to evaluate whether any of the event's organisers had committed specific offences outlined in the SASREA, which carry penalties of 5 to 20 years of imprisonment. In addition, she also had to assess whether the failure to fulfil responsibilities mandated by the legislation directly caused the resulting fatality.

The magistrate scrutinised the facts and absolved Glaxo Smith Kline of any wrongdoing. The inquest magistrate, however, determined that there was sufficient evidence to suggest prima facie criminal culpability on the part of the three parties involved in the project. The magistrate's findings against the three companies involved in the scaffolding erection, were based on several reasons:

1. The companies responsible for constructing and setting up the scaffolding should have reasonably anticipated that even moderate winds could cause it to collapse.
2. It was established that there had been no sign-off by a structural engineer, and the towers had not been adequately secured, leading to their dislodgment and subsequent injury to concertgoers.
3. Vertex demonstrated negligence and disregarded essential safety measures, such as securing the towers to a concrete platform or using weights and steel wires for stability.
4. Bothma Signs was fully aware of the wind conditions in Cape Town and the requirement for a safety file with a sign-off from a qualified person, yet they still neglected to fulfil these obligations.

5. Hirt & Carter could not rely on assurances from their subcontractor, Bothma Signs, regarding providing proper documentation and expertise.

Hirt & Carter sought a review of the magistrate's findings in the High Court, arguing that the magistrate had erred in holding them responsible for supervising and managing the erection of the towers, as this was the subcontractor's responsibility and was carried out by independent contractors. The High Court sided against Hirt & Carter, noting that they should have considered the requirement for proper certification and conducted a physical inspection of the structure. The court concluded that Hirt & Carter, having accepted liability for a safety compliance certificate, was obligated to ensure that the certificate complied with the necessary safety standards in form and substance.

Hirt & Carter's application for review and the setting aside of the magistrate's findings were dismissed by the High Court, prompting the company to appeal to the Supreme Court of Appeal for a review. In a concurring judgment, the Supreme Court of Appeal acknowledged that the magistrate had meticulously considered the involvement of the Hirt & Carter employee in addressing safety concerns and the factors known to both the employee and Hirt & Carter. Consequently, the Supreme Court of Appeal dismissed the application for review based on the following considerations:

1. The magistrate considered email correspondence that underscored the significance of obtaining a structural engineer's sign-off. Hirt & Carter's failure to even consider whether the appropriate certification was in place and their lack of insistence on physically inspecting the structure counted against them.

2. Bothma Signs was fully aware of the threat posed by Cape Town's wind and the necessity of a safety file with a sign-off from a qualified individual. However, they should have verified the presence of this safety file. The sign-off, carried out by Vertex workers who lacked professional qualifications, needed to be improved.

3. The magistrate correctly disregarded the argument that Hirt & Carter should be exonerated due to subcontracting Bothma Signs and Vertex. Based on the factual circumstances of the case, the magistrate reasonably concluded that the casualty resulted from an act or omission that prima facie constituted an offence on the part of Hirt & Carter.

In summary, the Supreme Court of Appeal supported the magistrate's thorough analysis of the Hirt & Carter employee's role in addressing safety issues and failing to obtain proper certification and ensure compliance with safety requirements by Bothma Signs. The court also affirmed that Hirt & Carter could not evade culpability by relying on the subcontracting arrangement. Ultimately, the magistrate's conclusion that the death resulted from an offence committed by Hirt & Carter was upheld.

Crowd control and management

On Saturday 29 July 2017, in the Carling Black Label fixture between Kaizer Chiefs and Orlando Pirates, a tragedy unfolded at the FNB Stadium; on this occasion, a stampede caused the death of two fans, and nineteen others sustained injuries.

Two plaintiffs also took legal action against the sponsor, the venue authority and the participating premiership soccer clubs. The plaintiffs alleged that whilst waiting in line to enter the stadium before the soccer match, a stampede occurred, which, according to the plaintiffs, resulted from poor crowd control measures and inadequate security personnel to control the large crowd.

Plaintiff particulars of claim

The plaintiffs alleged that they were pushed to the ground and trampled on and that the sole cause of the stampede was the result of the defendant's failure to:

1. Take positive steps to prevent any stampede and crowd behaviour by their prior conduct of organising such a game.

2. Take pre-emptive and cautious steps to control/combat/prevent crowd behaviour and any disorderly conduct that might expose soccer fans, in particular the plaintiff, to any bodily harm and loss of life as a result of an ensuing stampede.

3. Implement proper crowd control measures at any time during the hosting of the game.

4. Protect the soccer fans in attendance, in particular the plaintiff, from any form of violence, be it from a public or private source, at such a sporting event hosted by the defendants.

5. Eliminate, prevent and guard against hazardous conditions arising from unruly crowd behaviour and a stampede, thus putting the innocent public, particularly the plaintiff, in reasonably foreseeable harm's way when attending the soccer match.

6. Implement and comply with statutory, regulatory and standing orders on safety measures required in soccer matches in terms of the Safety at Sports and Recreational Act No. 2 of 2010.

7. Implement and ensure effective and efficient crowd control measures reasonably expected from them for hosting such a big event, albeit a friendly match, between the second and third defendants notorious for being crowd-pulling soccer rivals at the said stadium.

8. Take reasonably practicable steps not to create a dangerous situation of rowdy crowds when would-be spectators enter the stadium, during the match, and when leaving the stadium.

Venue authority plea

First defence: The plaintiffs do not have a valid claim due to their illegal conduct

In their plea, the venue authority claims that the stampede was caused by a patron illegally gaining access through an emergency gate between official entrance gates. The spectators forced the emergency gate open to gain (illegal) access to the stadium and, in the process, caused the stampede.

At the time of the incident, a security guard was deployed at the emergency gate to guard against illegal access. Regarding the applicable legislation, an emergency gate may not be locked during an event. One guard per emergency gate is the norm in the industry.

The venue authority believes that only valid ticket holders can, in principle (subject to proof of all other requirements), be entitled to claim compensation. In determining whether the right ticket holder would have a claim, differentiation must be made between a valid ticket holder who innocently ended up in the stampede and a valid ticket holder who participated in attempting to gain access to the stadium through the emergency gate. In these circumstances, only the right ticket holder who innocently ended up in the stampede will, in principle, have a claim.

Second defence: statutory and regulatory compliance

The event organiser and venue authority allegedly submitted a detailed pre-event risk assessment plan to the ESSPC, identifying the following risks: Forcing of inner perimeter emergency gates adjacent to turnstiles by groups of hooligan supporters during access pressure, resulting in overcrowding of the capacity stadium and a large crowd with general crowd management challenges; pressure on search areas, turnstiles, emergency gates, and stampedes at public transport nodes.

The abovementioned risks were categorised as a high probability of occurring at the event, and a joint SAPS and Private Security emergency response plan and an event access control and crowd management plan were prepared to deal with how the various role players were to handle these issues should they arise.

The event organiser and venue authority argued that these risks were identified in the pre-event risk assessment plan submitted seven weeks before the event, indicating that the event organiser and venue authority foresaw the potential challenges of large crowds.

That the submitted safety and security plans were in place is also a clear indication that the event organiser and venue authority, in foreseeing these possible risks, tried to take steps to prevent the threat from occurring, and alternatively identified steps to mitigate the same and to deal with the fallout should it be impossible to stop.

They argued that while a reasonable person in the shoes of the event organiser and venue authority would have foreseen that a stampede could occur, they would not have been able to prevent a charge, especially under the circumstances where several unruly, intoxicated fans attempted to gain access to the event via emergency gates without valid tickets.

The event organiser and venue authority plea claims that neither breached its duty of care, specifically in circumstances where they complied with (and went over and above) all regulatory requirements.

This matter is still to be decided and ruled upon.

Legislation

There is surprisingly a lot of legislation that impact sport and the hosting of sporting events (also see chapter 7). The various legislations include the National Environmental Management Act: Waste Act 59 of 2008; Hazardous Substances Act 15 of 1973; National Water Act 36 of 1998; The Occupational Health and Safety Act 85 of 1993; Animals Protection Act 1962; Environment Conservation Act 73 of 1989; National Noise Control Regulations; Foodstuffs, Cosmetics and Disinfectants Act 54 of 1972; as well as provincial and local government legislations, licenses or permits.

The negative effect of non-compliance

Several possible negatives may result from non-compliance. These include reputational damage to athletes, teams, and sports bodies; legal repercussions, fines, and sanctions; loss of public trust and diminished fan base; and potential impact on sponsorship deals and revenue streams.

Measures to mitigate compliance risk in sport

It is essential to implement robust policies and procedures and conduct regular risk assessments and audits. Additionally, it also necessary to provide comprehensive training and education to athletes and staff, establish effective whistleblower mechanisms, and collaborate with regulatory bodies and law enforcement agencies.

CHAPTER 12

ALTERNATIVE DISPUTE RESOLUTION IN SPORT

Jacques Faul

Introduction

Events have many role players that give effect to many rights and obligations. This will no doubt lead to disputes. This can be a major crisis and may even threaten the success of an event. Alternative Dispute Resolution (ADR) provides an alternative option to the normal legal processes. This is an important toolkit to address legal issues and a thorough understanding of the alternatives will assist in dealing with legal disputes.

Millions of rands could have been saved if disputes in sport had been mediated instead of going a formal legal route. The money could have been utilised to serve sport better. I have been blessed to study law and comprehend the value of sound legal advice and support.

However, mediation has the potential to save costs and keep the dirty laundry of sport out of the public domain. A lack of knowledge about alternative dispute resolution is one of the reasons why the option is not used very often. This chapter discusses all the alternative dispute resolution (ADR) options i.e.: negotiation, conciliation, mediation and arbitration.

Mediation is discussed in more detail, and I strongly recommend this option.

Training

I was privileged to attend the UCT/MiM Advocates & Attorneys and Other Qualified Legal Professionals Mediation Training Course. Experienced and qualified lecturers presented the course. It dramatically changed my perception of how to deal with conflict and disputes. This is especially true for the sporting industry. I have been a CEO in cricket for 20 years and immediately realised the tremendous value that facilitative mediation will add to the industry. At the Titans, we have established the Centre for Alternative Dispute Resolution in Sport and will align with this strategy.

Negotiation

Negotiations are discussions between parties to find a solution; this step should always be the first step. Starting with a letter of demand from your lawyer already muddy the water for a solution.

Disputes can be emotional, and parties are keen to show their legal muscle and negotiations are often disregarded. The final decision still lies with the parties. Senior management should play a leadership role in this regard. I strongly suggest a face-to-face meeting with senior decision-makers. E-mails seldom resolve these conflicts. It is further suggested that a phased approach to resolving disputes is standard operating procedure. This may follow the route of negotiation, conciliation, mediation and then a final step of litigation or arbitration.

Conciliation

This option is seldom used but should be the next step should negotiation fail. This involves having a conciliator assisting parties in finding a solution. The value of the process is that the conciliator may suggest solutions to the parties for consideration. The final decision still lies with the parties. A conciliator is an independent person who is able to assist the parties.

Mediation

If negotiation and conciliation fail, the next step should be mediation. This is strongly recommended before the parties enter a more formal legal route.

Education and training in dispute resolution

Many people involved in the event industry argue that dispute resolution is solely for the legal fraternity and should be referred to them. This is not true and there are various training options available to people who do not have a formal legal qualification. The fact that I have an LLM degree does come in handy but anyone can be trained as a mediator.

Rules of the court to deal with disputes

South Africa has a complex legal system that includes various courts to handle different types of legal disputes. It's important to note that laws and regulations can change for the courts to be more effective. Each province in South Africa has its own High Court that handles civil and criminal cases, as well as appeals from lower courts. The High Court has its own set of rules to deal with these matters.

The courts cannot handle the number of cases

The High Court in each province needs to resolve both civil and criminal matters. The courts cannot deal with the ever-increasing workload of cases and have thus amended their rules to encourage mediation before the courts are approached. This resulted in a rule change, namely Rule 41 (A).

Amendments to rules are announced under the Rules Board for Courts of Law Act 1985 (Act No. 107 of 1985). The new Rule 41 (A) refers to the amendment of rules regulating the conduct of the proceedings of the provincial and local divisions of the High Court of South Africa. On 7 February 2020 the Government Gazette[165] announced the new rule inserted after Rule 41. This dramatically affects the litigation landscape and forces parties to formally consider mediation and complete Form 27 as prescribed by the rule.

Joubert[166] states, *"Rule 41A prepares the ground for litigants to mediate before they venture to court. Subrule (2)(a) compels a plaintiff or applicant to file a prescribed Rule 41A Notice of agreeing or opposing mediation before summons or motions may be issued. Secondly, sub-rule (2)(b) compels the defendant or respondent to file a prescribed Rule 41A Notice of agreeing or opposing mediation before a plea or opposing papers may be issued. According to sub-rule (2)(c), the above notices must substantially follow Form 27 of the First Schedule. According to sub-rule (2)(d), the notices will be without prejudice and not filed with the Registrar. The purpose is not to disclose the parties' positions regarding mediation to the trial judge until the end of the trial. Suppose one or both parties decide to oppose mediation. In that case, they must clearly and concisely indicate reasons in their sub-rule (2) Notices that the case is or cannot be mediated."*

Mediation process

Mediation is a structured yet relatively informal process that can resolve disputes cost-effectively and quickly. A trained, experienced mediator will be equipped to address parties' anger and irrational behaviour to identify the real issues driving conflicts. Parties must sign an agreement to mediate and have settlement authority. The process remains voluntary. The process is confidential and without prejudice; it is further non-binding until a settlement agreement is signed to give it legal effect. The proceedings guarantee autonomy to the parties, and they determine the outcome. There are different forms of mediation, including:

- **Facilitative mediation**

    The facilitative mediator primarily focuses on helping the parties communicate effectively and understand each other's interests and needs. The mediator facilitates the negotiation process but does not offer opinions or solutions. They guide the parties through discussion and exploration of possible solutions. The emphasis is on empowering the parties to make their own decisions and reach a voluntary agreement.

- **Evaluative mediation**

    The evaluative mediator, in addition to facilitating communication, actively evaluates the legal merits of the case. This mediator may offer opinions, predictions, or assessments of how a court might decide the case based on legal principles. The goal is often to assist the parties in reaching a resolution that is legally sound and potentially aligned with what a court might decide.

- **Transformative mediation**

    Transformative mediation aims to empower parties by focusing on communication and recognition of each other's perspectives. The transformative mediator facilitates conversations that allow the parties to understand each other's needs and concerns. The mediator may also help parties recognise the impact of the conflict on their relationship. The central idea is to empower individuals to make their own decisions and to promote the recognition and understanding of each other's experiences, fostering a transformation in their relationship. This process refers to a facilitative approach and is not adjudicative in nature.

Mediation is tailored for sports disputes. The relationships between parties are vital in sport. Sports disputes, widely reported in the media, taint the sporting body's reputation. A swift resolution of disputes will have a less damaging effect in the eyes of sponsors and fans.

Mediation versus litigation

Litigation provides an outcome to a dispute. If parties think they have a strong case, they may favour this option. This may result in a recovery of only some legal costs and may be time-consuming. However, it is a well-known dispute option that has been used frequently.

Crawford[167] states that commercial mediation has several advantages over traditional litigation, noting that it is cheaper and may commence as soon as both sides are ready. "There is a prevalent attitude that during the business dialogue, people should take up positions and hold to them fiercely – a strict 'winner takes all' mentality. Litigation, which is essentially a process of escalating claim and counterclaim, encourages this approach. Litigation obscures the potential for constructive solutions offered through professional mediation."

Crawford elaborates on the other advantages of mediation:

- The process provides resolution without recourse to formal judgment.
- It brings parties together with an independent mediator in a neutral and confidential setting.
- With both parties' consent, they can produce legally binding agreements.
- The process can fix feelings.

It is very important to take note of these advantages as parties to disputes and their legal advisors may need to know the advantages of mediation versus litigation.

Arbitration and mediation in sport

Traditionally, most sporting disputes in South Africa were handled by the courts and the CCMA. The Memorandum of Incorporation of sporting federations could make provisions for internal mediation and arbitration processes. Sporting contracts will mainly provide alternative dispute resolution that may have mediation and arbitration clauses.

Mediation in sport is a new method for addressing disputes and conflicts. The Court of Arbitration for Sport (CAS) is based in Lausanne, Switzerland. It is a specialised court for sport. The regulations[168] state that under Articles S2 and S6, paragraphs 1 and 10 of the Code of Sports-related Arbitration, the International Council of Arbitration for Sport adopts the present mediation rules:

CAS Mediation Rules

(in force as from 1 September 2013; amended on 1 January 2016)

Pursuant to Articles S2 and S6 paragraphs 1 and 10 of the Code of Sports-related Arbitration, the International Council of Arbitration for Sport adopts the present Mediation Rules (the "Rules").

A. DEFINITIONS

Article 1

CAS mediation is a non-binding and informal procedure, based on an agreement to mediate in which each party undertakes to attempt in good faith to negotiate with the other party with a view to settling a sports-related dispute. The parties are assisted in their negotiations by a CAS mediator.

In principle, CAS mediation is provided for the resolution of contractual disputes. Disputes related to disciplinary matters, such as doping issues, match-fixing and corruption, are excluded from CAS mediation. However, in certain cases, where the circumstances so require and the parties expressly agree, disputes related to disciplinary matters may be submitted to CAS mediation.

Article 2

A mediation agreement is one whereby the parties agree to submit to mediation a sports-related dispute which has arisen or which may arise between them.

A mediation agreement may take the form of a mediation clause in a contract or a separate agreement.

B. SCOPE OF APPLICATION OF RULES

Article 3

Where a mediation agreement provides for mediation under the CAS Mediation Rules, these Rules shall be deemed to form an integral part of such mediation agreement. Unless the parties have agreed otherwise, the version of these Rules in force on the date when the mediation request is filed shall apply.

The parties may however agree to apply other rules of procedure.

C. COMMENCEMENT OF THE MEDIATION

Article 4

A party wishing to institute mediation proceedings shall address a request to that effect in writing to the CAS Court Office.

The request shall contain: the identity of the parties and their representatives (name, address, email address, telephone and fax numbers), a copy of the mediation agreement and a brief description of the dispute.

The day on which the mediation request is received by the CAS Court Office shall be considered as the date on which the mediation proceedings commence.

The CAS Court Office shall immediately inform the parties of the date on which the mediation commences, and shall fix the time limit by which the parties shall pay their share of the administrative costs and the advance of costs pursuant to Article 14 and Appendix I of the Rules.

If the parties agree to submit an ordinary/appeal arbitration procedure to mediation, the CHF 1,000 (one thousand Swiss francs) Court Office fee paid by the Claimant/Appellant in the arbitration procedure shall be credited to the mediation procedure and used to cover the administrative costs for the mediation.

If the advance of costs is not paid by both parties and if one party does not agree to pay the share of the other party(-ies), the mediation procedure is immediately terminated.

D. APPOINTMENT OF THE MEDIATOR

Article 5

The ICAS draws up the list of mediators available to be appointed in CAS mediation procedures.

The personalities whom the ICAS appoints appear on the list of mediators for a four-year period, and are thereafter eligible for reselection.

Article 6

Unless the parties have jointly selected a mediator from the list of CAS mediators, the mediator shall be appointed by the CAS President, after consultation with the parties, from among the list of CAS mediators.

In accepting such appointment, the mediator undertakes to devote sufficient time to the mediation proceedings to permit them to be conducted expeditiously.

The mediator shall be and must remain impartial, and independent of the parties, and shall disclose any facts or circumstances which might be of such nature as to call into question her/his independence in the eyes of any of the parties. Notwithstanding any such disclosure, the parties may agree in writing to authorise the mediator to continue his mandate.

In the event of an objection by any of the parties, or at her/his own discretion if she/he deems herself/himself unable to bring the mediation to a successful conclusion, the mediator shall cease her/his mandate and inform the CAS President accordingly, whereupon the latter will make arrangements to replace her/him, after consulting the parties and offering them the possibility to appoint another CAS mediator.

E. **REPRESENTATION OF PARTIES**

Article 7

The parties may be represented or assisted in their meetings with the mediator.

If a party is being represented, the other party, the mediator and the CAS must be informed beforehand as to the identity of such representative.

The representative must have full written authority to settle the dispute alone, without needing to consult the party she/he is representing.

F. **CONDUCT OF MEDIATION**

Article 8

Unless the parties have agreed to conduct the mediation in a particular manner, the mediator shall determine how the mediation will proceed, after consultation with the parties and taking due consideration of the CAS Mediation Guidelines.

Upon her/his appointment, the mediator shall establish the terms and timetable for submission by each party of a statement summarising the dispute, including the following details:

- a brief description of the facts and points of law, including a list of the issues submitted to the mediator with a view to resolution;
- a copy of the mediation agreement.

Where the parties agree to submit an ordinary/appeal arbitration case to mediation, the mediator may consider the request for arbitration/statement of appeal as one party's summary of its dispute and may invite only the other party to submit its summary of the dispute.

Each party shall cooperate in good faith with the mediator and shall guarantee her/him the freedom to perform her/his mandate to advance the mediation as expeditiously as possible. The mediator may make any suggestions she/he deems appropriate in this regard. The mediator may at any time communicate separately with the parties if she/he deems it necessary to do so.

G. ROLE OF THE MEDIATOR

Article 9

The mediator shall promote the settlement of the issues in dispute in any manner that she/he believes to be appropriate. To achieve this, the mediator will:

a. identify the issues in dispute;
b. facilitate discussion of the issues by the parties;
c. propose solutions.

However, the mediator may not impose a solution of the dispute on either party.

H. CONFIDENTIALITY

Article 10

The mediator, the parties, their representatives and advisers, and any other person present during the meetings between the parties shall sign a confidentiality agreement and shall not disclose to any third party any information given to them during the mediation, unless required by law to do so.

Unless required to do so by applicable law and in the absence of any agreement of the parties to the contrary, a party shall not compel the mediator to divulge records, reports or other documents, or to testify in regard to the mediation in any arbitral or judicial proceedings.

Any information given by one party may be disclosed by the mediator to the other party only with the consent of the former.

But for personal notes of the Mediator or the Parties, no record of any kind such as audio or video recording, transcript or minutes shall be made of the meetings.

Unless required to do so by applicable law and in the absence of any agreement of the parties to the contrary, the parties shall not rely on, or introduce as evidence in any arbitral or judicial proceedings:

a. views expressed or suggestions made by a party with respect to a possible settlement of the dispute;

b. admissions made by a party in the course of the mediation proceedings;

c. documents, notes or other information obtained during the mediation proceedings;

d. proposals made or views expressed by the mediator; or

e. the fact that a party had or had not indicated willingness to accept a proposal.

I. TERMINATION

Article 11

Either party or the mediator may terminate the mediation at any time. The mediation shall be terminated:

a. by the signing of a settlement by the parties;

b. by a written declaration of the mediator to the effect that further efforts at mediation are no longer worthwhile;

c. by a written declaration of a party or the parties to the effect that the mediation proceedings are terminated;

d. where one of the parties, or both, refuse(s) to pay its (their) share of the mediation costs within the time limit fixed pursuant to Article 14 of the Rules.

J. SETTLEMENT

Article 12

The settlement is drawn up by the mediator and signed by the parties and the mediator.

Each party shall receive a copy thereof. In the event of any breach, a party may rely on such copy before an arbitral or judicial authority. In the event of any breach, the parties may agree that the case be resolved by CAS arbitration, in accordance with the Code of Sports-related Arbitration.

A copy of the settlement is submitted for inclusion in the records of the CAS Court Office.

K. FAILURE TO SETTLE

Article 13

The parties may have recourse to arbitration when a dispute has not been resolved by mediation, provided that an arbitration agreement or clause exists between the parties.

The arbitration clause may be included in the mediation agreement. In such a case, the expedited procedure provided for under article R44, paragraph 4 of the Code of Sports-related Arbitration may be applied.

In the event of a failure to resolve a dispute by mediation, the mediator shall not accept an appointment as an arbitrator in any arbitral proceedings concerning the parties involved in the same dispute. However, if all parties have explicitly agreed so in writing once the mediation procedure is terminated, it is possible for the mediator to subsequently act as arbitrator for the same dispute and issue an arbitral award in accordance with the CAS Arbitration Rules ("Med- Arb procedure"). Such mediator can only act as an arbitrator if she/he is also on the list of CAS Arbitrators.

L. COSTS

Article 14

Each party shall pay the CAS administrative costs within the time limit provided in Article 4 of the Rules. In the absence of such payment, the mediation proceedings will not be initiated.

The parties shall pay their own mediation fees and expenses.

Unless otherwise agreed between the parties, the final costs of the mediation, which include the CAS administrative costs of CHF 1,000, the costs and fees of the mediator calculated on the basis of the CAS fee scale set out in Appendix I, and a contribution towards the CAS expenses will be borne by the parties in equal shares. At the outset of the mediation proceedings, the CAS Court Office shall require the parties to deposit an equal amount as an advance towards the costs of the mediation.

At the conclusion of the mediation, any portion of the advance of costs which is not used, shall be reimbursed to the parties in equal shares or in the proportion in which the parties paid the advance of costs.

It is unlikely that disputes in South Africa would find their way to CAS due to our relatively weak currency. As illustrated by the unsuccessful referral of the Caster Semenya case, CAS will probably deal with major and international disputes. The courts will deal with most South African conflicts. The Cricket South Africa (CSA) Members Council dispute with the Minister of Sport and the Interim Board resulted in enormous legal costs due to prominent legal firms providing costly consultations. Mediation would have saved money for CSA that could have been spent on the sport itself instead.

> Mironi[169] states that "due to the pivotal role arbitration has traditionally played in sport, the question posed in this article is not whether mediation should replace arbitration as a mainstream dispute resolution process. It only suggests that mediation should be institutionalised and used in appropriate sport-related disputes, primarily in contractual, commercial, and employment-related disputes emanating from sports organisation membership, as an alternative to going directly to arbitration or the courts. The article explores and analyses the limits of arbitration and the special advantage and potential contribution of mediation in sports disputes in terms of efficiency and flexibility, privacy and parties' autonomy, and better and more sustainable outcomes, enhancing access to justice, ability to deal with non-arbitrable disputes and preserving business and personal relationships."

Grabowski[170] states that mediation, a type of alternative dispute resolution that utilises a neutral outsider to facilitate a solution for a conflict between two parties, is seldom used in American professional sports disputes. However, the unique nature of such disputes and mediation's success in ending the 2012-13 National Hockey League labour lockout, indicate that mediation should be used much more often than the commonly used resolution methods of arbitration, litigation, and protracted negotiations. Mediation offers a fast, cost-saving way to settle virtually any conflict. Its confidential nature promotes open communication between the parties, which helps preserve, if not enhance, their working relationships. Although mediation will not fix every sports-related dispute, it could improve player management relations and performance, bolstering fans' confidence in professional sports.

Mediation has the potential to change the dispute resolution landscape in sport. As temporary custodians, sports administrators should act in the best interest of their sport and respect the industry as such. Through proper mediation processes, resources could be spent on promoting sport instead of on unnecessary legal battles.

Arbitration

Arbitration is not a more cost-effective option but has many other advantages. Arbitrators act as private judges, and the parties can agree on who will do the arbitration. The parties agree on the rules; they mostly follow the same rules as the courts. This makes it a formal legal process, but the parties are well aware of the rules that will be followed.

Arbitration will be much faster than litigation; you may wait months and sometimes even more than a year for a court date during a civil dispute. Arbitration proceedings are confidential, and this is a big plus for the parties as the media will be keen to report on significant disputes of the bigger sporting clubs and federations.

Why are some lawyers only sometimes keen on ADR?

Lawyers would mostly prefer arbitration as an ADR rather than any of the other options, including mediation. It would be wrong to assume that all lawyers will only recommend a legal route that provides the highest fee for them. Arbitration, as mentioned, will not be more cost-effective than the courts, but mediation will be. The reality is that if you successfully mediate, then you save drastically on your legal bill.

Lawyers can also rightly claim that they work under instruction, especially when a highly emotional client is in a fighting mood, and they don't want the client to feel that they don't believe in their case. It is also true that you sometimes have such a strong case that it will not be in your interests to follow the ADR route, although I would still suggest mediation to see if it cannot be settled outside of court.

Some lawyers argue that only arbitration brings about an outcome to the dispute. This is untrue, as the parties can draw up a binding contract at the conclusion of the other processes. This will provide enforceable rights.

Conclusion

Sport, like all other industries, will have disputes. The effective resolution of these disputes is usually reliant on good leadership. It is strongly recommended that sporting organisations exhaust other ADR options before entering into arbitration or other formal legal processes.

A better understanding of the available options will hopefully lead to a more cost-effective process. Experience has shown that many disputes are driven by emotion, impacting the chosen methodology and how to deal with it. Personal agendas and egos will not help in this regard.

Sports boards/managing committees and senior managers must be aware of the alternative dispute resolutions available to help solve the matter. Knowledge of these options will empower you to drive a process without relying only on legal advice.

CHAPTER 13

RACISM AND DISCRIMINATION IN SPORT

Jacques Faul

Introduction

Allegations of racism and discrimination may result in a major crisis for sporting organisations and people involved in sport. It may also have a devastating impact. This chapter investigates racism in sport and focuses on the recent reports on racism in cricket in South Africa and the UK. The aim is to provide lessons from these challenges and the reporting of allegations of racism and discrimination.

Suppose you do a basic desktop search on racism in sport. In that case, all sporting codes and federations have been challenged with allegations of racism and even institutionalised racism. All the major federations have anti-racism codes and rules. It is not just a South African issue but a worldwide societal issue. Civil society, individual players, athletes and organisations such as Black Lives Matter (BLM) have prominently engaged with the public to highlight racism in sport. Many sporting federations have resorted to formal enquiries and reports.

The chapter also highlights the role of the media and the need for balanced and fair reporting despite racism and discrimination being an emotional topic. The two most unjust behaviours countering the fight against racism and discrimination are to deny that it exists, as the first and the second is to use emotion and support for the fight against it to unfairly and dishonestly advance a toxic personal agenda. Sadly, I have had first-hand experience of both.

How to deal with allegations of racism and discrimination in sport

Sporting federations will most likely investigate allegations of racism and discrimination and require a process and a report. Some organisations do a once-off report on allegations, whilst others have annual reports. The latter acknowledges that the threat is ongoing and needs continuous monitoring. Surveys by players' associations provide a scientific assessment of the number of players who experience racism and discrimination or think that it is present within their sporting code.

The table below indicates only a few examples of reports on racism in sport.

Table 7: Reports on racism in sport

Report	Sporting Code	Country
• Race and Gender Equity in Sports	All sports	University of Central Florida USA
• "Kick it out "Annual"	Football/Soccer	UK
• Social Justice and Nation Building	Cricket	South Africa
• Racism in Scottish Cricket	Cricket	Scotland
• Evaluation report: Spectator Racism Project 2021-2022	All	Australia
• RFU survey	Rugby	UK
• ECB racism review	Cricket	UK
• YouGov	Soccer	Europe

It is clear from the few examples that it is a worldwide problem experienced by all codes in all countries. Sport is a microcosm of society, and there is enough scientific evidence to prove that discrimination and racism exist in society. You will be very naïve to think sport will be excluded from this.

Black Lives Matter (BLM)

The official BLM website[171] states that Black Lives Matter was founded in 2013 in response to the acquittal of Trayvon Martin's murderer. Black Lives Matter Global Network Foundation Inc., is a global organisation in the US, UK, and Canada, whose mission is to eradicate white supremacy and build local power to intervene in violence inflicted on black communities by the state and vigilantes. "By combating and countering acts of violence, creating space for Black imagination and innovation, and centring Black joy, we are winning immediate improvements in our lives."[172]

TePoela and Naurigh[173] note that on 25 May 2020, George Floyd was murdered by Minneapolis, Minnesota police officer Derek Chauvin. A 17-year-old bystander, Darnella Frazier, recorded his slow and methodical killing on her mobile phone when she posted the video to Facebook. The images of Floyd's gruesome death and Chauvin's cold resolve set off a wave of protests worldwide against anti-black racism.

The Floyd incident resulted in "individual voices, groups, organisations and businesses from all sectors of society cried out that 'Black Lives Matter', (BLM) in an about-face that turned swiftly from prior stances of silence or opposition."[174] Athletes, sports organisations, league officials and leading athletic apparel brands suddenly demanded change. They admitted fault for ignoring prior calls for criminal justice reforms and eradicating systemic racism and discrimination against black Americans. While anti-racism has been central in sporting organisations in Europe and within international organisations such as FIFA (the governing body for world soccer), the BLM protests appeared to take on a new urgency and potency. Many individual players, athletes and teams have since kneeled before a sporting event in solidarity with the BLM movement. This is not always received well, and some religious groups objected to this based on a religious argument.

Social Justice and Nation Building Hearings, Cricket South Africa 2021

During 2020, many ex-cricket players laid claims of racism in cricket during their playing days. This came on the back of a solid Black Lives Matter campaign. To make things worse, CSA has appointed me as acting CEO and Graeme Smith, as Director of Cricket. Smith appointed Mark Boucher as the head coach. We then appointed Jacques Kallis and Paul Harris as consultants with the Protea men's cricket team. Temba Bavuma was dropped from the test team to complete a perfect storm. We, including me, were politically naïve to think that this would be acceptable to your average black South African. There was an outcry from the press. This led to some opportunistic behaviour, including players guilty of corruption in disciplinary hearings. I have never seen the cricket community as divided based on race as in 2020.

Cricket South Africa

CSA had to do something about all the allegations. They opted first to have private hearings, which turned into public hearings that were streamed. The intentions of many were pure. However, some allegations were far-fetched or lies. We were the only organisation that ever called for such hearings. Anybody who felt they had experienced racism in cricket could come and testify.

How would it have turned out if a South African corporate or other sporting code had done the same? It was also a hospital pass from the former CSA board to the interim board. The interim board had no choice but to continue with the hearings initiated by the former board. It would have appeared that they are sweeping claims of racism under the carpet should they not allow the hearings to continue. Sadly, it did more harm than good to CSA as sponsors fled immediately, and it wasn't easy to attract new ones. In my humble opinion, it also did nothing for nation building. The process did provide a platform for people to tell their stories. It also highlighted that despite being a significantly transformed organisation, there were still claims of racism.

SJN Hearings

The Social Justice and Nation Building hearings (SJN), led by Advocate Dumisa Ntsebeza, aimed to investigate racial discrimination in cricket in South Africa. The hearings were initially going to be private, but this was later changed, and the hearings were streamed live on a platform and reported by some media almost immediately.

Media reporting

The media is vital in promoting sport and keeping sports federations on their toes. During the SJN, the reporting was not fair and balanced. There were clear agendas from some of the journalists. I know it was emotional, but some of the reporting was blatantly aimed at a personal agenda. Match fixers were treated as victims, with their allegations reported as facts. CSA testified comprehensively about the process followed, and unfortunately, like many other baseless allegations, it was not reported with the same vigour. Whenever a CEO admitted wrongdoing, it would lead the story with little reference to the rest of the testimony.

I often wondered if the media themselves learned some lessons too. The SJN report was silent about many of the allegations, and others were discredited by evidence. The cases against Smith and Boucher failed. I appreciate that some journalists wanted to provide a voice to those being discriminated against, but it still required balanced reporting. I concluded that journalists are also people who can be drawn into a crisis based on discrimination, and it is difficult for them to stay impartial. A senior reporter admitted that they probably got carried away by the hype created by the saga. I appreciated his honesty. Over the years, I have gotten to know most of the journalists involved in cricket, and they do an honest, great job. I know they were also divided on the issues.

South Africa has a sad, divided history; many sacrificed much for freedom. I thus have sympathy for some of the overreaction. Some people were opportunistic and keen to use the hype around SJN to clear their tainted reputations. It also did not help that senior CSA officials selectively leaked documentation to the media. Individuals involved in cricket were keen to present their narrative via the press.

It was a strange time for sport, but it highlighted that South Africa is still a very divided society. Emotions trumped rationality in many of the instances. This clearly indicates how people feel about topics such as racism and discrimination.

Rugby and other Sporting codes

Where CSA had formal public hearings, the other sporting codes responded with statements condemning racism. Rugby displayed a banner "RADAR", Rugby against Racism and Discrimination. Rugby has remained well supported by many South Africans and has signed lucrative sponsorship deals. The Springboks went on to win the rugby world cup in 2023. South Africans of all races celebrated them. Led by charismatic Siya Kolisi, the senior management team were otherwise all white and so was the acting CEO. This was similar to the management structure of CSA in 2019. The then CSA structure was severely criticised as being too white. The Springboks have never kneeled in support of the BLM movement.

Final Report

I interviewed David Becker[175] about the SJN process. Becker represented Graeme Smith as his lawyer. He agreed that the hearings provided a platform for people to voice their experiences of discrimination. However, he warns that the subject of crisis management is very often the cause of a review. This is for good reason. Useful lessons can be learned when reviewing processes that led to, or caused, a crisis or the management thereof.

History illustrates that when managing any crisis, it is important to adopt plans and procedures that are robust. Unfortunately, the SJN process, adopted by the board of Cricket South Africa (CSA) to investigate and manage incidents of racism in cricket, was not robust. This was largely due to the 'knee-jerk' reaction by individuals on the previous CSA board and the subsequent implementation of that process by the SJN Ombudsman appointed by the Board, Advocate Ntsebeza SC. The SJN process remains a relevant and interesting case study worthy of analysis.

Becker recalled that the extent that the SJN process was designed to determine "the causes, nature and extent of the racial discrimination and lack of transformation in cricket structures since Unification" and provide "a comprehensive report to the Board for its consideration on the activities and findings of the Ombudsman". However, there were a number of significant flaws raised by respondents in the process which greatly undermined the value of the process itself.

The SJN report, compiled by the Ombudsman, contained the 'tentative' findings of the Ombudsman following six months of hearings and the collection of written and oral submissions.

Following publication of the SJN Report, The Daily Maverick[176] conducted further investigations and on 16 December 2021, published an article on the final SJN Report stating:

> *The 235-page final report was submitted to the CSA board by the Ombudsman on 10 December. It was deeply critical of CSA and senior employees in that it claimed they engaged in prejudicial behaviour.*

It determines that CSA, current CSA director of cricket Graeme Smith and Proteas head coach Mark Boucher, as well as former star batter AB de Villiers, engaged in prejudicial conduct.

But in an 18-page letter sent to CSA on behalf of several of the respondents, the impartiality, independence and due process of the SJN—which cost CSA R7.5 million over six months—has been called into question.

"The conclusion that the findings made in the report are 'tentative' is concerning. Some of these 'findings' are very far-reaching and significant," the letter stated.

"Respectfully, how can a finding of racism, for example, be 'tentative'? Either it is a finding, or it is not a finding. If it is tentative (and if further work is required, as suggested by the Ombudsman in paragraphs 439 and 442 of his report to reach 'appropriate conclusions'), this report ought not to be accepted in its current form."

In a separate statement, Becker questions the dual role that lawyers Sandile July and Sandile Tom played as both legal advisors to the Ombud and then, as signatories to the complainants' Heads of Argument, legal submissions presented on behalf of a group of complainants at the closing of evidence.

"Questions have been rightfully asked about the dual role that the lawyers for the Ombudsman played, as it turned out that not only did they advise the Ombud, but at the same time drafted and submitted Heads of Argument on behalf of the complainants," Becker said.

"The apparent conflict is even more glaring when one considers that more than 250 paragraphs of the complainant's Heads of Argument have been simply cut and pasted word for word directly into the Ombudsman's report. This arguably undermines the independence of the Ombudsman and brings into question the integrity of the report and the process."

Commenting on the SJN Report two years later, Becker laments the lack of proper processes in the inquiry.

The moment the Ombudsman took upon his office the power and authority to make 'findings' rather than recommendations for the betterment of the sport, the inquiry became very problematic. In order to make 'findings', evidence must be properly presented and tested. Opportunities need to be provided for cross-examination. Despite having the authority to permit cross-examination, the Ombudsman did not allow it. Furthermore, proceedings were rushed. At times, respondents were asked to keep their oral evidence brief, in order to meet a particular timetable.

The Ombudsman acknowledged in his 'interim' report that "*This process was not capable of bringing about the outcome envisaged in the Terms of Reference due to the strictures of time*" and "*[t]his is a process that would have benefitted from more time*".

"This was deeply disappointing on its own, not least because of the great costs incurred. Yet the Ombudsman still proceeded to make 'tentative' findings of discriminatory conduct against certain individuals which were very significant and extremely prejudicial to those individuals," said Becker.

"The Ombudsman concluded in his report that 'We hope that CSA will be well advised to take on board and establish a process that will enquire (into) the grievances and reach appropriate conclusions'. Most commentators find this highly ironic, and rightly so, said Becker. "This is precisely what the Ombudsman was tasked to do. It left Cricket South Africa in an impossible position."

Becker raised further concerns. "Throughout the process—indeed even in the Ombudsman's Rules of Procedure—respondents were referred to as 'perpetrators' and complainants as 'victims', naturally raising questions of bias. In any independent process of adjudication, that should be avoided at all costs", said Becker.

Becker went on to lament, "On two occasions, the Ombudsman made findings of racism against individuals when the 'perpetrators' had not even been advised of the allegations against them. It is these sorts of flaws which undermined what could have been a useful process. In the end, unfortunately the new Board of Cricket South Africa were left with an incomplete report which was very costly, deeply flawed and which nonetheless made damaging, albeit 'tentative' conclusions. Sadly, all of this could have been avoided if better processes had been put in place."

Important lessons can and should be learned from this process. In particular, the successful management of any crisis requires the implementation of proper, well-considered processes. Good governance dictates that directors and executives follow due process, consider their duties of care, give due attention to conflicts of interests, properly document their decisions and provide for independent and robust processes of inquiry and adjudication.

Graeme Smith (Director of CSA appointed 2020)

I believe Graeme was unfairly targeted during the BLM saga in 2020. Following 'tentative' findings of discrimination against him in the SJN report, he was then also formally charged with racism by CSA as part of an arbitration process. Smith agreed to participate in the independent arbitration process before the highly respected advocate Hamilton Maenetje SC, to clear his name. He was later acquitted of all charges. He must have gone through significant personal trauma during this time. Playing credentials aside (Smith is the most successful test captain in the history of the game), he is a significant global brand with extensive income-generating ability. Allegations of racism would have been devastating for him. This amounted to a very personal crisis for Smith.

David Becker dealt with his defence. He followed a crisis management approach considering legal, commercial and PR issues at play. He had a small but highly effective group of experts advising on their field of expertise in this area. History will show that Becker and his team successfully protected Smith and his image. In 2022, Smith was appointed as the SA20 League Commissioner by CSA (the majority shareholder in the League). Smith hosted a very successful inaugural tournament in South Africa in 2023, to the great benefit of all cricketing stakeholders in South Africa. Despite enduring a personal crisis in having to fend off false and deeply offensive allegations, to his credit Smith has continued to provide great leadership and guidance to the game of cricket in South Africa and internationally. He sits on the MCC World Cricket Committee, an independent body comprised of senior current and former international cricketers and umpires from across the globe and remains a sought-after commentator.

Mark Boucher (Protea Coach appointed 2020)

During the SJN hearings, former Proteas player Paul Adams, made allegations that the players referred to him in a derogatory manner during an after-match informal gathering. He confirmed that these players included the then Proteas coach Mark Boucher. In particular, Adams alleged that he was the victim of a team song containing racial slurs. The allegations were leaked to the media, and it became a big story. The Proteas were playing a series in Ireland at the time.

Following 'tentative' findings of racism against Boucher in the SJN Report, CSA announced they would formally charge Boucher as part of a disciplinary process. Johann Rupert, the iconic South African businessman, publicly indicated that he would cover Boucher's legal costs. Adams refused to testify and his evidence was never properly tested. CSA withdrew all charges and the hearing never took place. In a formal statement, CSA said:

> *"Cricket South Africa (CSA) has concluded that there is no basis to sustain any of the disciplinary charges, including charges of racism, against Mark Boucher, the coach of the Proteas men's cricket team.*
>
> *CSA has formally and unreservedly withdrawn all of the charges and will make a contribution to Mr Boucher's legal expenses."*

CSA Board Chairperson Lawson Naidoo publicly defended the decision to charge Boucher. CSA was undoubtably placed in a difficult position following the 'interim' report from the SJN Ombudsman. To his credit, CSA Chief Executive Pholetsi Moseki stated:

> *"CSA appreciates that it has been very difficult for Mark to deal with these charges hanging over his head over the last few months. CSA regrets this. CSA is also appreciative of the fact that Mark has at all times conducted himself properly and professionally—refusing to be drawn into public debates about the charges and carrying out his duties with commitment and dedication."*

A Daily Maverick[177] article on 10 May 2022 concluded that "It appears the pursuit of Smith and Boucher was emotional rather than rational."

In 2023 Boucher was appointed the coach of the Mumbai Indians in the IPL. This is arguably the most prestigious coaching job in the world. His reputation as a cricket legend is still intact.

Titans and Northerns Cricket Union (SJN Hearings)

We at Titans prepared well for the hearings. Adv. Niel du Preez and Prof Rian Cloete are highly skilled lawyers. They were very supportive and brought a clinical, calm, and professional approach to our efforts.

Serious allegations were made against Northerns Cricket Union and Titans Cricket during the SJN process. These were related to, amongst other things, claims that we remunerated a player less because he is black African; and further claims that he experienced various discriminatory incidents as a player at Titans cricket. Sadly, this player ended a long, illustrious career at the Titans after pleading guilty to corruption-related charges brought by CSA under its Anti-Corruption Code. Another player claimed we did not contract him due to racism. There were serious allegations of discrimination and racism.

The board, under the leadership of Tebogo Siko (President) and Kabelo Khaas, board member and chairperson of the Transformation Committee, dealt with it honestly and transparently. We adopted an approach to learn from the SJN hearings whilst defending the organisation from false allegations. We were cleared in the SJN report but nonetheless embarked on a mission to ensure that discrimination would not be allowed on our watch. The organisation adopted two campaigns: "I Am Champion" and "A Team for All", pledging our stance against discrimination and for inclusivity. The educational efforts are, and will be, ongoing. There can be no place in the game for discrimination.

The efforts to address discrimination were sincere and not merely a PR exercise. We did an honest introspection, and despite being cleared of the allegations, we realised that as temporary custodians of the game, it is our duty to ensure cricket remains free from all forms of discrimination.

The aftermath (SJN)

There is little to show for all the pain, trauma and costs related to the SJN hearings. It provided a platform for people to speak out on their experiences, and in doing so I hope it brought them some healing. If the fact that nothing was implemented afterwards is an assessment of the SJN's success, then it failed as a process. The reasons for that are dealt with above. However, despite flaws in the process, I believe it indicated that racism and discrimination have tainted the game and still do so. This is despite cricket being transformed and spending millions developing the game at grassroots levels.

I was proud of the efforts of the Titans post-SJN. We decided that we would not waste this crisis, but rather use it to improve ourselves.

Declaration of interest

The case study on SJN was written from my perspective and as factual as possible. It is public knowledge that I had enemies at CSA during the hearings. Specific individuals were keen to accuse me of appointing Graeme Smith without following the correct procedure. During my testimony, I felt that the Ombudsman treated me fairly. I was relieved that Graeme Smith was acquitted of any wrongdoing. There was a witch hunt against Graeme Smith, Mark Boucher and myself. I felt sorry for Mark and Graeme; they have significant personal brands that attracted more media attention than I did. It was hurtful to read some baseless media reports and, in some cases, blunt lies. In some instances, these allegations were reported and stated as facts. CSA Anti-Corruption Officer Louis Cole and lawyer David Becker were also unfairly accused of conducting a race-based match fixing investigation on behalf of Cricket South Africa in 2016. The Ombudsman rightly found that there was no substance to these allegations. Unfortunately, there was little or no accountability for those who provided false and/or disingenuous allegations against many of the 'perpetrators'.

The Ombudsman praised me for my honesty in women's cricket. It was a traumatic experience for me and my family, and I was relieved when it was all over. I also accepted that this comes with the territory, and I am thankful and blessed to have been able to work in the industry I love for two decades. For the second time in my career, I received death threats and was the target of the extreme left and right of the South African political landscape.

The SJN could have been a much better process if some of the people involved did not have a selfish, toxic agenda. It could have been a more fruitful exercise if it had not been rushed. I had sympathy for Advocate Ntsebeza who was facing a very difficult task in uncharted territory, it must have been a daunting task.

Yorkshire County Cricket Club

Yorkshire County Cricket Club had a racial crisis starting in 2017. The following is a timeline reported by the Guardian[178]:

Aug 2017: Azeem Rafiq claims to have complained to Yorkshire's assistant coach, Richard Pyrah, and Martyn Moxon (the director of cricket) about being bullied by Tim Bresnan. He says he was advised to ignore it.

Aug 2018: Rafiq first complains about racism. The club holds a formal meeting to discuss his concerns. No further action is taken. He is released at the end of the season.

Sept 2020: Rafiq speaks publicly for the first time about his experience of racism during his professional career. Yorkshire chairman Roger Hutton says the county will formally investigate the claims, appointing local law firm Squire Patton Boggs to lead the inquiry. An independent panel is created to review their report.

Dec 2020: Rafiq launches legal action against Yorkshire, claiming he suffered "discrimination and harassment on the grounds of race".

Aug 2021: The panel's independent report is completed. Yorkshire apologises to Rafiq for "inappropriate behaviour" but denies institutional racism.

Sep 2021: A report summary is published, acknowledging seven of 43 allegations. The club admits Rafiq was a victim of "racial harassment and bullying". The full report is not published or provided to Rafiq. Julian Knight, chair of the parliament's digital, culture, media and sport committee, calls for "the report and its full findings" to be released.

Oct 2021: Rafiq is provided with a heavily redacted version of the report. Yorkshire announces that "no conduct or action taken by any of its employees, players or executives warrants disciplinary action".[179]

Nov 2021: Gary Ballance admits that he was one of those accused of using racist language toward Rafiq and says he "deeply regrets some of the language I used in my younger years". Michael Vaughan confirms that he is accused in the report of making an insensitive comment but denies doing so, saying: "I will fight to the end to prove I am not that person". Roger Hutton resigned as Yorkshire chairman, and Mark Arthur as chief executive, after most main sponsors withdrew from the club. The ECB suspends Yorkshire from hosting international cricket matches. Lord Kamlesh Patel replaces Hutton. They settled the employment tribunal case with Rafiq.

Dec 2021: Yorkshire's entire coaching team leaves the club. "Significant change is required at Yorkshire County Cricket Club, and we are committed to taking whatever action is necessary to regain trust," says Lord Patel.

February 2022: The ECB lifted its ban on international matches at Headingley in response to "the hard work and actions taken by Yorkshire County Cricket Club towards putting the club on a new path".

June 2022: The ECB charges Yorkshire and seven individuals: former England internationals Michael Vaughan, Tim Bresnan, Matthew Hoggard and Gary Ballance, the club's former captain and head coach Andrew Gale, and coaches Pyrah and John Blain, with bringing the game into disrepute; their cases to be heard by the body's Cricket Discipline Commission.

Gale withdraws his cooperation from what he describes as a "tainted" process. "I have no faith that a fair and just outcome will be the result if I engage in the process," he says. "I believe we are being put forward as scapegoats, and I will not cooperate in that process."

Nov 2022: The CDC hearings are delayed after Rafiq's lawyer successfully argues that they should not be held behind closed doors.

Dec 2022: Rafiq returns to the DCMS, where he accuses the ECB of attempting to discredit him. "Thirteen months on from me opening my heart out, all that's changed is that me and my family have been driven out of the country," he says.

Feb 2023: Bresnan, Hoggard, Pyrah and Blain join Gale in withdrawing cooperation from the CDC hearings. With Ballance admitting the charges against him and Yorkshire agreeing with the ECB after admitting four charges of bringing the game into disrepute, Vaughan is the only party charged to remain involved in the process.

March 2023: CDC hearings go ahead in London, with the verdict announced on Friday, 31 March. Vaughan is cleared, but Bresnan, Hoggard, Pyrah, Blain and Gale are found liable for their alleged use of racist and discriminatory language.

The Guardian[180] further reports on 28 July 2023 that Yorkshire has been fined £400,000 and given a 48-point deduction in that year's County Championship by the ECB's Cricket Discipline Commission as a result of allegations of racism and discrimination at the club over 17 years.

The club would not appeal the decision, ending the turmoil related to the racism saga.

The club admitted four charges, with separate fines levied for each. The mishandling of their initial report into Rafiq's experiences brought an £80,000 fine; the deliberate mass deletion of emails and documents relating to that report brought a £50,000 fine, and for repeatedly failing to act upon allegations of racist behaviour and for failing to address "the systemic use of racist or discriminatory language" between 2004 and 2021, they were fined £135,000.

There was an added cost to Yorkshire other than the fines when a tribunal found that cricket staff, including former head coach Andrew Gale, were wrongly sacked following the Azeem Rafiq racism scandal and are now in line to receive huge payouts.

Chapter 13: Racism and Discrimination in Sports

Titans have an exchange programme with Yorkshire, and I got to know Mark Arthur and Lord Patel. Both made a very favourable impression on me during our interactions. The personal trauma individuals experience during such an ordeal should not be underestimated. Solving the challenges of racism allegations and the process to follow is complex. Yorkshire experienced a significant crisis with a drastic negative impact.

ECB report on racism and discrimination

Euronews[181] reported on the report on racism and discrimination in English cricket. The Independent Commission for Equity in Cricket (ICEC) was commissioned in November 2020 as part of the ECB's wide-ranging effort to address allegations of discrimination and improve equality, diversity and inclusion in cricket.

Cindy Butts chaired the commission. The ICEC received more than 4,000 submissions from people at all levels. Half said they experienced discrimination in the previous five years. But the figures were higher when separated by ethnicity: 87% of people with Pakistani and Bangladeshi heritage, 82% of people of Indian origin, and 75% of Black contributors.

The extensive report pointed out "entrenched" racism in all levels of English cricket alongside a highly sexist environment for female cricketers.

Institutional racism, sexism and class-based discrimination continue to infect English cricket, a report published by the Independent Commission for Equity in Cricket has found.

Among its findings, racism was "entrenched" in the English game, women were treated as "second-class citizens," and cricket was a rare option in state schools. Then, if anybody wanted to complain about the problems, the ICEC said the system was confusing and unsuitable. The report calls for "decisive action" and makes 44 recommendations and several sub-recommendations.

The Cricketer[182] notes the recommendations:

1. **The ECB (England Cricket Board) should make "an unqualified public apology for its failings and those of the game it governs"**

   The report's authors say the governing body should acknowledge the existence of racism, sexism, elitism and class-based discrimination and recognise its impact. They also call for an apology for a historic failure to support women's and girls' cricket and black cricketers.

2. **A 'State of Equity in Cricket' report should be published every three years**

   The ICEC report suggests their report should be the initial benchmark as part of an ongoing process to evaluate the game.

3. **The ECB should, within 12 months, publish a set of cultural values to guide all individuals participating in cricket under its jurisdiction.**

   The ICEC commissioners say these guidelines "should form the basis of a game-wide values and behaviours framework which is explicit about the culture the game aspires to build and the behaviours it expects and rejects".

4. **The ECB should commit to regular 'culture health checks'**

   A facility should also be put in place allowing those who participate in cricket in England and Wales to submit testimony about their experiences.

5. **The ECB should, within six months, commit to racial literacy training for its executive and board, and the executives of the first-class counties, women's regional teams and the MCC**

   This training should be regularly updated and refreshed, the report says, "to build competency in leading EDI (Equity Diversity and Inclusion) in cricket".

6. **The ECB should commit to being an anti-racist, anti-sexist and anti-classist organisation**

   The report states that the governing body should encourage all cricket organisations within its network to do likewise.

7. **The ECB should adopt a clear and consistent strategic approach to issues of EDI**

   The report is scathing about commercial or PR issues subsuming or being the driving force for EDI initiatives. It stresses that the ECB commercial and PR imperatives should not dictate EDI progress. It calls for clear and present acceptance of and admission to discrimination where it occurs. And it demands that the onus to identify discrimination should not fall on those from minority backgrounds.

8. **The ECB should substantially increase funding for EDI initiatives, particularly at recreational and talent pathway level**

9. **The ECB should comply with the Public Sector Equality Duty where possible**

   PSED (Public Sector Equality Duty) is a duty on public authorities to consider or think about how their policies or decisions affect people who are protected under the Equality Act.

10. **Within the next six months, the ECB should appoint a chief equity, diversity and inclusion officer - at board level**

    The report calls for this individual to have a "singular focus on EDI".

11. **Within the next 12 months, the ECB commits to an investigation into the decline in participation in cricket among the black community**

    The report also calls for an action plan to reinvigorate participation in this demographic, increased central funding for the ACE Programme, financial support for "black-led" grassroots clubs, and a commitment to a project similar to the South Asian Action Plan.

12. **Within 12 months, the ECB should commit to an in-depth examination of the class barriers that exist in cricket**

    The report calls for the ECB to develop a specific action plan to remove these barriers.

13. **The ECB should introduce gender-based budgeting into their next business cycle**

    "Spending and investment decisions can have very different impacts on women and men, because of different starting points, needs and priorities," the report reads.

    "The analysis conducted to inform decision-making should adopt an intersectional approach that considers race, class and gender."

14. **The ECB should "at pace" increase the levels of investment in the core infrastructure and operations of the women's and girls' game**

15. **An overhaul of women's pay, so that by 2029 men's and women's cricketers are paid equally domestically, and internationally by 2030**

    Equality in working conditions should be levelled immediately, according to the report, while the identification of salaries should be standardised across genders.

    The "pay" mentioned in the report relates to average pay.

    The report states that rookie contracts should be introduced for the women's regional structure by 2024, while The Hundred should pay its male and female players equally by 2025.

16. **Equal representation for the women's regional teams within the ECB governance structure**

    The report states that the eight regions should each hold a vote within the ECB membership, in line with the first-class men's counties, county boards and the MCC. This will align men's and women's representation.

17. **The ECB's articles of association should be amended within six months to highlight its responsibilities in relation to EDI (Equity Diversity and Inclusion)**

    "It should be a fundamental 'objective' for the ECB to promote and deliver EDI in professional and recreational cricket," the report says.

It also calls for references to "upholding spirit and tradition" of the game to be updated with an emphasis on EDI, and calls for the scrapping of the annual reappointment of directors.

18. **From 2024, the annual fixtures between Eton and Harrow, and Oxford and Cambridge should no longer take place at Lord's**

    ICEC proposes that the Eton-Harrow and Oxford-Cambridge matches at Lord's replace the "national finals' days for state school competitions for boys and girls, as well as a national finals' day for competitions for men's and women's university teams.

19. **The ECB should place a greater emphasis on EDI when allocating, suspending, cancelling and reinstating high-profile matches**

    "There is clear evidence that being allocated such matches, or having the right to host them, is a powerful tool to encourage compliance," the report says.

    The report suggests making EDI compliance a "gateway criterion" for awarding major matches.

20. **The County Partnership Agreement, County Governance Framework, and Regional Host Agreements should have stronger and firmer EDI commitments when they are next updated**

    The report calls for formal and specific ethnicity targets for each first-class county and county board, reflective of their respective county's demographics, and financial incentives for counties that meet their targets.

21. **There should be sanctions for counties which fail to reach EDI targets within the next County Partnership Agreement**

22. **An independent regulatory body should be established within the next 12 months**

    The report is damning on the potential conflicts of interest due to the ECB being both promoter and regulator of cricket in England and Wales.

    "The new body should be a subsidiary company with its own ring-fenced budget, and its own legal counsel and investigatory staff," the report says. Those involved in the regulatory body should have "specific experience of investigating discrimination complaints".

23. **There should be a single set of regulations and non-regulatory standards across the cricket administered by the ECB**

24. **The definition of "regulatory matters" should be updated**

    The report calls for only matters relating to discipline and integrity to fall under the "regulatory" sub-head. ICEC proposes the Cricket Discipline Commission to continue to be the body that hears cases relating to regulatory affairs.

25. **Redefine "non-regulatory matters" as all other rules and standards**

    The new regulatory body should investigate breaches of EDI directives to avoid conflicts of interest between the ECB as promoter and its commercial objectives.

26. **All ECB operational and strategic decisions should be made after consideration for the impact of those decisions from an EDI perspective**

27. **An improvement of the ECB's executive management's diversity within two years**

    The report calls for "demonstrable progress" in this timeframe and the establishment of "longer-term targets".

28. **The ECB should report on EDI complaints annually**

    ICEC states that counties should be required to report key information about complaints to the ECB. The commission also calls for a best-practice complaints procedure to be conceived and implemented across the network.

29. **A game-wide volunteer strategy relating to EDI should be established**

    "The strategy should make clear how volunteers will be trained and supported to develop their EDI knowledge and skills, including specific training on discrimination and sexual harassment," the report says.

30. **The ECB should make centralised training relating to EDI complaints available to all cricket clubs, leagues and organisations**

31. **Leading figures of cricket clubs, leagues and organisations should be accountable for failures to uphold "high standards of behaviour"**

    The report calls for "mandatory reporting obligations" for officials.

32. **Changes to the Cricket Discipline Commission (CDC)**

    The report states that anyone working in the professional game should fall under the jurisdiction of the CDC, while sanctioning powers of the commission should be strengthened.

    CDC panels must have specific experience in matters relating to EDI, while panel members should be paid and administrative expenses reimbursed.

    Chairs of the CDC should be appointed by the ECB using expert external recruitment, while the CDC chair should appoint panel members using the same process. Each should serve two four-year terms at most.

33. **The ECB's anti-discrimination code should be updated**

    Socio-economic status should also be considered, the report says, while the code should "explicitly cover victimisation and make clear that it would be grounds for disciplinary action".

The ICEC panel calls for greater clarity in how charges are made, by whom and the criteria whereby they are decided. They call for consistency in the complaints-handling process, and clear and accessible guidance on best practice following the receipt of a complaint.

34. **The introduction of an informal complaints' submission process**

    Suggestions from the panel include mediation and "Freedom to Speak Up Guardians", who support those who otherwise may not report issues relating to discrimination.

35. **An overhaul of the schools' talent pathway to ensure more meritocratic selection**

    The report is damning of the influence of a select group of private schools on the cricket pathway in England and Wales.

    ICEC calls for a State Schools Action Plan within 12 months, including the reallocation of central funding below under-14 level to "level the playing field".

    The report proposes that the State Schools Action Plan become enforceable by introducing it into the County Partnership Agreement.

36. **Children from low socio-economic backgrounds and those at state schools should be able to enter talent pathways without charge**

    The report condemns the costs associated with entering talent pathways at a young age, and the impact it has on drop-out rates among those from certain sectors of society.

    ICEC says these changes need to be implemented in time for the 2024-25 winter training pathway.

37. **The ECB and counties should proactively broaden where they source talent from**

    Among the sub-criteria proposed by ICEC are the scrapping of schools' nominations and the introduction of widescale open trials, with scouts being sent into state schools and local clubs, the increased recognition of non-traditional cricket formats as a potential talent pool, and considerable funding increases for free, year-round cricket provision in deprived areas.

38. **The introduction, by 2025, of accessible county and national-level T20 competitions for state school boys' and girls' cricket teams at under-14 and under-15 level**

39. **A more robust and systematic approach for talent identification by the counties**

    The report is damning about the pathway's inherent bias within the talent identification sector. It calls for a "charter of best practice" to be established. It also calls for conflicts of interest among selectors to be declared and for those who have privately coached young players to be barred from selection decisions.

> ICEC wants to introduce bias training for all decision-makers on the pathway, and for selection decisions to be supported by documentary evidence.
>
> Furthermore, the report requires an appeals process to be established for those who feel selections have been discriminatory.
>
> 40. **Selection for inter-county representative cricket should not begin before under-14 level**
>
> 41. **County age-group coaches should be tasked with taking cricket into state schools between under-10 and under-13 levels**
>
>   Additionally, the report calls for increased ECB funding for "Chance to Shine" in state secondary schools. It also requires that counties should encourage local clubs to make facilities available for schoolchildren.
>
> 42. **The ECB and wider game should develop a system to regularly collate and monitor EDI data with respect to entry into and progression through the talent pathway**
>
> 43. **Recommendations to government**
>
>   The report calls for UK government to collect and monitor data on cricket participation in state schools, require and resource "significantly higher" levels of cricket in state schools, and work with private schools to gift a minimum number of free coaching hours to local state school pupils.
>
> 44. **A detailed response from the ECB to the ICEC report within three months**
>
>   ICEC states that the ECB should establish a fully independent steering group to monitor the governing body's work within six months. That group should publish a follow-up report in 2025. The report also calls for the ECB to provide regular updates on EDI progress to the Department for Culture, Media and Sport select committee.

Lessons

The lessons learned about racism and discrimination in sport in general and from SJN, Yorkshire, and the ECB report, can be summarised as follows:

1. The process established for any review process must be clear and legally sound.
2. Avoid involving people with a toxic personal agenda; this will impact the credibility of the process.
3. The process should be sufficiently resourced and enough time allowed to be dealt with thoroughly.
4. All involved in the process of investigation should be truly independent. Not only should it be free from bias, but it must be free from the perception of bias in order to maintain credibility.

5. Despite the recommendations of an inquiry, the labour practices should be followed as described in the various acts should this require you to charge people.
6. Not all allegations are true; some people will use the hype for personal gain. Allegations of racism and discrimination can destroy careers and lives. Where findings are to be made of any nature, evidence must be provided under oath and properly tested by way of cross-examination.
7. The media must report in a fair and balanced manner.
8. Clear recommendations must be made and implemented.
9. Continuous monitoring must take place.
10. Educational efforts to address inclusivity must be ongoing at all levels of sports.

Conclusion

Racism and discrimination are a reality in society and, thus, also in sport. It should be tackled in an honest, responsible way. The impact on a sporting organisation can be drastic. Sporting organisations should entrench ongoing monitoring and education at all levels. By its very design, sport can unite societies and people.

Fairness should be at the centre of all procedures investigating claims of racism or discrimination, and one should guard against being carried away by emotion.

CHAPTER 14

CRISIS MANAGEMENT PLAN

Jacques Faul

Introduction

The final chapter provides examples of crisis management plans and templates that sporting organisations may use. Each sporting organisation needs a Crisis Management Plan to prepare for a crisis.

The ability to execute the plan is essential. The plan included below is the one used by Titans Cricket and SuperSport Park and is based on existing and commonly used plans. It provides a good structure to deal with a crisis.

Shamansouri & Hashemi-Minabad Plan

Ezzatolah Shamansouri and Hashemi-Minabad[183] are two Iranian academic commentators in the field of Physical Culture and Tourism. Their research relates to crisis management in sport. They developed the following crisis management strategic plan.

The figure below looks busy and complex; however, it provides a clear roadmap to deal with a crisis in sport.

Crisis management strategic plan

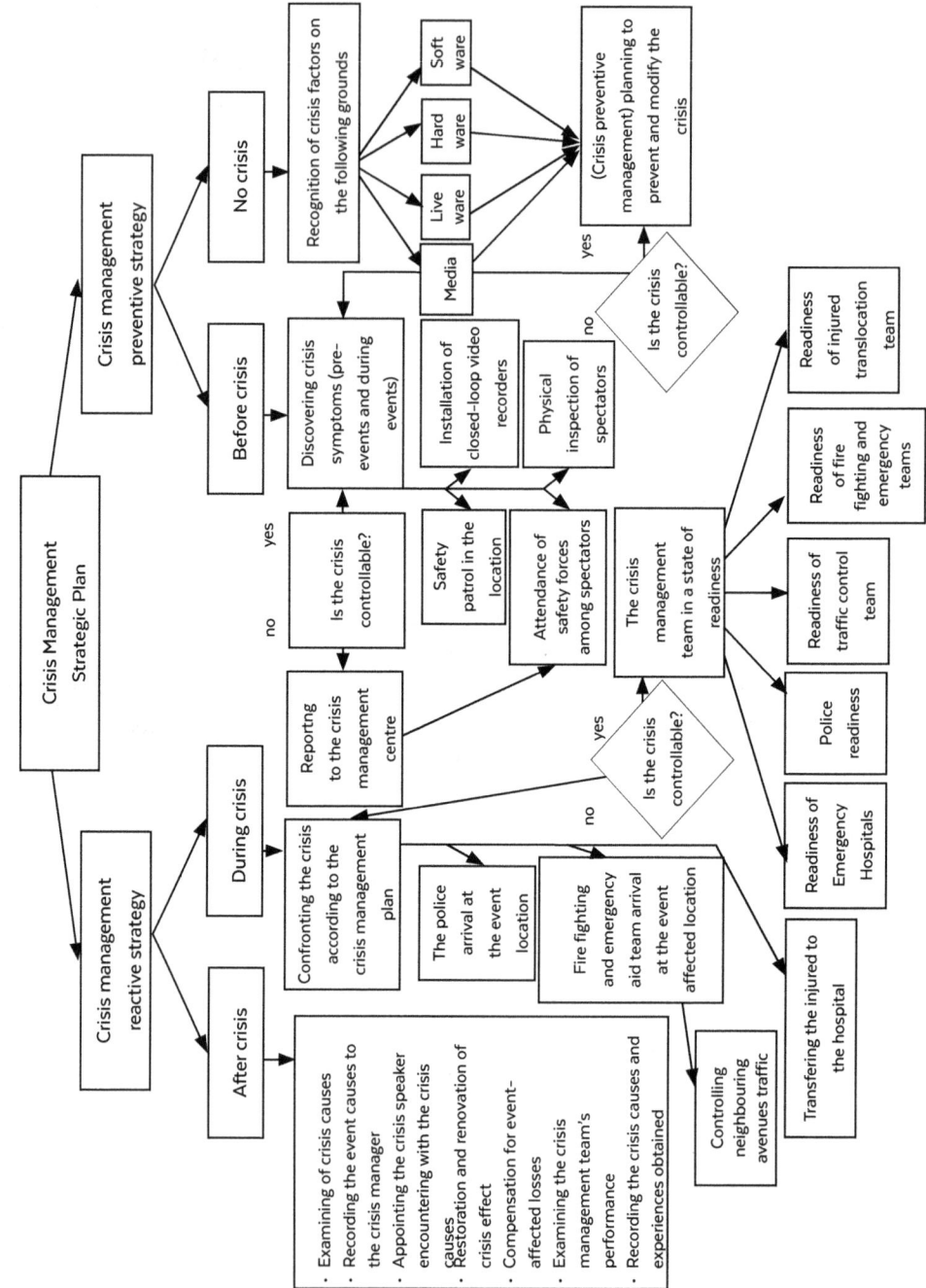

Figure 4: Crisis Management strategic Plan

The figure illustrates actions varying from no crisis, before, during, and after the crisis and provides good guidance for a venue in crisis.

ANNEXURE A: CRISIS MANAGEMENT PLAN

Crisis Classification

Level 1: A serious crisis that will require implementing a complete crisis plan.	The crisis classification may be upgraded or downgraded at any time.
Level 2: It could potentially be a severe crisis but requires analysis as per the crisis plan and initial media response. It needs to be monitored to see if it must be upgraded or downgraded.	Assess seriousness based on: • Legal impact • Duty of care • Noncompliance and governance • Reputation
Level 3: The incident can be handled by management and can be managed internally.	
Level 4: The incident can be handled on a departmental level.	Scoring to determine level: 4 – very serious 3 – serious 2 – uncertain 1 – not serious 0 – little or no impact

	Score
Legal	
Duty of Care	
Noncompliance and governance	
PR	
Reputation	
	Total

Level 1 = 15+
Level 2 = 10 – 14
Level 3 = 5 – 9
Level 4 = below 4

CRISIS MANAGEMENT TEMPLATE

AIPIL: Analysing, Initial Response Plan, Planning, Implementing, Learning

Analysing

Actions	Considerations
Is there a threat of a crisis? How can it be mitigated?	Impact/Likelihood
If it is a crisis, what is the level of the crisis?	Possible reputational damage. Financial implications. Duty of care implications. Legal implications.
Implementations according to crisis classification.	
Do we have the internal capacity to deal with the crisis?	
What are facts, and what is still uncertain?	
Analyse possible mitigating action.	
Analyse stakeholder sequence communication.	Key stakeholders to be informed first.

Initial Response Plan

Actions	Considerations
Who needs to be informed first?	You don't have to design a final plan at this stage, just an initial response. An introductory holding statement will suffice. Do not get drawn into speculation.
Establish a crisis committee and project name.	
Establish a crisis communication committee.	

Prepare a holding statement.
 	
• Immediate steps to mitigate:
  1 Legal implications
  2 Duty of care obligations	

Annexure

Planning

Actions	Considerations
Plan the communication strategy.	Use the template for the communication plan.
Timetable for planning meetings: • Crisis management meetings • Crisis communication committee meetings • Briefing meetings with staff • Briefing meetings with sponsors • Briefing meetings with the board • Briefing meetings with the media	
Crisis committee to plan mitigation steps.	

Implementing

Actions	Considerations
Implement crisis plan and mitigating steps.	Assess impact, and don't be afraid to make adjustments.
Actions and implementations will flow from the scheduled meetings.	Resist the temptation to schedule too many additional meetings.
Stay within the initial planned structure.	

Learning

Actions	Considerations
A formal report of lessons learnt needs to be compiled with recommendations on the following:	
Future early detection	'Don't waste a good crisis'
Preventative measures	
Effectiveness of committee	
Reputational damage	
Financial impact	
Duty of care	
Recommended change in policies or standard operating procedures	

COMMUNICATION PLAN TEMPLATE

Date:	
Description of crisis:	
Crisis Communication Plan: Code name:	
Crisis team:	
Chairperson:	
Members:	
The communications team:	
The lead/spokesperson:	
Members:	
Procedure & Process	
During a crisis, we will follow these steps to craft our response statement and get the communications team on the same page. 1. Determine meeting schedule and venue(s). 2. Copies of the response plan, prepared statements and crisis & communication team contact information. 3. Media contact lists (print and digital versions). 4. Social media, monitoring sites and web login information. 5. Convene the communications team to act on communications-related strategic objectives. 6. Develop a specific communication plan relevant to the actual circumstances of the crisis. It includes: a. Identifying and prioritising our audiences. b. Communication mechanisms for each audience (email, phone call, etc.). c. Responsibilities and timelines for each task. d. Stakeholder communication sequence plan.	

7. Assign a team member to create a timeline of the actual events related to the crisis and any responses given and actions taken.
8. Notify key stakeholders of the determined sequence.
9. Fill out the Crisis Factsheet.
10. Craft key messages related to the actual circumstances (and refine/adapt them as needed).
11. Identify and prepare the spokesperson most appropriate for the situation.
12. Use key messages to prepare possible response statements for telephone, email, text messages, website, social media, and crisis site inquiries.
13. Make sure your crisis response meeting venue is properly set up with copies of the crisis communications response plan, the response statement and contact information for all crisis management and communications team members.
14. Assign responsibility to create and maintain phone and email logs of news organisations/reporters/bloggers/websites covering the crisis and any other key personnel, clients, vendor partners, etc., who may be inquiring about the situation.
15. Remind staff of existing media (social and traditional) policies. Only authorised staff may communicate with the media. All queries must be referred to them.
16. Set predetermined times for updates on the crisis to staff members.
17. Provide staff with key messages to communicate to people functionally associated with them, such as suppliers and sponsors.
18. Set predetermined times for communicating updates to the media. Honour these commitments.
19. Make sure those affected by the crisis are updated regularly.

Crisis Factsheet

Event code name:	
Communication goals:	

Details:

What happened?
When did it happen?
Who is involved?
Who is affected?
How did it happen?

Do we have credible sources of information? What additional facts are needed to put the event into perspective? What is currently being done? What is the potential legal risk? What is the potential PR risk? What is our duty of care? Who should be informed first?
Information that has been confirmed: source, date, & time
Information that is still unknown
Messaging templates The communications team will use the following templates if unprepared for a crisis. Only include definitive facts and not speculative details; verify *everything* you say. Ensure that the statement is authentic and appropriate for the situation. The holding statement should always include the following: • A factual headline • The date and time • The location of the incident • Basic details that have been confirmed • When the company was made aware of the issue • Actions your organisation is taking that you are willing to make public • An expression of compassion or empathy (if appropriate) • Details on when further updates will be provided **The holding statement should never include:** • Details that are unconfirmed or uncertain • Any speculation • A response to unsubstantiated rumours • Statements of blame or finger-pointing • Names of victims in the case of death

HOLDING STATEMENT - GENERIC

We have recently been informed that a [what happened] at [location] involving [who] occurred today at [time]. The incident is under investigation, and more information is forthcoming.

HOLDING STATEMENT - OFFENSIVE STATEMENT OR ACTION BY EMPLOYEE

Accusation only:

We are saddened and disappointed by the recent allegations surrounding the [incident/accusation] with/against [employee].

[Company] is committed to being a safe and inclusive workplace. We're still assessing the situation and these accusations. In the meantime, we sincerely apologise to all those affected or upset by these accusations.

HOLDING STATEMENT - LAWSUIT

We cannot comment on ongoing litigation, but [company] is committed to [statement that does not divulge information or opinion about the lawsuit]. Our legal team is studying the relevant documents.

HOLDING STATEMENT - NEGATIVE RESULT IN A LEGAL MATTER

Our lawyers are studying the procedure's outcome; we cannot comment now.

HOLDING STATEMENT - INJURY AT STADIUM/SPORTS EVENT

We can confirm that a spectator/employee/contractor has sustained an injury during an event held on __ at__. We are currently investigating the incident. We wish the injured a speedy recovery. The safety of fans is of the utmost importance for the stadium.

HOLDING STATEMENT - DEATH AT A SPORTING EVENT

It is with shock that we confirm the tragic death(s) of a person(s) at (event and date). The investigation of this tragedy is our highest priority. I would like to express our sincere condolences to the family and friends of the deceased.

HOLDING STATEMENT - SPECTATOR DISCOMFORT

We have become aware of claims/incidents by spectators that (mention) occurred during the event (date, place). A positive fan experience is of the utmost importance to us. We are investigating these incidents and apologise to all affected by this.

Key messages
TARGET AUDIENCE MESSAGE
National Federation Sponsors Employees Public/community Media Board

Evolvement and improvement of the crisis management plan

The above is an example of a crisis management plan that can be tailored to the needs of the organisation and adjusted over time. The holding statements should only be used as a guide.

All staff involved should receive training on the plan and how it should be rolled out. A proper crisis management plan will structure your efforts and guide you when panic is most likely to set in.

Conclusion

Sporting organisations should have mechanisms in place to prevent disaster/crisis situations, together with early detection scanning. However, if a significant crisis is at hand an organisation needs as a bare minimum, a standard crisis management plan.

ENDNOTES

1. Kahperd Convention in Louisville Kahperd Journal, 2012.
2. Stoldt, 2012.
3. Seeger *et al.*, 2003.
4. Coombs, 2010.
5. Seeger & Ulmer, 2002.
6. Zamoum & Gorpe, 2018.
7. Pfaltzgraff, R.L. Jnr., 2008.
8. Coombs, 2010.
9. Mitroff & Anagnos, 2001.
10. Coombs, 2010.
11. Zamoum & Gorge, 2018.
12. Milašinoviæ & Kešetoviæ, 2008.
13. Shipway, Miles & Gordon, 2021.
14. Peyton and Acharya., 2023.
15. Weir, 2013.
16. Cohen, K, (ESPN), 2020.
17. Calacus, 2022.
18. Cantillon, 2022.
19. Hollander & Nolte, 2023
20. Koehn, 2022.
21. Robbins et al. 2015.
22. Indian Express, 2021.
23. Topper & Lagadec, 2013.
24. Shipway, Miles & Gordon, 2021.
25. David Becker Interview, 2023.
26. Freeman, 1984.
27. Bryson, 1995:27.
28. Eden & Ackermann, 1998:117.
29. Brenner, 1995.
30. Donaldson & Preston, 1995.
31. Institute of Directors, 2016
32. Parmar et al., 2010.
33. Hult et al., 2011:49.
34. Jones, 1995.
35. Donaldson & Preston, 1995.
36. Jones, 1995.
37. Clarkson, 1995.
38. Jones & Wicks, 1999.
39. Parmar et al., 2010.
40. Hult et al., 2011:49.
41. Walters & Kitchin, 2009.
42. Interview with Anant Sarkaria, 2023.
43. Mitroff & Anagnos, 2001.
44. Seeger, Reynolds & Day, 2020.
45. Institute of Directors SA, 2016:12.

46 Cloete, 2005:59.
47 Louw, 2010:171-173.
48 Louw, 2010:159-161.
49 Basson & Loubser, 2000:Ch4-2.
50 Cloete, 2005:60.
51 Ibid, 61.
52 Davis, 2013:171.
53 King IV Report™, 2016.
54 Delport, 2016:54(1) – 54(2A).
55 Ibid, 54(3).
56 Ibid, 54(4).
57 Louw, 2010:69-70.
58 Ibid, 2010:156.
59 Ibid, 2010:60-61.
60 Basson & Loubser, 2000:Ch4-26.
61 Ndoro and Another v South African Football Association and Others (16/16836), 2018.
62 Gardiner, 2012:270-272.
63 Louw, 2010:29.
64 Blackshaw, 2013:945.
65 Compliance Institute SA, 2018.
66 Lavalette, 2020.
67 Compliance Institute SA (GACP), 2018.
68 Reuters, 2016.
69 Rollin, 2015.
70 Associated press, 2018.
71 McLean, 2014.
72 Frosdic, 1997.
73 Taylor, 1998:102.
74 Tarlow, 2017.
75 Ibid.
76 Hugo Kemp Interview, 2023.
77 Bowley, Rein, Scholtz & Boffard, 2004.
78 Shipway, Miles & Gordon, 2021.
79 Ibid.
80 De Klerk & De Klerk, 2022.
81 Arvidsdotter et.al., 2016.
82 De Klerk & De Klerk, 2020.
83 De Klerk & De Klerk, 2022.
84 De Klerk & De Klerk, 2020.
85 Al-Dahash, Thayaparan & Kulatunga, 2016.
86 Canada, Heath, Money, Annandale, Fischer & Young, 2007.
87 Knox & Roberts, 2005.
88 James & Gilliland, 2012.
89 Olsson, 2010.
90 Sisco, 2010.
91 James & Gilliland, 2012.
92 American Psychological Association, 2013.
93 James & Gilliland, 2012.

94 Flannery & Everly, 2000.
95 National Child Traumatic Stress Network [NCTSN], 2010.
96 Oliver, 2019.
97 Ibid.
98 Ibid.
99 Ibid.
100 National Child Traumatic Stress Network, (NCTSN), 2010.
101 Debiec, 2018.
102 McClelland & Gilyard, 2019.
103 Ibid.
104 Ibid.
105 Ibid.
106 Ibid.
107 Ibid.
108 Debiec, 2018.
109 Ibid.
110 Ibid.
111 Ibid.
112 Ibid.
113 Ibid.
114 Ibid.
115 American Psychological Association., 2023.
116 De Klerk & De Klerk, 2022.
117 Debiec, 2018.
118 McClelland & Gilyard, 2019.
119 Ross, 2017.
120 Dooley, Wilkinson & Sweeny, 2019.
121 McLean, Gaul & Penco, 2022.
122 Dooley, Wilkinson & Sweeny, 2019.
123 Ibid.
124 Ibid.
125 McLean, Gaul & Penco, 2022.
126 Thomas, S. *et al.*, 2022.
127 Schimelpfening, 2023.
128 Ibid.
129 Schimelpfening, 2023.
130 Schimelpfening, 2023.
131 James & Gilliland, 2012.
132 Ahmad, 2019:452-455.
133 De Klerk & De Klerk, 2022.
134 Brymer, M. *et al.*, 2006.
135 James & Gilliland, 2012.
136 Ibid.
137 Ibid.
138 Ibid.
139 Ibid.
140 Brymer, Layne, Jacobs, Pynoos, Ruzek, Steinberg & Watson, 2006.
141 James & Gilliland, 2012.

142 Ibid.
143 Lakeman, 2019.
144 Proctor, C. et al., 2015
145 Lakeman, 2019.
146 Harvard Health Publishing, 2020.
147 Ibid.
148 Swiner, 2023.
149 Ibid.
150 Mirgain & Singles, 2016.
151 Ibid.
152 Mirgain & Singles, 2016.
153 Hull University Teaching Hospitals, 2021. 5-4-3-2-1.
154 Hull University Teaching Hospitals, 2021.
155 Kaiser Permanente, 2021.
156 Ibid.
157 Ibid.
158 Carona & Fonseca, 2021:424-426.
159 Beck Institute, 2021.
160 Ibid.
161 Naz & Gul, 2016:130-141.
162 Ibid.
163 Ibid.
164 Allen, S., 2018.
165 Government Gazette, 2020.
166 Joubert, 2020.
167 Crawford, 2019.
168 CAS Mediation Rules, 2021.
169 Mironi, 2017.
170 Grabowski, 2014.
171 Black Lives Matter. 2024.
172 Ibid.
173 Tepoela & Nauright, 2021.
174 Ibid.
175 David Becker Interview, 2023.
176 Ray, 2021.
177 Ray, 2022.
178 Burnton, 2023a.
179 Ibid.
180 Ibid.
181 Euronews, 2023.
182 The Cricketer, 2023.
183 Shamansouri & Hashemi-Minabad 2010.

BIBLIOGRAPHY

Acharya, B., & Peyton, N. 2023. Oscar Pistorius: From 'blade runner' hero to convicted murderer. *International Business Times*. Available at: https://www.ibtimes.com/oscar-pistorius-blade-runner-hero-convicted-murderer-3682350 (Accessed: 03 October 2023).

Ahmad, N.S. 2019. Crisis intervention: Issues and challenges. *Advances in Social Science, Education and Humanities Research*, 304, pp. 452-455.

Al-Dahash, H., Thayaparan, M., & Kulatunga, U. 2016. Understanding the terminologies: Disaster, crisis and emergency. Available at: https://www.arcom.ac.uk/-docs/proceedings/9ac79958d9024495cd81e13909ed08cb.pdf (Accessed: 10 October 2023).

Allen, S. 2018. The Science of Gratitude. *Search Issue Lab*. Available at: https://search.issuelab.org/resource/the-science-of-gratitude.html (Accessed: 10 October 2023).

American Psychological Association. 2013. *Trauma*. Available at: http://www.apa.org/topics/trauma/ (Accessed: 10 October 2023).

American Psychological Association. 2023. *Stress effects on the body*. Available at: https://www.apa.org/topics/stress/body (Accessed: 10 October 2023).

1986 Edinburgh Commonwealth Games were on Brink of being cancelled: Report. 2013. *Business Standard*, 25 August. Available at: https://www.business-standard.com/article/news-ani/1986-edinburgh-commonwealth-games-were-on-brink-of-being-cancelled-report-113082500107_1.html (Accessed: 23 May 2023).

Arvidsdotter, T., Marklund, B., Kylén, S., Taft, C., & Ekman, I. 2016. Understanding persons with psychological distress in primary health care. *Scandinavian Journal of Caring Sciences*, 30(1), pp. 687-694.

Associated Press. 2018. Cameroon stripped of right to host 2019 Africa Cup of Nations. *The Guardian*, 30 November. Available at: https://www.theguardian.com/football/2018/nov/30/cameroon-stripped-right-host-africa-cup-of-nations-2019?CMP=share_btn_link (Accessed: 03 May 2023).

Basson, J.A.A., & Loubser, M.M. 2000. *Sports and the Law in South Africa*. Durban: LexisNexis Butterworths.

Beck Institute. 2021. *Essentials of CBT: Online course*. https://beckinstitute.org/training/online-training/ (Accessed: 23 May 2023).

Black Lives Matter. 2024. About. Available at: https://blacklivesmatter.com/about/ (Accessed: 23 May 2023).

Blackshaw, I. 2013. Match fixing in sport: a top priority and ongoing challenge for sports governing bodies. *De Jure Law Journal*, 46(4), p. 945.

Botha, M.M. 2008. Can whistle-blowing be an effective good governance tool? *Tydskrif vir Hedendaagse Romeins-Hollandse Reg*, 71, p. 482.

Bowley, D.M., Rein, P., Scholtz, H.J., & Boffard, K.D. 2004. The Ellis Park Stadium Tragedy. *European Journal of Trauma*, 30(1), pp. 51-55. doi:10.1007/s00068-004-1230-2.

Brenner, S.N. 1995. Stakeholder Theory of the Firm: Its Consistency with Current Management Techniques. In J. Näsi (ed.). *Understanding Stakeholder Thinking*. Helsinki: LSR-Julkaisut Oy, pp. 75-96.

Brymer, M., Layne, C., Jacobs, A., Pynoos, R., Ruzek, J., Steinberg, A., & Watson, P. 2006. *Psychological first aid: Field operations guide* (2nd ed.). Los Angeles, CA: The National Child Traumatic Stress Network and National Center for PTSD.

Bryson, J. 1995. *Strategic Planning for Public and Non-Profit Organizations*. San Francisco, CA: Jossey-Bass.

Burnton, S. 2023a. Azeem Rafiq and Yorkshire: timeline of a county cricket crisis. *The Guardian*, 31 March. Available at: https://www.theguardian.com/sport/2023/mar/31/azeem-rafiq-and-yorkshire-timeline-of-a-county-cricket-crisis?CMP=share_btn_link (Accessed: 03 October 2023).

Burnton, S. 2023b. Yorkshire fined £400,000 and docked points over cricket racism scandal. *The Guardian*, 28 July. Available at: https://www.theguardian.com/sport/2023/jul/28/yorkshire-fine-points-deductions-over-racism-scandal-cricket (Accessed: 03 October 2023).

Calacus. 2022. Lessons learnt from the Top Sports Crises of 2022. *Calacus Sports PR Agency*. Available at: https://calacus.com/calacus-blog/2022/12/15/lessons-learnt-from-the-top-sports-crises-of-2022 (Accessed: 03 October 2023).

Canada, M., Heath, M. A., Money, K., Annandale, N., Fischer, L., & Young, E. L. 2007. Crisis intervention for students of diverse backgrounds: School counsellors' concerns. *Brief Treatment and Crisis Intervention*, 7(1), pp. 12-24.

Cantillon, M. 2022. Premiership Rugby's ongoing crisis: Why are clubs like Wasps and Worcester Warriors struggling? *Sky Sports*. Available at: https://www.skysports.com/rugby-union/news/12321/12718790/premiership-rugbys-ongoing-crisis-why-are-clubs-like-wasps-and-worcester-warriors-struggling (Accessed: 03 October 2023).

Carona, C., & Fonseca, A. 2021. Socratic questioning put into clinical practice. *BJPsych Advances*, 27(6), pp. 424-426.

CAS Mediation Rules. *Rules - Tribunal Arbitral du Sport / Court of Arbitration for Sport*. Available at: https://www.tas-cas.org/en/mediation/rules.html (Accessed: 27 June 2021).

Clarkson, M.B.E. 1995. A stakeholder framework for analyzing and evaluating corporate social performance. *Academy of Management Journal*, 20(1), pp. 92-118.

Cloete, R. 2011. *Introduction to Sports Law*. Durban: LexisNexis Butterworths.

Cloete, R. (ed). 2005. *Introduction to Sports Law in South Africa*. Durban: LexisNexis Butterworths.

Cohen, K. 2020. Timeline of Lance Armstrong's career successes, doping allegations and final collapse. *ESPN*. Available at: https://africa.espn.com/olympics/cycling/story/_/id/29177227/line-lance-armstrong-career-successes-doping-allegations-final-collapse (Accessed: 10 October 2023).

South Africa. 2008. *Companies Act 71 of 2008*. Available at: https://www.gov.za/ss/documents/companies-act (Accessed: 10 October 2023).

Compliance Institute SA. 2019. *Generally accepted compliance practice framework (GACP)*. Compliance Institute Southern Africa. Available at: https://www.compliancesa.com/generally-accepted-compliance-practice-framework-gacp (Accessed: 03 October 2023).

Coombs, W.T. 2010. *Parameters for crisis communication - The Handbook of Crisis Communication*. Oxford: Wiley/Blackwell, pp. 17 - 53.

Courtroommail. 2018. *Today in History-Oscar Pistorius gets 5 years in prison for girlfriend's death*. Available at: https://www.courtroommail.com/today-in-history-oscar-pistorius-gets-5-years-in-prison-for-girlfriends-death/ (Accessed: 03 October 2023).

Crawford, D. 2019. Why mediation is always the better way to solve problems. *Belfast Telegraph*. Available at: https://www.belfasttelegraph.co.uk/news/northern-ireland/why-mediation-is-always-the-better-way-to-solve-problems/37852836.html (Accessed: March 13, 2023).

Davis, D. (ed). 2013. *Companies and other Business Structures in South Africa Southern Africa*. Cape Town: Oxford University Press.

De Klerk, M., & De Klerk, W. 2020. Crises containment management in South African schools: A critical review. *Journal of Psychology in Africa*, 30(6), pp. 599-604.

De Klerk, M., & De Klerk, W. 2022. Developing a Model for Crises Containment Management in South African Schools. *Scientific Research*, 13(8), pp. 2385-2400. https://doi.org/10.4236/ce.2022.138151.

Debiec, J. 2018. Memories of trauma are unique because of how brains and bodies respond to threat. *The Conversation*. Available at: https://theconversation.com/memories-of-trauma-are-unique-because-of-how-brains-and-bodies-respond-to-threat-103725 (Accessed: 03 October 2023)

Delport, P. 2016. *Henochsberg on the Companies Act 71 of 2008*. Durban: LexisNexis.

Demirtas, O., & Karaca, M.A. 2020. *Handbook of Leadership Styles*. New Castle: Cambridge Scholars Publishing.

South Africa. Department of Sport and Recreation. 1998. *South African Sports and Recreation Act 110 of 1998*. Available at https://www.gov.za/documents/national-sport-and-recreation-act (Accessed: 03 October 2023).

Dobrauz, G. 2023. *Good governance and compliance in sports*. PWC. Available at: https://www.pwc.ch/en/insights/good-governance-and-compliance-in-sport.html (Accessed: March 13, 2023).

Donaldson, T. & Preston, L.E. 1995. The stakeholder theory of the corporation: concepts, evidence and implications. *Academy of Management Review*, 22(1), pp. 65-92.

Dooley, M. K., Wilkinson, D., & Sweeny, K. 2020. Social support during stressful waiting periods: An inductive analysis. *Qualitative Psychology*, 7(3), pp. 228-244. https://doi.org/10.1037/qup0000143.

Doubek, J. 2022. 50 years ago, the Munich olympics massacre changed how we think about terrorism. *NPR*, 4 September. Available at: https://www.npr.org/2022/09/04/1116641214/munich-olympics-massacre-hostage-terrorism-israel-germany (Accessed: 07 February 2024).

Eden, C. & Ackermann, F. 1998. *Making Strategy: The Journey of Strategic Management*. London: Sage.

The extensive report pointed out "entrenched" racism in all levels of English cricket alongside an extremely sexist environment for female cricketers. 2023. *Euronews*, 27 June. Available at: https://www.euronews.com/2023/06/27/institutional-racism-and-sexism-infects-english-cricket-says-report (Accessed: March 13, 2023).

Flannery, R. B., & Everly, G. S. 2000. Crisis intervention: A review. *International Journal of Emergency Mental Health*, 2(2), pp. 119-126.

Freeman, R.E. 1984. *Strategic Management: A Stakeholder Approach*. Cambridge: Cambridge University Press.

Frosdic S. 1997. *Cultural Complexity in the British Stadium Safety Industry*. Oxford: Butterworth Heinemann

Fry, E.M. 2017. Crisis Communication, Sports And Twitter: How Baylor University And Its Fans Used Tweets To Communicate During The 2015-2017 Sexual Assault Scandal. Unpublished master's thesis. Columbia: University of Missouri. Available at: https://core.ac.uk/download/pdf/288007914.pdf (Accessed: 03 October 2023).

Gardiner, S. 2012. *Sports Law*. 4th edition. London: Routledge.

Getz, D. 1997. *Event Management and Event Tourism*. New York: Cognizant.

Ginige, K., Amaratunga, D., & Haigh, R. 2018. Mapping Stakeholders Associated with Societal Challenges: A Methodological Framework. *Procedia Engineering*, 212(2018), pp. 1195-1202. https://doi.org/10.1016/j.proeng.2018.01.154.

South Africa. Department of Justice and constitutional Development. 2007. *Amendment of Rules Regulating the Conduct of the Proceedings of the Magistrates' Courts of South Africa*. Available at: https://www.justice.gov.za/legislation/notices/2020/20200207-gg43000rg11038gon107-RulesBoard_MC.pdf (Accessed: 10 October 2023).

Grabowski, M. 2014. Both Sides Win: Why Using Mediation Would Improve Pro Sports. *Harvard Journal of Sports & Entertainment Law*, 5(2), pp. 189-214.

Harvard Health Publishing. 2020. *Relaxation techniques: Breath control helps quell errant stress response*. Available at: https://www.health.harvard.edu/mind-and-mood/relaxation-techniques-breath-control-helps-quell-errant-stress-response (Accessed: 10 October 2023).

Hellriegel, D., Slocum, J.W., Jackson, S.E., Louw, L., Saude, G., Amos, T., Klopper, H.B., Louw, M., Oosthuizen, T., Perks, S. & Zindiye, S. 2017. *Management*. Cape Town: Oxford University Press.

Hollander, W. & Nolte, L. 2023. *The Management of Sport in South Africa*. Randburg: KR Publishing.

Coombs, T. 2010. Crisis communication and its allied fields, in Coombs, T. & Holladay, S. J. (eds.) *The Handbook of Crisis Communication*. Chichester, Oxford: Wiley-Blackwell, pp. 54-64.

Hull University Teaching Hospital. 2021. *5-4-3-2-1 Grounding Technique*. Available at: https://www.hey.nhs.uk/wp/wp-content/uploads/2021/09/CPS_54321.pdf (Accessed: 10 October 2023).

Hult, G.T.M., Mena, J.A., Ferrell, O.C. & Ferrell, L. 2011. Stakeholder marketing: a definition and conceptual framework. *Academy of Marketing Science Review*, 1(1):44-65.

Indian Express. 2021. *ICC CEO Manu Sawhney resigns amid inquiry over conduct*. Available at: https://indianexpress.com/article/sports/cricket/icc-ceo-manu-sawhney-resigns-amid-inquiry-over-conduct-7395560/ (Accessed: 03 October 2023).

Institute of Directors SA. 2016. King IV Report on Corporate Governance for South Africa. Available at: https://www.adams.africa/wp-content/uploads/2016/11/King-IV-Report.pdf (Accessed: 10 October 2023).

ITV News. 2021. *New Year honours: Figen Murray, Daniel Craig and William Roache recognised*. Available at: https://www.itv.com/news/granada/2021-12-31/new-year-honours-figen-murray-daniel-craig-and-william-roache-recognised (Accessed: 03 October 2023).

James, R.K., & Gilliland, B.E. 2012. *Crisis intervention strategies*. Belmont, CA: Brooks/Cole, Cengage Learning.

Ko, C., Ma, J., Bartnik, R., Haney, M. H., & Kang, M. 2018. Ethical leadership: An integrative review and future research agenda. *Ethics & Behavior*, 28(2), 104-132.

Jones, T.M. & Wicks, A.C. 1999. Convergent stakeholder theory. *Academy of Management Review*, 24(2), pp. 206-219.

Jones, T.M. 1995. Instrumental stakeholder theory: A synthesis of ethics and economics. *Academy of Management Review*, 20, pp. 404-437.

Jones, T.M., Felps, W. & Bigley, G.A. 2007. Ethical theory and stakeholder-related decisions: the role of stakeholder culture. *Academy of Management Review*, 32(1), pp. 137-155.

Joubert, J. 2020. Mediation Rule 41A of the High Court. *LexisNexis*. Available at: https://www.lexisnexis.co.za/lexis-digest/resources/covid-19-resource-centre/practice-areas/mediation-and-arbitration/mediation-rule-41a-of-the-high-court (Accessed on 27 June 2021).

Kaiser Permanente. 2021. *Examining the evidence: A more detailed method*. Available at: https://thrive.kaiserpermanente.org/care-near-you/northern-california/redwoodcity/wp-content/uploads/sites/9/2021/03/webex-4.22-Examining-the-Evidence-detailed.pdf (Accessed: 03 October 2023).

King, K. 2012. 2012 Kahperd Convention in Louisville. *Ky Shape*. Available at: https://kyshape.org/wp-content/uploads/2017/03/JournalFall2013.pdf (Accessed: 03 October 2023).

Knox, K. S., & Roberts, A. R. 2005. Crisis intervention and crisis team models in schools. *Children & Schools*, 27(2), pp. 93-100.

Koehn, N. 2020. Real Leaders Are Forged in Crisis. *Harvard Business Review*, 3 April. Available at: https://hbr.org/2020/04/real-leaders-are-forged-in-crisis (Accessed: 03 October 2023).

Lakeman, R. 2019. *The Mental State Examination*. Available at: https://testandcalc.com/richard/resources/Teaching_Resource_Mental_Status_Examination.pdf (Accessed: 03 October 2023).

Landman, A. 2001. A charter for whistle blowers: a note on the Protected Disclosures Act 26 of 2000. *Industrial Law Journal*, 22(37).

Lavalette, T. 2020. Troubled Cricket South Africa's Crisis Intensifies After The Entire Board Steps Down. *Forbes*, 27 October. Available at: https://www.forbes.com/sites/tristanlavalette/2020/10/27/troubled-cricket-south-africas-crisis-intensifies-after-the-entire-board-steps-down/?sh=25a8abe16e6b (Accessed: May 2023).

Leisering, K. 2022. What is compliance? Definition, basics & tips to get started. *EQS Group*. Available at: https://www.eqs.com/compliance-blog/what-is-compliance/ (Accessed: 03 May 2023).

Louw, A.M. 2010. *Sports Law in South Africa*. Netherlands: Wolters Kluwer.

McClelland, D., & Gilyard, C. 2019. *Calming trauma - How understanding the brain can help.* Phoenix Society for Brain Survivors. Available at: https://www.phoenix-society.org/resources/calming-trauma (Accessed: 24 May 2023).

McLean, D. 2014. Lost Edinburgh: 1986 commonwealth games. *The Scotsman.* Available at: https://www.scotsman.com/arts-and-culture/lost-edinburgh-1986-commonwealth-games-1530073 (Accessed: 24 May 2023).

McLean, L., Gaul, D., & Penco, R. 2022. Perceived social support and stress: A study of 1st year students in Ireland. *International Journal of Mental Health and Addiction,* 21, pp. 2101-2121.

Milašinoviæ, S. & Kešetoviæ, Z. 2008. *Crisis And Crisis Management – A Contribution To A Conceptual & Terminological Delimitation.* Scientific Review Article. Available at: https://core.ac.uk/download/pdf/288007914.pdf (Accessed: 03 October 2023).

Mirgain, S.A. & Singles, J. 2016. *Progressive muscle relaxation.* US Department of Veterans Affairs. Available at: https://www.va.gov/WHOLEHEALTHLIBRARY/docs/Progressive-Muscle-Relaxation.pdf (Accessed: 10 October 2023).

Mironi, M. 2017. The promise of mediation in sport-related disputes. *International Sports Law Journal,* 16, pp. 131-154. Available at: http://mediation-moves.eu/wp-content/uploads/2018/06/The-Promise-of-Mediation-in-Sport-Publication.pdf (Accessed: 10 October 2023).

Mitroff, I.I. & Anagnos, G. 2001. *Managing crises before they happen: What every executive and manager needs to know about crisis management.* New York: AMACOM.

National Child Traumatic Stress Network [NCTSN]. 2010. *Psychological first aid: Field operations guide.* 2nd ed. Available at: https://www.ptsd.va.gov/professional/treat/type/PFA/PFA_2ndEditionwithappendices.pdf (Accessed: 10 October 2023).

Naz, S., & Gul, S. 2016. Translation and validation of Tennessee Self Concept Scale. *Journal of Behavioural Sciences,* 26(1), pp. 130-141.

Ndoro and Another v South African Football Association and Others. 2018. Gauteng High Court, (16/16836). *Southern African Legal Information Institute.* Available at: https://www.saflii.org/za/cases/ZAGPJHC/2018/74.html (Accessed: 10 October 2023).

News - black lives matter (no date) *Black Live Matter.* Available at: https://blacklivesmatter.com/news/ (Accessed: 10 October 2023).

Oliver, B. 2019. *All trauma is not the same: Big T vs little t and how to treat them.* Nexus Recovery. Available at: https://nexusrecoveryservices.com/blog/big-t-vs-little-t-trauma/ (Accessed: 10 October 2023).

Olsson, E. K. 2010. Defining crisis news events. *Nordicom Review Journal,* 31(1), 87-101.

Parmar, B.L., Freeman, R.E., Harrison, J.S., Wicks, A.C., Purnell, L. & De Colle, S. 2010. Stakeholder theory: the state of the art. *The Academy of Management Annals,* 3(1), pp. 403-445.

Peyton, N. & Acharya, B. 2023. Oscar Pistorius: from "Blade Runner" hero to convicted murderer. *Times Live.* Available at: https://www.timeslive.co.za/news/south-africa/2023-03-31-timeline-oscar-pistorius-from-blade-runner-hero-to-convicted-murderer/ (Accessed: 03 October 2023).

Pfaltzgraff, R.L. Jnr. 2008. *Crisis Management: Looking Back and Looking Ahead.* Speech presented at the Crisis Management Conference: Athena 2008. The Hellenic Ministry of National Defence, 2 July, 2008.

South Africa. 2004. *Prevention and combating of corrupt activities act 12 of 2004.* Available at: https://www.gov.za/documents/prevention-and-combating-corrupt-activities-act-0 (Accessed: 10 October 2023).

Proctor, C., Tweed, R., & Morris, D. 2016. The Rogerian Fully Functioning Person: A Positive Psychology Perspective. *Journal of Humanistic Psychology,* 56(5), pp. 503-529. Available at: https://doi.org/10.1177/0022167815605936 (Accessed: 10 October 2023)

Ray, C. 2021. More problems for Cricket SA as Social Justice and Nation Building findings are branded "flawed". *Daily Maverick*, 16 December. Available at: https://www.dailymaverick.co.za/article/2021-12-16-more-problems-for-cricket-sa-as-social-justice-and-nation-building-findings-are-branded-flawed/ (Accessed: 10 October 2023).

Former Safa Boss Nematandani banned over match-fixing. 2016. *Reuters*. Available at: https://www.reuters.com/article/soccer-fifa-south-africa-idINKBN13X1LL (Accessed: 23 May 2023).).

Rollin, J. 2015. 2015 FIFA corruption scandal. *Encyclopædia Britannica*. Available at: https://www.britannica.com/event/2015-FIFA-corruption-scandal (Accessed: 03 October 2023).

Ross, D. 2017. How trauma affects the brain: Doctors' notes. *Toronto Star*. Available at: https://www.thestar.com/life/health_wellness/analysis/2017/12/04/how-trauma- affects-the-brain-doctors-notes.html (Accessed: 03 October 2023).

Schimelpfening, N. 2023. Dialectical Behavior Therapy [DBT]: Definition, techniques, and benefits. *Verywell Mind*. Available at: https://www.verywellmind.com/dialectical-behavior-therapy-1067402 (Accessed: 03 October 2023).

Seeger, M. & Ulmer, R. 2002. A post-crisis discourse of renewal: The cases of Malden Mills and Cole Hardwoods. *Journal of Applied Communication Research*, 30(2), pp. 126-142. doi:10.1080/00909880216578.

Seeger, M.W., Snellnow, T.L. & Ulmere, R.R. 2003. *Communication and organizational crisis*. CT, Praeger: Westport.

Seeger, M., Reynolds, B. & Day, A. 2020. Crisis and emergency risk communication: Past, present, and future. In: Frandsen, F. & Johansen, W. ed. *Crisis Communication*. Berlin, Boston: De Gruyter Mouton, pp. 401-418. https://doi.org/10.1515/9783110554236-019

Shipway, R., Miles, L. & Gordon, R. 2021. *Crisis and disaster management for sport*. S.l.: Viella: Routledge.

Sisco, H. F. 2010. *Crisis definition and response: Understanding non-profit practitioner perspectives*. Prism Online PR Journal. Available at: https://www.researchgate.net/publication/46280169_Crisis_definition_and_response_Understanding_non-profit_practitioner_perspectives (Accessed: 03 October 2023).

South Africa. 2010. *Safety at Sports and Recreational Events Act 2 of 2010*. Available at: https://www.gov.za/documents/acts/safety-sports-and-recreational-events-act-2-2010-27-may-2010 (Accessed: 03 October 2023).

South Africa. 1997. *South African Institute for Drug-Free Sport Act 14 of 1997*. Available at: https://www.gov.za/documents/south-african-institute-drug-free-sport-act (Accessed: 10 October 2023).

Stoldt, G.C., Dittmore, S.W., & Branvold, S.E. 2012. *Sport public relations: Managing stakeholder communication*. Champaign, IL: Human Kinetics.

Swiner, C.N. 2023. *What is box breathing?* Available at: https://www.webmd.com/balance/what-is-box-breathing (Accessed: 10 October 2023).

Taylor, R., & Plumely, E., 1998. Question session: where do we go from here? In *Sports stadiums, after Hillsborough*. Paper presented at a sport council, 1998, p. 102.

TePoel, D. & Nauright, J. 2021. Black lives matter in the Sports World. *Sport in Society*, 24(5), pp. 693-696. doi:10.1080/17430437.2021.1901392.

ICEC's 44 recommendations on cricket's EDI problems: A summary. 2023. *The Cricketer*, 27 June. Available at: https://www.thecricketer.com/Topics/ecb/icec_44_recommendations_crickets_edi_problems_summary.html (Accessed: 10 October 2023).

Thomas, S., Kanske, P., Schäfer, J., Hummel, K. V., & Trautmann, S. 2022. Examining bidirectional associations between perceived social support and psychological symptoms in the context of stressful event exposure: a prospective, longitudinal study. *BMC Psychiatry*, 22 (736), pp. 1-13.

Topper, B. & Lagadec, P. 2013. Fractal crises - A new path for crisis theory and management. *Journal of Contingencies and Crisis Management*, 21, pp. 4-16. Wiley Online Library. Available at: https://onlinelibrary.wiley.com/doi/10.1111/1468-5973.12008 (Accessed: 03 October 2023).

Uslu, O. 2019. The general overview to leadership theories from a critical perspective. *Marketing and Management of Innovation*, 1, pp. 161-172. Available at: https://www.researchgate.net/publication/332106314_General_Overview_to_Leadership_Theories_from_a_Critical_Perspective (Accessed: 10 October 2023).

Veldsman, T.H. & Johnson, A.J. 2016. *Leadership. Perspectives from the front line*. Randburg: KR Publishing.

Walters, G., & Kitchin, P. 2009. *Stakeholder Management and Sport Facilities: A Case Study of the Emirates Stadium*. Available at: https://www.semanticscholar.org/paper/Stakeholder-Management-and-Sport-Facilities%3A-A-Case-Walters-Kitchin/aaf22d175f05fc0e43d14d72428d51625e4e63d8/figure/1 (Accessed: 03 October 2023).

Weir, K. 2013. Nike halts Pistorius deal to protect brand. *Reuters*, 21 February. Available at: https://www.reuters.com/article/us-safrica-pistorius-nike-idUKBRE91K0G020130221 (Accessed: 03 October 2023).

Williams, K. 2016. The Oppressive Seeds of the Colin Kaepernick Backlash. *The Conversation*, 7 October. Available at: https://theconversation.com/the-oppressive-seeds-of-the-colin-kaepernick-backlash-66358 (Accessed: 03 October 2023).

Zamoum, K. & Gorpe, T.S. 2018. Crisis management: A historical and conceptual approach for a better understanding of today's crises. In Holla, K., Titko, M. & Ristvej, J. (eds). *Crisis Management - Theory and Practice* [Preprint]. London: IntechOpen Limited, pp 203-217. doi:10.5772/intechopen.76198.

INDEX

A

African Cup of Nations (AFCON), 84
AIPIL: Analysing, Initial Response Plan, Planning, Implementing, Learning, 158
allegations of racism and discrimination, 135, 146, 154
alternative dispute resolution, 123, 127, 133
arbitration, 111, 123-124, 127-128, 130, 132-134, 141
arbitration and mediation in sport, 127
assess well-being, 101, 103
Athletics South Africa (ASA), 67

B

Black Lives Matter (BLM), 135-136
Boston Marathon, 91
Bradford City Stadium Fire, 90
brand and communication, 38
breathe, recentre and distract, 101, 104
building a relationship, 41

C

captains of industry as stakeholders, 48
CAS Mediation Rules, 127-128
characteristics of great sports leaders, 37
club cricket, 1-2
Columbia 1980, 90
communicating during a crisis, 55-56, 58
compliance and risk management in sport, 80
compliance in sport and risk appetite and tolerance, 78
conciliation, 123-124
Confederation of African Football (CAF), 29, 84
controlling body, 113-114, 116
corporate compliance, 78
corporate governance, 13, 67-69, 79
Council of Southern Africa Football Associations (COSAFA), 29
Cricket Discipline Commission (CDC), 151
Cricket South Africa, 1, 4, 23, 61, 67, 79-80, 133, 137, 139, 141-142, 144
Cricket South Africa (CSA), 1, 4, 67, 133, 139, 142
crises in sport, 1, 17-18, 27, 42, 90
crisis and individual athletes and players, 20
crisis classification, 157-158
crisis communication, 30, 53-56, 58-59, 65, 158-160
crisis in sport, 43, 111, 155
crisis management plan, 40, 155-157, 164
crisis management strategic plan, 156
crisis related to events, 87
crisis scenario planning, 92
crisis theory, 39
critical elements of a crisis communication plan, 53-54
crowd control and management, 112, 119
crowd management in sport, 92
cultivate compliance, 94

D

danger of not responding to the media, 64
declaration of interest, 144
defining stakeholder management, 45
definition of governance in sport, 67
Dialectic Behaviour Therapy (DBT), 101
disaster management centre, 116

E

education and training in dispute resolution, 124
effective communication plan, 53
Ellis Park disaster, 112
emergency services, 92, 116
empirical approach, 46-47
essential services personnel, 116
Ethical issues and challenges, 74
event day physical inspection, 93
event organiser, 113-114, 116-117, 120-121
examining the evidence, 100, 107
ex-players and officials, 49

F

Fédération Internationale de Natation (FINA), 75
Federation of International Football Association (FIFA), 29
FIFA World Cup Qatar, 24

financial crisis, 25

G

Glasgow, 90
global sporting events on governance, 72
good governance in sport, 67-68
governance in sport, 67-68
Graeme Smith, 137, 139-141, 144

H

history of crisis management theory, 17

I

illegal conduct, 120
immediate safety, 100-102
Importance of Effective Crisis Communication, 54
inclusivity and diversity, 68
Independent Commission for Equity in Cricket (ICEC), 147
Institute of Directors in South Africa (IDSA), 79
International Boxing Association (IBA), 24
International Cricket Council (ICC), 67
International Olympic Committee (IOC), 24, 72
International Sporting Event (ISE), 88
International Sporting Venue (ISV), 88

J

James Sutherland, 31
journalist's perspective, 59

K

King IV and compliance, 79
King IV: Principle, 46
Klerksdorp High School (KHS), 2

L

Lance Armstrong, 20, 22, 36
Le Mans, 90
lead time management, 94-95
leadership and governance, 42
leadership during crisis management, 38

leadership mistakes during a crisis in sport, 43
leading through a crisis, 37
learning from others in a crisis, 15
Legal compliance in event planning, 112
legislation, 69, 73-74, 82, 113-117, 120-121
Lenin Stadium Moscow, 90
Lima Peru, 90
Lions cricket, 3-4
LIV golf, 24
lobbying groups and activists, 48

M

Mark Boucher, 137, 140, 142, 144
measures to mitigate compliance risk in sport, 121
media reporting, 9, 21, 23, 138
mediation, 111, 123-134, 152
mediation process, 125
mediation versus litigation, 126
medical personnel, 116
mega sport crises, 19
mental wellness, 97
metro police and traffic police, 116

N

National Commissioner, 114
National Stadium in Guatemala City, 91
negative effect of non-compliance, 121
negotiation, 4, 111, 123-125
Nepal, 91
Netball South Africa (NSA), 67
non-compliance in sport, 84
North West cricket, 3
North West Cricket Board (NWC), 2
North West Cricket CEO, 3
Northerns Cricket Union (NCU), 63
North-West University (NWU), 56

O

Oscar Pistorius, 20-21

P

philosophy for a sporting organisation, 48
players' associations, 49, 135

Premier Soccer League (PSL), 29
pressure from the media, 43
Progressive Muscle Relaxation (PMR), 104
protecting your soul through crisis management, 100

R

racism and discrimination, 135, 137-139, 144, 146-147, 153-154
racism and discrimination in sport, 135, 153
recent crises in world sport, 24
regulatory compliance, 78, 80, 84, 112, 120
role of social media in crisis communication, 53, 56
rugby and other sporting codes, 139
rules of the court to deal with disputes, 124

S

Sandpaper Gate, 31
SAPS, 114-115, 120
scanning and mapping of stakeholders, 50
security business and a security officer, 115
security service provider, 115
SJN hearings, 142-144
Social Justice and Nation Building hearings, 63, 138
Social Justice and Nation Building hearings (SJN), 138
South African Football Association (SAFA), 67
South African Institute for Drug-Free Sport (SAIDS), 75
South African legal position, 112-113
South African Rugby Union (SARU), 67
South African Sports Confederation and Olympic Committee (SASCOC), 71
sporting organisations, 23, 25, 37, 46, 50, 52-53, 134-135, 137, 154-155, 164
sports governance, 74-75
sports governing bodies, 70, 74
sports leaders, 37-39
stadium owner, 114
stadium/event disasters, 90
stakeholder engagement, 45, 50-51
stakeholder power and interest, 50
stakeholder strategy, 48
stakeholder theory, 46-47

stakeholders and events, 51
stakeholders during a crisis, 49-50, 54
Standard Operating Procedure (SOP), 88, 93
state security services, 115
statutory and regulatory compliance, 120
stewards or marshals, 116
strategic leadership, 40
strategic partners and alliances, 41
strategy and crisis, 15

T

terrorist attack, 19-20, 91, 95
Tiger Woods Case Study, 35
Titans and Northerns Cricket Union (SJN Hearings), 143
Titans Cricket, 8, 143, 155
toxic leadership, 39
transparency, accountability and responsibility, 68
Turnaround strategies, 11

U

understanding stakeholder management, 46

V

venue authority, 113-114, 119-121

W

world cups – major events, 64
worst-case scenario, 29

Y

Yorkshire County Cricket Club, 145-146

Z

Zimbabwe cricket, 9